What the critics are saying about

THE JEWELER'S EYE

WILLIAM F. BUCKLEY, Jr.
THE JEWELER'S EYE

A BERKLEY MEDALLION BOOK
PUBLISHED BY G. P. PUTNAM'S SONS
DISTRIBUTED BY BERKLEY PUBLISHING CORPORATION

For Harry Elmlark

ACKNOWLEDGMENTS

My thanks to the proprietors of: the *Columbia Teachers College Record*, *West Magazine*, *National Review*, the *Saturday Evening Post*, the *New York Times*, *Esquire*, *Book Week*, *TV Guide*, *Commonweal*, and the Washington Star Syndicate, for whom I originally wrote the material in this book.

G. P. PUTNAM'S-BERKLEY MEDALLION EDITION, JULY, 1969

G. P. Putnam's Sons
200 Madison Avenue
New York, N.Y. 10016

Berkley Publishing Corporation
200 Madison Avenue
New York, N.Y. 10016

BERKLEY MEDALLION BOOKS ® TM 757,375

Printed in the United States of America

Cover photograph © Philippe Halsman

CONTENTS

Introduction

The material in this book has been published before in
various journals and newspapers and was brought together
at the urging of Walter Minton, the president of the
illustrious House of Putnam, to whom I am most grateful
for his initiative. William Targ, the editor-in-chief of Putnam's, undertook to read everything I have written (over
my own signature) in five years, excluding books and
speeches, and as of this writing has survived the ordeal,
though he cannot be pronounced as finally cured until
1972—at which point I shall perhaps be equipped to subject him to another massive dose of opinions. Needless to
say, I am awed by his industry. I have been afraid to ask
him what are his own political sympathies, lest it should
prove that he is a committed liberal, and Mr. Minton
guilty of cruel and unusual punishment. In any event, I do
thank him for his kind and intelligent attentions, and I am
sure he would want me to say that he is no more responsible for the final arrangements of the book than he is for the
author's opinions.

I shall not attempt to suggest, let alone to impose, a
synthesis on a book that comments on so many people,
things, and ideas. The title is, of course, a calculated effrontery, the relic of an impromptu answer I gave once to
a tenacious young interviewer who, toward the end of a
very long session, asked me what opinion did I have of
myself. I replied that I thought of myself as a perfectly
average middle-aged American, with, however, a jeweler's
eye for political truths. I suppressed a smile—and
watched him carefully record my words in his notebook.
Having done so, he looked up and asked, "Who gave you
your jeweler's eye?" "God," I said, tilting my head
skyward just a little. He wrote *that* down—the journalism

9

schools warn you not to risk committing anything to memory. "Well,"—he rose to go, smiling at last—"that settles *that!*" We have become friends.

The moral, of course, is at one's own expense. Those who give opinions regularly must either put themselves forward as impostors or else confess quite openly that they are the very best opinions going. That is not to say, of course, that they are the result of one's own thought, created *ex nihilo*. Mine most assuredly are not: I lean most heavily on other men, living and dead, men whose ideas, should I find myself at variance with them, it would cause me great anxiety, indeed would bring me to doubt deeply the wisdom of continuing in my profession. If I felt that I were losing my faith, I would lie down until I got over it. That is thought by most people to be very un-American. I consider that it is very wise, provided you are certain, as I am, of the superiority of other people's thinking to your own, and know who those others are. To be sure, everyone receives other people's opinions differently. Everyone is his own alembic. But I thought to hang onto the notion of the jeweler's eye, because I like to stress that I think some ideas are better than others, and of course, since I am free to choose between them, I traffic in the better ones, in preference to the others. The jeweler knows value; that is his trade. I cherish the little story Mary McCarthy passed along in her book on Venice. It was during the age of Savonarola, and the zealot's henchmen had gathered together to burn in the public square at Florence a huge assortment of profane works of literature and art. A Venetian jeweler was seen to jot down in his notebook a figure for every book, painting, or artifact piled onto the heap. And then, just as the torch was about to be applied, he approached the executioner and offered him, cash, 56,872 florins for the lot. Needless to say, I advance this book as not for burning, profane though the opinions are in the eyes of the contemporary Savonarolas—to whom I am always prepared to extend amnesty, upon the showing of contrition and the promise to reform.

W. F. B.

Stamford, Connecticut,
January, 1968

I. What Is Conservatism?

NOTES TOWARD AN EMPIRICAL
DEFINITION OF CONSERVATISM

October, 1963

I am asked most frequently by members of the lecture audience two questions, to neither of which have I ever given a satisfactory answer. The first is asked by those who share my feelings that the world is in crisis and the nation imperiled: "What can I do?" I don't know, and I haven't the stomach to contrive an aphoristic answer. The second question, asked alike by friendly and hostile listeners, is "What is conservatism?" Sometimes the questioner, guarding against the windy evasiveness one comes to expect from lecturers, will add, "preferably in one sentence." On which occasions I have replied, "I could not give you a definition of Christianity in one sentence, but that does not mean that Christianity is undefinable." Usually that disposes of the hopes of those who wish a neatly packaged definition of conservatism which they can stow away in their mind alongside (or replacing?) the definitions of astrology, necrophilia, xenophobia, and philistinism. Those who are obstinate I punish by giving, with a straight face, Professor Richard Weaver's definition of conservatism as "a paradigm of essences towards which the phenomenology of the world is in continuing approximation"—as noble an effort as any I have ever read. The point is, of course, that we are at the stage dangerously close to mere verbal gambiting. I have never failed, I am saying, to dissatisfy an audience that asks the meaning of conservatism.

Yet I feel I know, if not what conservatism is, at least

11

who a conservative is. I confess that I know who is a conservative less surely than I know who is a liberal. Blindfold me, spin me about like a top, and I will walk up to the single liberal in the room without zig or zag and find him even if he is hiding behind the flowerpot. I am tempted to try to develop an equally sure nose for the conservative, but I am deterred by the knowledge that conservatives, under the stress of our times, have had to invite all kinds of people into their ranks to help with the job at hand, and the natural courtesy of the conservative causes him to treat such people not as janissaries, but as equals; and so, empirically, it becomes difficult to see behind the khaki, to know surely whether that is a conservative over there doing what needs to be done, or a radical, or merely a noisemaker, or pyrotechnician, since our ragtag army sometimes moves together in surprising uniformity, and there are exhilarating moments when everyone's eye is right. I have, after all, sometimes wondered whether I am myself a true conservative. I feel I qualify spiritually and philosophically; but temperamentally I am not of the breed, and so I need to ask myself, among so many other things, how much it matters how one is temperamentally. There are other confusions.

Whittaker Chambers, for instance, distinguished sharply between a conservative and a "man of the Right." "You," he wrote me on resigning as an editor of *National Review,* "are a conservative, and I know no one with better title to the word. But I am not one, never was. I call myself, on those occasions when I cannot avoid answering the question, a man of the Right." I reflected on that letter, needless to say, as would you if you were the editor of a journal from which Whittaker Chambers had just withdrawn, and remarked an interesting thing: In the five-year history of the journal, Chambers was the only man to resign from its senior board of editors explicitly because he felt he could no longer move within its ideological compass; and yet he never wrote a piece for us (or in the last dozen years of his life, that I know of, for anyone else) that was out of harmony with the thrust of *National Review*'s position.

Oh, yes, people withdraw, and write and denounce you, and swear green grass will never grow over your grave on

12

account of this or that offensive article or editorial or book review; but these losses are merely a part of the human attrition of outspoken journalism. They prove nothing, in our case, that has anything to do with ideological fecklessness. What I am saying is that notwithstanding the difficulty in formulating the conservative position, and the high degree of skepticism from our critics before *National Review* was launched, *National Review*'s position was, I believe, instantly intelligible, from the very first issue. *He would probably say that anyway* (the skeptic will charge), *it being in his and the journal's interest to say so.* But I make that statement on empirical grounds, as I propose to make others in this essay on the meaning of conservatism, which will reason a posteriori from the facts to the theory—and which will be based exclusively on my own experiences as editor of *National Review*. Since I shall not allude to it again, let me say so now unambiguously: This essay is about the experiences of *National Review* and their bearing, by the processes of exclusion, on a workable definition of contemporary conservatism. I do not by any means suggest that *National Review* is the only functioning alembic of modern conservatism, merely that it is the only one whose experiences I can relate with any authority, and that its experiences may be interesting enough to be worth telling.

Roughly the same group of men, representing the same vested interests in certain ideas and attitudes, continue to be the major participants in *National Review*. The magazine found instantly and expanded an audience which seemed intuitively to grant and to understand the happy eclecticism of the magazine's guiding ideas; whereas the critics, whose delighted line at the beginning was one or another variant on the theme: "This country needs a conservative magazine, and having read *National Review,* we *still* say what this country needs is a conservative magazine," finally, except for the bitter-enders, gave up, and began to refer to *National Review* as, plain and simple, a "conservative journal." Others, who, as I say, refuse to give up, will continue to refer to it only after a ritualistic pejorative: "the McCarthyite *National Review,*" "the ultrarightist *National Review,*" etc. But it being so that in language the governing law is usage, it is by now predictable that those who feel Peter Viereck or

13

Clinton Rossiter or Walter Lippmann are the true architects of American conservatism are bound to enter the ranks of eccentricity, like the right-wing gentlemen who, because they continue to insist on referring to themselves as "liberals," have difficulty communicating with the rest of the world, which for two generations now has understood liberalism to mean something else, beginning, roughly, from the time Santayana observed that the only thing the modern liberal is concerned to liberate is man from his marriage contract.

Since this is to be an empirical probe, based, apologetically, on my personal experience as editor of *National Review,* I shall speak about people and ideas with which *National Review* has had trouble making common cause. In 1957, Whittaker Chambers reviewed *Atlas Shrugged,* the novel by Miss Ayn Rand wherein she explicates the philosophy of "Objectivism," which is what she has chosen to call her creed. Man of the right, or conservative, or whatever you wish to call him, Chambers did in fact read Miss Rand right out of the conservative movement. He did so by pointing out that her philosophy is in fact another kind of materialism—not the dialectical materialism of Marx, but the materialism of technocracy, of the relentless self-server, who lives for himself and for absolutely no one else, whose concern for others is explainable merely as an intellectualized recognition of the relationship between helping others and helping oneself. Religion is the first enemy of the Objectivist, and after religion, the state—respectively, the "mysticism of the mind," and "the mysticism of the muscle." "Randian Man," wrote Chambers, "like Marxian Man, is made the center of a godless world."

Her exclusion from the conservative community was, I am sure, in part the result of her desiccated philosophy's conclusive incompatibility with the conservative's emphasis on transcendence, intellectual and moral; but also there is the incongruity of tone, that hard, schematic, implacable, unyielding dogmatism that is in itself intrinsically objectionable, whether it comes from the mouth of Ehrenburg, or Savonarola, or Ayn Rand. Chambers knew that specific ideologies come and go, but that rhetorical totalism is always in the air, searching for the

14

ideologue-on-the-make; and so he said things about Miss Rand's tone of voice which, I would hazard the guess, if they were true of anyone else's voice, would tend to make it *eo ipso* unacceptable for the conservative. ". . . the book's [*Atlas Shrugged*'s] dictatorial tone . . . ," Chambers wrote, "is its most striking feature. Out of a lifetime of reading, I can recall no other book in which a tone of overriding arrogance was so implacably sustained. Its shrillness is without reprieve. Its dogmatism is without appeal . . . resistance to the Message cannot be tolerated because disagreement can never be merely honest, prudent, or just humanly fallible. Dissent from revelation so final can only be willfully wicked. There are ways of dealing with such wickedness, and, in fact, right reason itself enjoins them. From almost any page of *Atlas Shrugged,* a voice can be heard, from painful necessity, commanding: 'To a gas chamber—go!' The same inflexibly self-righteous stance results, too, in odd extravagances of inflection and gesture. . . . At first we try to tell ourselves that these are just lapses, that this mind has, somehow, mislaid the discriminating knack that most of us pray will warn us in time of the difference between what is effective and firm, and what is wildly grotesque and excessive. Soon we suspect something worse. We suspect that this mind finds, precisely in extravagance, some exalting merit; feels a surging release of power and passion precisely in smashing up the house." *

As if according to a script, Miss Rand's followers jumped *National Review* and Chambers in language that crossed the *i*'s and dotted the *t*'s of Mr. Chambers' point. (It is not fair to hold the leader responsible for the excesses of the disciples, but this reaction from Miss Rand's followers, never repudiated by Miss Rand, suggested that her own intolerance is easily communicable to other Objectivists.) One correspondent, denouncing him, referred to "Mr. Chambers's 'break' with Communism"; a lady confessed that on reading his review she thought she had

* Several years later, a graduate student in philosophy, a disciple of Hayek, von Mises, and Friedman, analyzed the thought and rhetoric of Miss Rand and came to similar conclusions. Miss Rand, he wrote (2, References), is "hate blinded," "suffocating in her invective."

"mistakenly picked up the *Daily Worker*"; another accused him of "lies, smears, and cowardly misrepresentations"; still another saw in him the "mind-blanking, life-hating, unreasoning, less-than-human being which Miss Rand proves undeniably is the cause of the tragic situation the world now faces. . . ."; and summing up, one Objectivist wrote that "Chambers the Christian communist is far more dangerous than Chambers the Russian spy."

What the experience proved, it seems to me, beyond the unacceptability of Miss Rand's ideas and rhetoric, is that no conservative cosmology whose every star and planet are given in a master book of coordinates is very likely to sweep American conservatives off their feet. They are enough conservative and anti-ideological to resist totally closed systems, those systems that do not provide for deep and continuing mysteries. They may be pro-ideology and unconservative enough to resist such asseverations as that conservatism is merely "an attitude of mind." But I predict on the basis of a long association with American conservatives that there isn't anybody around scribbling into his sacred book a series of all-fulfilling formulas which will serve the conservatives as an Apostles' Creed. Miss Rand tried it, and *because* she tried it, she compounded the failure of her ideas. She will have to go down as an Objectivist; my guess is she will go down as an entertaining novelist.

The conservative's distrust of the state, so richly earned by it, raises inevitably the question: How far can one go? This side, the answer is, of anarchism—that should be obvious enough. But one man's anarchism is another man's statism. *National Review*, while fully intending to save the nation, probably will never define to the majority's satisfaction what are the tolerable limits of the state's activity; and we never expected to do so. But we got into the problem, as so often is the case, not by going forward to meet it, but by backing up against it.

There exists a small breed of men whose passionate distrust for the state has developed into a theology of sorts, or at least into a demonology, to which they adhere as devotedly as any religious fanatic ever attempted to adhere to the will of the Lord. I do not feel contempt for the endeavor of either type. It is intellectually stimulating to

16

discuss alternatives to municipalized streets, as it is to speculate on whether God's wishes would be best served if we ordered fried or scrambled eggs for breakfast on this particular morning. But conservatives must concern themselves not only with ideals, but with matters of public policy, and I mean by that something more than the commonplace that one must maneuver within the limits of conceivable action. We can read and take pleasure in the recluse's tortured deliberations on what will benefit his soul. Bernanos' *Diary of a Country Priest* was not only a masterpiece; it was also a best seller. And we can read with more than mere amusement Dr. Murray Rothbard's suggestion that lighthouses be sold to private tenants who will chase down the beam in speedboats and collect a dollar from the storm-tossed ship whose path it illuminates. Chesterton reminds us that many dogmas are liberating because, however much damage they do when abused, it cannot compare with the damage that might have been done had whole peoples not felt their inhibiting influence. If our society seriously wondered whether or not to denationalize the lighthouses, it would not wonder at all whether to nationalize the medical profession.

But Dr. Rothbard and his merry anarchists wish to *live* their fanatical antistatism, and the result is a collision between the basic policies they urge and those urged by conservatives who recognize that the state sometimes is, and is today as never before, the necessary instrument of our proximate deliverance. The defensive war in which we are engaged cannot be prosecuted by voluntary associations of soldiers and scientists and diplomats and strategists, and when this obtrusive fact enters into the reckonings of our state haters, the majority, sighing, yield to reality, whereas the small minority, obsessed by their antagonism to the state, would refuse to give it even the powers necessary to safeguard the community. Dr. Rothbard and a few others have spoken harshly of *National Review*'s complacency before the twentieth-century state in all matters that have to do with anti-Communism, reading their litanies about the necessity for refusing at any cost to countenance the growth of the state. Thus, for instance, Ronald Hamowy of the University of Chicago complained about *National Review* in 1961: ". . . the Conservative movement has been straying far under *National*

17

Review guidance . . . leading true believers in freedom and individual liberty down a disastrous path . . . and that in so doing they are causing the Right increasingly to betray its own traditions and principles."*

And Henry Hazlitt (*3,* References), reviewing Dr. Rothbard's magnum opus, *Man, Economy, and State,* enthusiastically for *National Review,* paused to comment, sadly, on the author's "extreme apriorism," citing for instance, Dr. Rothbard's opinion that libel and slander ought not to be illegalized and that even blackmail, " 'would not be illegal in the free society. For blackmail is the receipt of money in exchange for the service of not publicizing certain information about the other person. No violence or threat of violence to person or property is involved.' . . . when Rothbard wanders out of the strictly economic realm, in which his scholarship is so rich and his reasoning so rigorous, he is misled by his epistemological doctrine of 'extreme apriorism' into trying to substitute his own instant jurisprudence for the common law principles built up through generations of human experience."

"Extreme apriorism"—a generic bull's-eye. If *National Review*'s experience is central to the growth of contemporary conservatism, extreme apriorists will find it difficult to work with conservatives except as occasional volunteers helping to storm specific objectives. They will not be a part of the standing army, rejecting as they do the burden of reality in the name of a virginal antistatism. I repeat I do not deplore their influence intellectually, and tactically, I worry not at all. The succubi of Communism are quite numerous enough and eloquent enough to be counted upon to put their ghastly presences forward in ef-

---

* On behalf of the magazine I answered in part (*1,* References), "The American conservative needs to proceed within the knowledge of history and anthropology and psychology; we must live in our time. We must indeed continue to cherish our resentments against such institutionalized impositions upon our prerogatives as social security. But we must not, if we are to pass for sane in this tormented world, equate as problems of equal urgency, the repeal of the social security law, and the containment of the Soviet threat. The problems of assigning priorities to the two objectives is not merely a problem of intellectual discrimination, but of moral balance."

18

fective protest against the marriage of any but the most incurable solipsist to a set of abstractionist doctrines the acceptance of which would mean the end of any human liberty. The virgins have wriggled themselves outside the mainstream of American conservatism. Mr. Hamowy, offering himself up grandly as a symbol of the undefiled conservative, has joined the Committee for a Sane Nuclear Policy.

We ran into the John Birch Society—or, more precisely, into Robert Welch. Mr. Welch's position is very well known. Scrubbed down, it is that one may reliably infer subjective motivation from objective result—*e.g.,* if the West loses as much ground as demonstrably it has lost during the past twenty years to the enemy, it can only be because those who made policy for the West were the enemy's agents. The ultima ratio of this position was the public disclosure—any 300-page document sent to hundreds of people can only be called an act of public disclosure—that Dwight Eisenhower is a Communist. (To which the most perfect retort—was it Russell Kirk's? —was not so much analytical as artistic: "Eisenhower isn't a Communist—he is a golfer.")

In criticizing Mr. Welch, we did not move into a hard philosophical front, as for instance we did in our criticisms of Miss Rand or of the neoanarchists. Rather, we moved into an organizational axiom, the conservative equivalent of the leftists' *pas d'ennemi à gauche*. The position has not, however, been rigorously explicated or applied. Mr. Welch makes his own exclusions; for instance, Gerald L. K. Smith, who, although it is a fact that he favors a number of reforms in domestic and foreign policy which coincide with those favored by Mr. Welch (and by *National Review*), is dismissed as a man with an *idée fixe,* namely, the role of Perfidious Jew in modern society. Many right-wingers (and many liberals, and all Communists) believe in a *deus ex machina.* Only introduce the single tax, and our problems will wither away, say the followers of Henry George. . . . Only expose the Jew, and the international conspiracy will be broken, say others. . . . Only abolish the income tax, and all will be well. . . . Forget everything else, but restore the gold standard. . . . Abolish compulsory taxation, and we all shall be free. . . . They are called nostrum peddlers by some; certainly they are obsessed. Because whatever virtue there is in what they call for—and some of their proposals strike me as highly desirable, others as mischievous—no one of them can begin to do the whole job, which continues to wait on the successful completion of the objectives of the Committee to Abolish Original Sin. Many such persons, because inadequate emphasis is given to their pandemic insight, the linchpin of social reconstruction, are dissatisfied with *National Review*. Others react more vehemently; our failure to highlight *their* solution has the effect of distracting from its unique relevance and so works positively against the day when the great illumination will show us the only road forward. Accordingly, *National Review* is, in their eyes, worse than merely useless.

The defenders of Mr. Welch who are also severe critics of *National Review* are not by any means all of them addicts of the conspiracy school. They do belong, however inconsistently, to the school that says that we all must work together—as a general proposition, sound advice. Lenin distinguished between the sin of sectarianism, from which suffer all those who refuse to cooperate with anyone who does not share their entire position, right down to the dependent clauses, and the sin of opportunism, the weakness of those who are completely indiscriminate about their political associates.

The majority of those who broke with *National Review* as the result of our criticisms of Mr. Welch believe themselves to have done so in protest against *National Review*'s sectarianism. In face, I believe their resentment was primarily personal. They were distressed by an attack on a man who had ingratiated himself with them and toward whom their loyalty hardened in proportion as he was attacked. So their bitterness ran over, and now it is widely whispered that *National Review* has been "infiltrated."

The questions we faced at *National Review* were two. The first, to which the answer was always plainly no, was whether Mr. Welch's views on public affairs were sound. The editors knew from empirical experience that they were not. Enough of us had recently been to college, or were in continuing touch with academic circles, to know that the approaches to the internal security and to foreign relations that have been practiced by successive administrations after the Second World War are endorsed by the overwhelming majority of the intellectuals of this country; therefore, any assumption that only a Communist (or a fool, as Mr. Welch allowed) could oppose the House Committee on Un-American Activities or favor aid to Poland and Yugoslavia must deductively mean that the nation's academies are staffed, primarily, by Communists (or fools). It is not merely common sense that rejects this assumption, but a familiarity with the intricate argumentation of almost the entire intellectual class (who, of course, are not fools, at least not in the sense in which Mr. Welch uses the word).

The second question then arose—whether it was necessary explicitly to reject Mr. Welch's position as an unrealistic mode of thought. And that had to be answered by asking whether at the margin it contributed or not to the enlightenment of right-wing thought. The answer was not as obvious as one might suppose. Ironically, the assumptions that reason will prevail and that logic and truth are self-evident—the constituent assumptions of those who believe that that syllogism is correct which says: "(a) We were all-powerful after World War II; (b) Russia is now as powerful as we are; therefore, (c) we willed the enemy's ascendancy" (the essence of Mr. Welch's methodology)—argued in favor of leaving Mr. Welch alone. Thus might one reason if one believed that the truth will triumph: If Mr. Welch merely succeeds in drawing people's attention, which otherwise would not be drawn, to public events; if he scourges them to read about and think about public affairs, then those same people, though introduced to public concern by Mr. Welch, will by the power of reason reject, upon examination, Mr. Welch's specific counsels and graduate as informed members of the anti-Communist community.

But reason is *not* king (and many of those who have shrunk from Mr. Welch have done so less because on reflection they repudiate his analysis than because public scandal of a kind has in fact attached to discipleship in a movement dominated by a man with a very special set of views which reality rejects). And so it seemed necessary to say what one hoped would be obvious: that the Welch view is wrong, that it is wrong irrespective of the many personal virtues of Mr. Welch, and wrong irrespective of

21

how many people who were otherwise politically lethargic are now, thanks to Mr. Welch, politically animated.

In consequence, *National Review* was widely criticized for "throwing mud" at Mr. Welch (a curious way to refer to the act of throwing at Mr. Welch his own statements!), and some battle lines (and some necks) were broken. Whom did we actually alienate? A body of people? A body of thought? I tend to think not, for the reasons I have suggested. If we alienated those who genuinely believe in *pas d'ennemi à droite,* why do these same people (a) applaud Mr. Welch's exclusion of Gerald L. K. Smith and (b) proceed to exclude us? It is no answer to the latter inconsistency that the penalty of turning against someone on your side excuses the turning away against the offender, and Mr. Welch, while failing to be consistent on point (a) above, *was* consistent in respect of (b). Aside from a few aggrieved references to *National Review*'s naïveté and to the Communists' need of conservative front men to implement the smear of the John Birch Society, he has not, as yet anyway, excluded us from the anti-Communist community.

For this reason I tend to put down our encounter with Mr. Welch as having no philosophical significance in an empirical probe of the contemporary locus of American conservatism—except to the extent it can be said that *National Review* rejects as out of this world what goes by the name of the conspiracy view of history. Most of the followers of Mr. Welch who broke with *National Review* on account of our criticisms of him showed themselves, by the inconsistency of their own position, to have acted primarily out of personal pique—to which, of course, they are entitled. But perhaps this brief analysis is relevant, if only because it explains why *National Review*'s noisiest collision did not serve any great purpose in the construction of an empirical definition of conservatism.

A few years ago, Max Eastman, the author and poet, wrote sadly that he must withdraw from the masthead of *National Review:*

"There are too many things in the magazine—and they go too deep—that directly attack or casually side-swipe my most earnest passions and convictions. It was an error in the first place to think that, because of political agree-

22

ments, I could collaborate formally with a publication whose basic view of life and the universe I regard as primitive and superstitious. That cosmic, or chasmic, difference between us has always troubled me, as I've told you, but lately its political implications have been drawn in ways that I can't be tolerant of. Your own statement in the issue of October 11 (1958) that Father Halton labored 'for the recognition of God's right to His place in Heaven' invited me into a world where neither my mind nor my imagination could find rest. That much I could take, although with a shudder, but when you added that 'the struggle for the world is a struggle, essentially, by those who mean to unseat Him,' you voiced a political opinion that I think is totally and dangerously wrong. . . ."

Can you be a conservative and believe in God? Obviously. Can you be a conservative and not believe in God? This is an empirical essay, and so the answer is, as obviously, yes. Can you be a conservative and despise God and feel contempt for those who believe in Him? I would say no. True, Max Eastman is the only man who has left the masthead of *National Review* in protest against its pro-religious sympathies, but it does not follow that this deed was eccentric; he, after all, was probably the only man on *National Review* with that old-time hostility to religion associated with evangelical atheism—with, *e.g.*, the names of Theodore Dreiser, Upton Sinclair, Henry Mencken, and Clarence Darrow, old friends of Eastman. If one dismisses religion as intellectually contemptible, it becomes difficult to identify oneself wholly with a movement in which religion plays a vital role, and so the moment came when Max Eastman felt he had to go, even while finding it difficult to answer the concluding observation I made to him: "I continue to feel that you would be at a total loss as to what to criticize in the society the editors of *National Review* would, had they had the influence, establish in America."

Mr. Eastman's resignation brought up an interesting point, to which I also addressed myself in my reply to my old friend:

"You require that I take your letter seriously, and having done so I must reproach myself rather than you. For if it is true that you cannot collaborate formally with me then it must be true that I ought not to have collaborated

23

formally with you; for I should hate for you to think that the distance between atheism and Christianity is any greater than the distance between Christianity and atheism. And so if you are correct, that our coadjutorship was incongruous, I as editor of *National Review* should have been the first to spot it and to act on it. All the more because my faith imposes upon me more rigorous standards of association than yours does."

I know now, several years after this exchange of letters, that my point here, that the reciprocal of the proposition that a God hater cannot associate fully with a Christian, is not in fact true—for reasons that are not easy to set down without running the risk of spiritual or philosophical condescension. But the risk must be taken, and I choose the Christian, rather than the secular, formulation because, although the latter can very handily be made—see, *e.g.*, Eric Voegelin's "On Readiness to Rational Discussion" (*4*, References)—it remains debatable in a way that the Christian formulation does not. The reason why Christian conservatives can associate with atheists is that we hold that, above all, faith is a gift and that, therefore, there is no accounting for the bad fortune that has beset those who do not believe or the good fortune that has befallen those who do. The proreligious conservative can therefore welcome the atheist as a full-fledged member of the conservative community even while feeling that at the very bottom the roots do not interlace, so that the sustenance that gives a special bloom to Christian conservatism fails to reach the purely secularist conservatism. Voegelin will argue on purely intellectual grounds, taking as his lesson the Socratic proposition that virtue can be taught, but only if virtue is defined as knowledge. Socrates defined knowledge, Voegelin reminds us, as transcendental cognition, as, in fact, requiring the ability to see far enough into the nature of things to recognize transcendence, a view he elaborated in *Protagoras*.

The God hater, as distinguished from the agnostic (who says merely that he doesn't know) or simply the habitual atheist (who knows there is no God, but doesn't much care about those who disagree), regards those who believe in or tolerate religion as afflicted with short-circuited vision. Their faith is the result of a combination of intellectual defectiveness and psychological immaturity, leading to the use of analysis and rhetoric which Max Eastman "can't be tolerant of."

The agnostic can shrug his shoulders about the whole thing, caring not whether, in his time, the conflict between the pro-religious and antireligious elements within conservatism will be resolved. There are so many other things to do than think about God. "Are you anything?" a lady flightily addressed at her dinner table a scholarly gentleman and firebrand conservative who has always managed to nudge aside questions or deflect conversational trends that seemed to be moving into hard confrontations involving religion. He smiled. "Well, I guess I'm not *nothing*," and the conversation went on pleasantly. Max Eastman *is* nothing, and he can no more resist the opportunity to incant his nonbelief than the holy priest can resist the opportunity to proselyte—and so the tension.

Mr. Eastman, like many other programmatic conservatives, bases his defense of freedom primarily on pragmatic grounds. Erik von Keuhnelt-Leddihn once remarked that Friedrich Hayek's *Constitution of Liberty* seemed to be saying that if freedom were not pragmatically productive, there would be no *reason* for freedom. It appears to be the consensus of religious-minded conservatives that ordered freedom is desirable quite apart from its demonstrable usefulness as the basis for economic and political association. The research of the past ten years on Edmund Burke appears to have liberated him from the social pragmatists by whom he had been co-opted. Not to stray too far from the rules of this discussion, I cite a poll a few years ago which showed that the great majority of the readers of *National Review* think of themselves formally as religious people, suggesting that conservatism, of the kind I write about, is planted in a religious view of man.

Though as I say only a single resignation has been addressed to *National Review* in protest against the magazine's friendliness to religion, there is much latent discord, particularly in the academic world, centering on the question, not so much of whether God exists or doesn't (only a few continue to explore the question consciously, let alone conscientiously, and most of the latter are thought of as infra dig), but on the extent to which it is proper to show toward religion the intellectual disdain the God haters believe it deserves. Russell Kirk was not allowed inside the faculty of a major university in which, *mirabile dictu,* conservatives (specifically, libertarians) had control of the social science department—because of his "religiosity." The Mt. Pelerin Society, an organization of free-market economists and laymen, has recently trembled over inscrutable personal issues; but somewhere there, in the interstices of the strife, is a hardening of positions relating to religious differences, or differences over religion, which sometimes express themselves, loosely, in arguments between "traditionalist" and "libertarian" conservatism.

Though I say the antagonism is here and there seen to be hardening, I have grounds for optimism, based not merely on *National Review*'s own amiable experiences with all but the most dedicated atheists, but on the conviction that the hideousness of a science-centered age has resulted in a stimulation of religious scholarship and of all of those other impulses, intellectual and spiritual, by which man is constantly confounding the most recent wave of neoterics who insist that man is merely a pandemoniac conjunction of ethereal gases. The atheists have not got around to answering Huxley's self-critical confession that neither he nor his followers had succeeded in showing how you can deduce Hamlet from the molecular structure of a mutton chop.

I repeat what is obvious: These are merely notes, though not I hope altogether desultory, suggesting where are some of the confines of contemporary conservatism, the walls it runs up against and bounces away from. The freeway remains large, large enough to accommodate very different players with highly different prejudices and techniques. The differences are now tonal, now substantive, but they do not appear to be choking each other off. The symbiosis may yet be a general consensus on the proper balance between freedom, order, and tradition.

REFERENCES

1. Buckley, W. F., Jr., " 'National Review': Criticism and Reply," *New Individualism Review,* 1961, *1* (No. 3), 3-11.

2. Goldberg, B., "Ayn Rand's 'For the New Intellectual,'" *New Individualism Review,* 1961, *1* (No. 3), 17-24.
3. Hazlitt, H. "The Economics of Freedom," *National Review,* 1962, *13,* 231-232.
4. Voegelin, E., "On Readiness to Rational Discussion," in A. Hunold (ed.), *Freedom and Serfdom: an Anthology of Western Thought* (Dordrecht, Holland), 1961, pp. 269-284.

WHAT THE PROFESSORS ARE SAYING

January 25, 1966

It is a matter deeply disturbing to ever so many people that the conservative movement was not terminated on the day that Lyndon Johnson beat Barry Goldwater so decisively at the polls. It was very generally supposed that the electorate had once and for all spoken on the subject and that, therefore, the only realistic thing a conservative could do was to fold up his tent and hitchhike along with history.

It is, of course, clear by now that no such accommodation is intended by conservatives, either because they are fanatics, who will not learn from experience, or because they believe that the conservative critique of modern society continues to be relevant. Let us leave the question moot, but in any case agree on the fact, which is that conservatives survived the debacle of 1964 and, however weakened on a national scale, continue to press their views.

What distinguishes, in the political order, a conservative from a liberal these days? The conservative, just to consider his position on issues that recently have come to the forefront, believes (a) that the United States as a collectivity has the right and the duty to commit the state and its citizens to whatever actions are necessary abroad in order to secure the defenses of our own country; (b) that the passion for federal activity in place of local activity has reached a point of mania, as for instance when we see the federal government undertaking educational and urban renewal programs which individual communities and states could easily do in their own behalf; and (c) that the ideological and political vested interests, for instance, some of the civil righters and some of the monopoly labor unions, are exercising an inordinate leverage on public affairs.

The sociologist is deeply in thrall to certain words and concepts which are found in great concentration in Professor Richard Hofstadter's works. For instance, we learn that "the entire right-wing movement [is] infused at the mass level with the fundamentalist style of mind." "Fundamentalist" is a bad word, bad enough in religion, of course, but also very bad in politics, and we are to understand that the conservative's opposition to deficit financing and certain welfarist programs relates not to any rational objection to deficit financing (on the ground that it will cause great social pain when carried to extremes) or to state welfarism (on the ground that it is in many ways a highly sophisticated means of hurting the poor people for the benefit of the lower middle classes). . . .

No, Professor Hofstadter glumly concludes, the survival of conservatism in America doesn't have to do with a rational approach to modern problems, but to a whole lot of other things. The conservative, he says, doesn't merely set out to vote for his own economic best interests. Indeed, says the professor, most conservatives aren't even qualified to know what it is that inures to their best interests; the fact of the matter is they are dominated by extrarational prejudices—"among them the sheer weight of habit and party loyalty, ethnic origins and traditions, religious affiliations and religious styles, racial and ethnic prejudices, attitudes towards liberty and censorship, feelings about foreign policy quite unrelated to commercial goals of dubious relationship to the national interest."

It is a pity that such as Professor Hofstadter cannot bring themselves to meditate on the conservative critique without lapsing into the sociological doodles which are a substitute for the hard thought necessary to understand why so much of America continues to resist the liberal orthodoxy.

It isn't a matter of stupidity—Professor Hofstadter is manifestly an intelligent man. It is a matter of years and years of conviction that that which is not espoused by Professor Hofstadter and his ideological colleagues is not worth analyzing, but rather diagnosing.

THE DEBATE DROOPS

June 28, 1966

On the assumption that we will not for the rest of our lives debate only the question of the South Vietnamese war, it is relevant to ask how goes the general debate between conservatives and liberals on the subject of the government's role in the economy. It is the unhappy conclusion of a very brilliant and highly composed economist at the University of Chicago that the debate goes very poorly indeed. The gentleman in question, George J. Stigler, is himself a conservative, but he assigns in a superbly useful paper called "The Unjoined Debate," about equal blame between conservatives and liberals for the failure of that debate to move forward.

At the rhetorical or bombastic level, the liberals he finds more guilty, as witness for instance their increasing tendency to dispose of a position different from their own as extremist. But clearly not all conservatives who, say, supported the candidacy of Senator Goldwater, are extremists; wherefore, Mr. Stigler observes, "the believer in democracy, or even more basically a believer in the dignity of man, has a moral obligation to seek to remove differences of opinion among groups by honest argument."

The author separates into four divisions the neglected areas of purposive debate:

There is, to begin with, the preservation of liberty. The conservatives take the position that an increase in the state's power involves a necessary decrease in the individual's freedom, while the liberals rejoin that such freedoms as the individual has lost are insubstantial—indeed, that no basic liberties are seriously infringed today. The conservative will point, say, to the building he cannot build without conforming to the municipal code or the public school he cannot teach at, even though he is qualified to teach at a great university. The liberal counters that these are minor inconveniences, considering the

29

necessity, if only to guard the safety of one's neighbors, of well-built houses and the residual benefits to poor students of uniform teaching codes. Professor Stigler believes that conservatives should make their case more concretely—"the seeds-of-destruction talk is sheer indolence parading as prophecy."

Concerning the humanitarian treatment of the needy, the conservative has historically stressed the efficiency of the free economic system, and this was a great semantic error, because he might better have stressed the word "humanitarian," rather than "efficient," since, in the economic context, they are exactly synonymous. *I.e.,* an efficient system distributes welfare in a way that an inefficient system does not. "It is fair to say," Stigler concludes, "that the conservative is compassionate for the great mass of the population which is moderately affected by each public policy, whereas the liberal is compassionate for the special, identifiable group which is most benefited or injured by the policy in question." Conservatives tend to worry about the higher cost of bread for everyone, while liberals rejoice in the higher income that subsidies make possible for the farmers.

Which impinges on the third division between conservatives and liberals—namely, the competence of the state. Not nearly enough work has been done, maintains Professor Stigler, on the factual question of whether the government's charitable impulses actually bear fruit. Are there fewer business failures on account of the Securities and Exchange Commission? Better trains on account of the ICC? What the liberals especially need to examine is the increased tendency of government to be guided by bloc-interest legislation: import quotas for the oil lobby, monopoly immunities for the labor unions, that kind of thing.

And finally, there is the question of the competence of the individual. Can he look after himself? Not completely. But far more than the liberal generally supposes. "Competition is the consumer's patron saint," maintains Professor Stigler, and that is true whether the consumer buys a box of shredded wheat or a large automobile.

Some will find the Stigler approach a little sedate for their taste, but it is a refreshing change from the volleys of

30

exchanged and desultory abuse, the eternally unresolved debate. It might well be that history will only determine that the questions proved moot. But they could be less so if, say, the conservatives got busy sharpening their critique and if the liberals could bring themselves to answer such criticisms Mr. Stigler has so lambently formulated.

II. The Flowering of Liberalism

THE *GLAMOUR* POLL

December 24, 1966

In a recent issue, *Glamour* magazine thought to probe the general feelings about this and that among the major movie and drama critics, thinking to throw light on whether the critics' prejudices are (a) uniform and (b), if so, whether they tend to correspond with the people's prejudices.

The poll is not uninteresting, even though there are few surprises. Without consulting the dozen top critics, anyone tuned in on the *Zeitgeist* would pretty well guess what the ladies and gentlemen would say, though to be sure there are the interesting exceptions. Concerning only one question was there absolute unanimity: "Do you prefer (check one) Robert Kennedy or William Buckley?" Every single one of the critics, even the nonconformists, the anarchists, and the solopsists, chose Robert Kennedy. Chalk one up for me, and say not the struggle naught availeth.

For a while there, as I scanned the entries after that question, my heart pounded, fearing the vote would not be unanimous, for I saw a concentration of qualifying type appended to one answer. It turned out to be Dwight Macdonald's, *Esquire*'s movie critic and the world's general critic, who was gracious enough to be impartial in his disapproval, citing Dr. Johnson's uneasiness at being asked to "settle the precedence between a flea and a louse"—but, under the strain of having to make the choice, he ticked off the name RFK.

Mr. Macdonald did not otherwise feel a strain in selecting between alternatives, preferring, one assumes robustly,

Trotsky over Stalin (he might have been vexed if Ho Chi Minh had been thrown in), *Newsweek* over *Time*. San Francisco over Los Angeles, radio over TV—and, perhaps most significant of all, cats over dogs. Birds of a feather, as Dr. Johnson used to say.

The poll is to a considerable extent sheer entertainment, but it serves, of course, to make yet another redundant demonstration of the homogeneity of opinion, particularly concerning matters of political interest, among our governing cultural elite. For instance, there is no one at all who is "enthusiastic" about Lyndon Johnson, a slight one is prepared to let go as, at best, statistically negligible.

One critic (for *Status* magazine, not surprisingly) came out foursquare ("dislike strongly") against government subsidies of the arts, greatly distinguishing himself from his colleagues. Indeed there seemed to be great hope for this critic, and I traced his vote profile analysis, panting hopefully. He soared easily over Beecher's Brook (he "dislikes strongly" Allen Ginsberg) and other formidable hurdles (he likes bullfights and is neutral on Drs. Masters and Johnson)—only to find him beached on the shoals of Ronald Reagan, of whom he "disapproves," like everyone else, except a brave two or three critics who class themselves as "neutral."

Strawinthewindwise, there is the interesting popularity contest between *Time* magazine and *Newsweek*—which *Newsweek* wins handily, almost 2 to 1. For those who need a key to that one, it works this way: *Time* is more literate, but nothing is more sinful than literacy if the prejudices aren't predictably right, and *Time* is sometimes reactionary—*e.g.*, on Vietnam, patriotism in general, and religion. *Time* is also more feline, and cats don't like cattiness outside their own fraternity (the movie reviewer of *Time* magazine is one of the shrewdest observers and inventive verbalists in the business).

Besides, it can be fashionable to take ·the slightly less popular of the two available choices—*e.g.*, which do you prefer, color or black-and-white TV, to which the "in" answer is, of course, black and white. But only Richard Schickel of *Life* magazine prefers Los Angeles to San Francisco, which may be a tribute to his taste, his perversity, or the influence of Mrs. Schickel.

Everyone prefers Trotsky over Stalin, except a few who

write in Lenin. (A curious absence of wisecracks in response to that curious question.) Jung has it all over Adler, the Beatles over the Stones, Simone Signoret over Ann-Margret (confession: Who is the lady?); *Batman* and *Peyton Place* are tied; General de Gaulle no one is enthusiastic about, but only the semistalwart *Status* reviewer dislikes him strongly.

One thing more, not exactly surprising. Dostoevski wins in a walk over Tolstoi. Indeed, no one voted for Tolstoi (nor would I have, given the choice). But then no one would have been more indifferent to the results of such a poll than Tolstoi, or more contemptuous of the idea of it than Dostoevski, who would have found so many contemporary intellectuals well cast as underground men.

RICHARD GOODWIN AND THE GREAT SOCIETY

August 26, 1965

Richard Goodwin's attempt a couple of weeks ago to explain the meaning of the Great Society deserves more attention than it has gotten because indeed it was, as the New York *Times* said, "the most sophisticated and revealing commentary to date."

Mr. Goodwin is the bright young thing inherited by President Johnson from President Kennedy. He rose to prominence from the ashes of the Bay of Pigs as an expert, nobody quite knew how, in Latin American affairs. It is he who reputedly conceived the idea of the Alliance for Progress and who paused at a meeting of the Organization of American States in 1961 at Punta del Este to chat with Che Guevara, causing the eyebrows to lift in all the chancelleries of the world. He could get away with that kind of thing because he is very young, and his brashness is one of his most engaging weapons. At one point he is said to have overdone it with JFK, who put him in the deepfreeze, whence he emerged, leaving Latin America to Thomas Mann, as big thinker for Lyndon Johnson.

I do not mean to sound disrespectful of Mr. Goodwin, because I am not. I merely fear him. His concept of the Great Society is as authentic as anybody's because he is suspected (see, for instance, Theodore White's *The Making of a President*) of having invented the confounded thing, whose principal exegete he logically is. The key phrase, for cryptographers who desire to learn the meaning of the society that is supposed to shape our future, is the following, which you will see repeated time after time:

"The Great Society is concerned not with the quantity of our goods but the quality of our lives." The phrase has that dreadful singsong assonance built on quasi-antitheses which is the hallmark of New Frontier rhetoric. ("We must not negotiate out of fear, but we must not fear to negotiate.")

Notwithstanding that it is evolving more as a slogan than as an answer to the riddle of humanity, what it does mean is that the government of the United States, under Lyndon Johnson, proposes to concern itself with the quality of American life. And this is something very new in the political theory of free nations. The quality of life has heretofore depended on the quality of the human beings who gave tone to that life, and they were its priests and poets—not its bureaucrats.

Mind you, Mr. Goodwin realizes that the growth in the quantity of government (and, I might add, the diminution in its quality) in the generation since it began coming out of the walls, has led to the disturbing phenomenon of a sense of individual impotence. The American people, Mr. Goodwin realizes, feel sort of useless and even a little afraid. Thus, the Great Society must "ensure our people the environment, the capacities, and the social structures which will give them a meaningful chance to pursue their individual happiness."

He then confesses the need for the restoration of community responsibility. "As we advance we will inevitably place more and more emphasis on local responsibility . . . only in this way can we give Americans the chance to look to their own efforts for the enrichment of their own lives. The very process of looking to others damages the chance for individual action which will give fuller meaning to our lives." In the few weeks since Mr. Goodwin wrote those words, the Great Society has deprived the local communities of the right to set their own voting rights standards, of the right to allow a man to work without joining a union, and of the right to veto poverty projects if the governor finds them badly designed for that state.

As he looks about him, Mr. Goodwin is a little bit

despondent at the dearth of ideas on just how to structure a society which will give every individual that happiness over the quality of himself that the Great Society expects of him. "Today, with the exception of a few men— men like Ken Galbraith, and Michael Harrington and Paul Goodman"—American society simply isn't coming through. Thus, Mr. Goodwin names a sort of cultural-economic *dirigiste,* a doctrinaire socialist, and an anarchist as the voices of freshness. And then Mr. Goodwin concedes it will take a long time before the Great Society is finally established, which is good news for all of us living today.

McNAMARA'S NEWSPEAK

May 26, 1966

Secretary McNamara's use of English is odd. It certainly isn't idiomatic, and yet it isn't by any means Bureaucratic-Exact, or even Just Plain Functional. I fear there is a trace of Newspeak in it. Consider a paragraph or two from his address to the newspaper editors in Montreal a week ago. The Secretary is talking about the two senses in which the United States military can help the rest of the world, the first and obvious being direct military assistance.

"The second—and perhaps less understood category of military assistance in a modernizing nation—is training in civic action. 'Civic Action' "—Mr. McNamara paused to explain—"is . . . one of those semantic puzzles. Too few Americans—and too few officials in developing nations—really comprehend what military civic action means. Essentially, it means using indigenous military forces for non-traditional military projects—projects that are useful to the local population in fields such as education, public works, health, sanitation, agriculture—indeed, anything connected with economic or social progress."

The above passage is by no means easy to understand. What is "non-traditional military projects"? Does he think that is the same as "traditionally non-military projects"? Why should civic action be a semantic puzzle? Or did McNamara mean that "military civic action" is a semantic

36

puzzle? It is worse than that. Syntactically it is an abomination. So is it conceptually.

Mr. McNamara weighed in, as usual, with his statistics, and it transpires that, among other things, during the past four years "United States-assisted civic action programs" have provided "dental care to approximately four million people." And McNamara's clincher: "What is important is that all this was done by indigenous men in uniform. Quite apart from the developmental projects themselves, the program powerfully alters the negative image of the military man as the oppressive preserver of the stagnant status quo."

There is a terrible congestion of nonsense in the sentences herein quoted, and the implications are enough to take one's breath away. A country's military should concern itself exclusively with the national defense. The whole of the military tradition is not otherwise bearable in a free society. The discipline, the automatic obedience, the rigid hierarchies—these are the paraphernalia of the battlefield, not of the schoolroom, or highway construction company, or dentist's office. If a country's soldiery haven't enough to do to keep them profitably engaged, let them imitate the Swiss system, which circulates its citizens back and forth from farm to barracks with very little confusion, but with never any ambiguity: The man is a soldier or a civilian. Never half of each. Never a semantic puzzle.

Secretary McNamara went on to urge that all American youth give two years of their life to service to the country. He used the word "voluntary," but others (e.g., Senator Javits) have already called for compulsory service. McNamara called on those who do not qualify for service in the military to join the Peace Corps or participate in the poverty program. Now one wonders whether the instinct to duty which all Americans feel, or should feel, will evolve into what Secretary McNamara would then call "military civic duty."

One of the reasons why what McNamara calls "semantic puzzles" are confused and confusing is that language tinkering is the way to circumnavigate great and sound traditions. In this case, McNamara, using the language of Orwell, seems to be introducing into respectability the

37

idea that Americans should be drafted to perform "anything connected with economic or social progress."

MALCOLM MUGGERIDGE
ON THE ESTABLISHMENT

September 9, 1965

A half dozen years ago the term was utterly unknown. I remember using it once in a lecture at the National War College and noting the blank bewilderment on the faces of all those bright young colonels and commanders and GS 15's. "The Liberal Establishment"—what on earth is that? Then Richard Rovere wrote an article on the subject, half in fun, half serious, and the question began to intrude into the public consciousness: Is there such a thing as a Liberal Establishment?

What does the term mean? It means a loose and spontaneous association of the people who occupy most of the command posts in our society, who tend to react the same way to certain kinds of stimuli, and who—because they are the style setters of the age—pretty well succeed in planting their axioms on the public thought process. For instance? For instance, Tshombe is not quite okay, and Boumediene is not quite not okay.

M. Stanton Evans, the illustrious young editor of the Indianapolis *News,* has now written a book called, very simply, *The Liberal Establishment.* It tries to give the answer to why we end up feeling sort of suspicious about a Tshombe—and sort of tolerant toward a Boumediene. He piles example on example of the kind of thing the Liberal Establishment is a sucker for. Needless to say he has not, in performing this valuable work of contemporary sociology, endeared himself to members of the Liberal Establishment, who, for reasons altogether understandable, do not like to think of themselves as in any way predictable, particularly when their predictability is shown, as by Mr. Evans, to result from a continuing moral lesion.

By definition, it is a risky thing to expose any Establishment—because an Establishment does not merit the name unless it has the power to govern opinion and to discipline the mutinous. Under the circumstances, references to Mr. Evans' book by the British critic Malcolm Muggeridge, who reviews it in the current issue of *Esquire* magazine, are quite remarkable. Now Mr. Muggeridge is a very complicated man—not exactly a liberal, but on the other hand not by any stretch of the imagination a conservative. He is an aristocratic iconoclast, who on one occasion even took on the Queen of England ("frumpy, frowzy, and banal"). But notwithstanding his helplessness if there is an unbroken icon in the house, he has one of the sharpest eyes in the business and is unsurpassed as a social critic.

Mr. Muggeridge does not doubt at all that the West is ruled by a Liberal Establishment which "ruthlessly, and where necessary corruptly and unscrupulously, seeks to perpetuate itself." He gives a couple of examples, to be sure mostly old hat. "Who, for instance," he asks, "could have been less liberal than the late Stalin? Yet he enjoyed in his day the adulation or at any rate the tolerance of most of the liberal intelligentsia of the West, from André Gide to Bernard Shaw. . . . In my time as a newspaper correspondent in Moscow," he continues, "the most assiduous and untruthful champion the Soviet Government had was the late Walter Duranty of the *New York Times*. The same newspaper's man in Cuba was, it seems, initially strong for Castro." What lessons does he draw from the liberals' strange attraction to their enemies? "We liberals are so made that anyone who wants to murder us is a hero and anyone foolish enough to be on our side is a villain. We despise a Tshombe who, by the large, would seem to be well disposed toward us, and venerate an Nkrumah, who hates our guts and never hesitates to say so."

And he concludes his analysis with a soaring piece of overstatement which I shall nevertheless pass along: "Liberalism will be seen historically as the great destructive force of our time; much more so than communism, fascism, nazism, or any of the other lunatic creeds which make such immediate havoc. Compared with the long-term consequences of a Gilbert Murray, a Bertrand Russell, a Mrs. Eleanor Roosevelt, Hitler was an ineffectual dreamer, Stalin a Father Christmas, and Mussolini an Arcadian shepherd. It is liberalism which makes the Gaderene swine so frisky; as mankind goes to their last incinerated extinction the voice of the liberal will be heard proclaiming the realization at last of life, liberty, and the pursuit of happiness."

Well. Boys will be boys, and, concededly, the typewriter presents awful temptations to those who know how to program a great big shock for the reader. (I am glad I am not the editor of *Esquire,* with the responsibility for . . . "Dear Mr. Jones: I assure you that Mr. Muggeridge did *not* mean to compare Eleanor Roosevelt to Adolf Hitler. . . .") But after you have wrung out the naughty-boy lather, you have, from a very famous and acute critic, a formal recognition of the important phenomenon isolated by Mr. Evans in his important book: There is such a thing as a Liberal Establishment. And anyone who seeks to understand what is going on nowadays ought to have a look at this enlightening volume.

HARVEY SCHECHTER
ON LIBERAL ANTI-COMMUNISM

May 6, 1962

Every time the sun sets, our knowledge of Communism evaporates just a little bit. Unless we work hard, day after day, to replenish our dissipating reserves, those of us who have known tend to forget, and those who never knew— the generation coming out of childhood—tend to grow up in ignorance of all those gruesome data about the nature of the enemy we face. "It is particularly discouraging," Harvey Schechter writes in the New York *Times Sunday Magazine,* "to hear young people making the kinds of statements about the Soviet Union and the Communists which were the vogue a generation ago—statements which haunt us in the Sixties like voices from the past."

The complaint comes from a strange quarter. Usually, writers for the New York *Times* are busy pooh-poohing those who complain of a national ignorance about Communism. And the title of Mr. Schechter's article, moreover, is "The Liberals Have Helped the Radical Right." It is his thesis that there has been "a tragic failure by liberals to understand their own responsibility for the current state of affairs." The result, he observes, is that organizations the liberals disapprove of have taken over as the most conspicuous teachers of anti-Communism. He cites, for instance, Dr. Fred Schwarz's Christian Anti-Communist Crusade.

Mr. Schechter, himself a liberal, must be complimented for his courage in frankly confessing the liberals' grave dereliction. He has the courage to say that while it is true that some conservatives "are inclined to see Communists everywhere, some liberals are inclined to see Communists nowhere." Recently at a meeting of Californians concerned with civil liberties, he found that some of his associates hadn't the least idea how to distinguish between Communist objectives and liberal objectives. There are liberals, he says, who believe that Communists are simply an overbred species of liberals. (As a matter of fact, there are conservatives who believe the same thing.) "Liberals have failed their own movement and the whole community by their failure to educate the American public in a sane and sober manner about the true character of the Communist conspiracy."

Mr. Schechter is, of course, right. Professor Peter Viereck wrote a book twenty years ago identifying the "shame" and the "glory" of the intellectuals. Their glory was the speed with which they identified the Nazi menace. Their shame was the reluctance they have always shown in turning on the Communists.

What the Vierecks and the Schechters fail to examine is precisely that aspect of the problem that haunts American anti-Communist conservatives. We ask ourselves: Is it merely neglect that has caused the liberals to wage anti-Communism so incompletely? Or are there other causes, of a mysterious nature, which account for the continuing blindness of the liberals to the Communist problem? Does James Roosevelt clamor for the abolition of the House Committee on Un-American Activities merely because he is stupid? Do liberals glide into the Fair Play for Cuba Committee merely because they are gullible? Do professors of political science and international relations agitate against nuclear tests because of their ignorance of politics and diplomacy?

The melancholy answer is that we have here not merely an accidental blindness of the kind one might hope to cure by putting potent drops, distilled by the anti-Communist department of the New York *Times,* into their eyes; it is a

41

deep psychological problem which in our time has caused the paralysis of the liberal will when faced with the tensest problems of anti-Communist political warfare.

The French social philosopher Jules Monnerot once sighed that the West is incapable of effectively opposing Communism because "the Right cannot understand, and the Left is infected." M. Monnerot does not suggest that the liberals are pro-Communist, but rather that in their response to Communism they have always been, and always will be, distracted from their purpose by the Communists' disingenuous self-identification with goals which they pretend to share along with the left liberals: civil rights, state socialism, anticapitalism, anticolonialism, anti-religion, the superordination of life over against any of the ideals in whose behalf death, heroism—great wars, even—have been considered tolerable sacrifices.

Why do liberals, one wonders, continue to rail against the anti-Communist schools of Dr. Fred Schwarz? Even Mr. Schechter, while deploring the state of American ignorance about Communism, cannot resist disdaining Dr. Schwarz, whom he identifies as "an Australian physician who has traded his stethoscope for a microphone."

One wishes the liberals would trade their quarrels against anti-Communist conservatives, against General Franco and Chiang Kai-shek, against Presidents Diem and Fuentes, for quarrels against the Communists and those who abet them. But we are asking them to pick a quarrel with themselves.

WHAT'S HAPPENING
TO LEFT ANTI-COMMUNISM?

January 19, 1967

Someone recently charged that no committee composed primarily of American liberals has ever protested the barbarities of the Vietcong. I received this information skeptically, but on poking around found that it appears to be true. What has happened to the anti-Communist left?

The question is explicitly asked, and some answers are proferred, in a fascinating essay by Max Geltman, published in the current issue of *National Review*. Mr. Geltman is a liberal scholar and publisher whose special field of interest is the anti-Semitism of the left, which, he has tried over the years to demonstrate, is the prime source of that disease. (Recently he cited the results of an inquiry into French anti-Semitism which show that among political groupings anti-Semitism is highest in the French Communist Party.)

Mr. Geltman reminds us of how it used to be, during the late thirties, the forties, and the early fifties. In those days among the toughest anti-Communist critics were liberals and socialists, most of whom wrote at one time or another for the *New Leader,* a weekly social-democratic magazine sponsored for the most part by New York labor unions, and for *Partisan Review,* the highbrow quarterly, whose editors, now as then, are William Phillips and Philip Rahv.

Just twenty years ago the crisis of the day had to do with Iranian oil—whether to intervene to protect Iran from going over to the Soviet Union, which hungered for the vast deposits of Iranian oil. The fellow travelers quickly took their places, and the chorus went up against interference with Iran, in favor of the idea of socializing oil—but it was all too much for the editors of the *Partisan Review* who published a sham-withering editorial heard 'round the liberal world. As one rereads it, in 1967, one wonders why it isn't equally relevant today, substituting South Vietnam for Iran, Red China for Russia, Ho Chi Minh for Stalin:

"Yes indeed," wrote the aroused liberals sarcastically, "Russia must be secure even if we have to sacrifice the security of all her neighbors. What about Iran's security?

"The longer [Stalin] can operate in Europe, the more democrats he can shoot. Thanks in large part to his various Fifth Columns abroad, who consciously or unconsciously succeed in misleading public opinion. The 'liberals' of PR, the Nation, the New Republic, have always required easy whipping boys . . . every argument they use to justify intervention in Spain is a valid argument for intervention in Russia. Spain is totalitarian? Beside Stalin's monolithic police state Franco's fascism is a pretty amateur affair.

"It is clear that [these] liberals are embarked upon nothing less than a policy of appeasement of Russia. . . . A second feature of this new appeasement is the consistent
43

attack upon the State Department. . . . But perhaps the grossest ingredient in this new dish of appeasement is the constant 'liberal' shout of war. If war is not inevitable, does it not become a man's duty to cry stinking fish and face up to the inevitability?

"The services [of these liberals] are probably . . . spontaneous and 'pure.' But this does not mitigate their guilt for a campaign of concealment, misrepresentation, and deception in the interests of a foreign power. We are long since familiar with the fact that the Communist Party is a Fifth Column. These 'liberals,' have become a more potent and dangerous Fifth Column since they succeed in deceiving a good many more people."

That editorial really tore it, and the editors were blamed and praised all over the world. The prestigious John Dewey moved into the controversy, identifying himself completely with the editors and adding that "it is a pleasure to have plain speaking beautifully phrased" (Dewey was never much as a literary critic).

How things are changed! At last spring's international P.E.N. convention, the writers refused to seat the delegates from Spain and Portugal, but smothered the Soviet delegation with togetherness, and joined with Arthur Miller in helping to table a modestly worded resolution protesting continuing anti-Semitism in the Soviet Union. There were writers at that convention who had applauded the anti-Communist tocsin sounded by the *Partisan Review*'s editors twenty years ago, but now they go along with the same acts they then condemned. The arguments they isolated, scorned, penetrated, finally won them over, attesting to the acuity of their own warning that these were the most dangerous arguments of all, so dangerous they finally infected the pathologists who first identified them.

HATE AMERICA

March 18, 1967

Further on the question: Who are the new pro-Communists?—further evidence that the new breed is negatively defined. They are not so much pro-Communist as anti-American. But since they work at anti-Americanism feverishly and at anti-Communism not at all, the vector of their analysis and passion is pro-Communist.

The current issue of *Partisan Review,* the quarterly omnium-gatherum of literature leftists, features a symposium simply called "America," which might better have been called "Hate America." To give you an idea, the *New Yorker*'s archliberal Richard Rovere is, in that company, the voice of smug reaction.

Just about everyone in the symposium seems to be agreed that the United States is irredeemably a racist country. "As some Negroes begin to move beyond civil rights into the need for radical changes in education, housing and employment policies," writes the critic Nat Hentoff, echoing the views of the majority, "the fundamentally racist character of the majority of the white adult population is unmistakably revealed. In September 1966, Senator Eastland observed: 'The sentiment of the entire country now stands with the Southern people.' There wasn't much hyperbole in his satisfaction." Mr. Hentoff wants to run Dr. Benjamin Spock for President. (If they'd let babies vote, Spock might do well.)

Boy, do they hate LBJ! Paul Jacobs, the labor writer, urges American youth as their highest duty to let it be known "that the America of President Johnson is not the only America there is." Jack Newfield, the *Village Voice*'s most agonized conscience, says that LBJ's "egotism, deceitfulness, pettiness, vindictiveness, provincialism are poisoning the country. To see the President on the 7 o'clock news each night, and know he is lying again, does more damage to us than any specific policy."

And always, right after a criticism of LBJ, there follows, as inexorably as the day follows the night, the friendly reference to Bobby—"I don't know whether Robert Kennedy would end the war, wage a more grassrootsy War on Poverty, or send more federal registrars into the rural South, but I do think his intelligence, candor, wit and activism would have a beneficial effect. His style and character could unify, inspire, energize people, rather than disgust, alienate and embarrass them."

And then there is the critic and novelist Susan Sontag, a sweet young thing, who puts it this way: "When [and if] the man in the White House who paws people and scratches [himself] in public is replaced by the man who dislikes being touched and finds Yevtushenko 'an interesting fellow,' American intellectuals won't be so disheartened."

The said Miss Sontag is the most expressive of the spokesmen of discontent. "Today's America, with Ronald Reagan the new daddy of California and John Wayne chawing spareribs in the White House, is pretty much the same Yahooland that Mencken was describing. . . . The quality of American life is an insult to the possibilities of human growth. . . . If the Bill of Rights were put to a national referendum as a new piece of legislation, it would meet the same fate as New York City's Civilian Review Board. Most of the people in this country believe what Goldwater believes, and always have. But most of them don't know it. Let's hope they don't find out."

Is it just America that they hate? No, not really. It is the West. "The truth is that Mozart, Pascal, Boolean algebra, Shakespeare, parliamentary government, baroque churches, Newton, the emancipation of women, Kant, Marx, Balanchine ballets, et al., don't redeem what this particular civilization has wrought upon the world. The white race is the cancer of human history. . . ."

Miss Sontag, whose sense of humor is about as well developed as King Kong's, unguardedly concedes that American culture is "making grey neurotics of most of us," to which the appropriate answer (she means most of us who write for *Partisan Review*) is, alas, not altogether reassuring for a sane American. Because *PR*'s zoo is an influential lot. "Americans know," Miss Sontag informs us, "[that] their backs are against the wall, that 'they' want to take it away from 'us.' And I must say America deserves to have it taken away." An authentic voice of the new pro-Communism.

NO MORE COMRADES

September 9, 1967

A brilliantly informed editor of an august national publication mused at lunch that surely the national torment over Vietnam traces to the global unintelligibility of Lyndon Johnson's position. If Vietnam is a local affair, we have no more business dying there than we do dying for the freedom of Biafra. If it is a part of an international enterprise of which we are intended as the strategic victims, then by all means we must be prepared to die there, in order to interdict a major salient that might otherwise reach across the Pacific to our own continental shoreline.

But Mr. Johnson, whose habit of mind is schizophrenic in so many things, confuses us. It isn't only our unctuous bridge building to Eastern Europe and Russia, though that is confusing enough if we meditate on the excruciating paradox that machinery Made in America is used to make products to sustain the Vietcong army. It goes beyond that, to the point of a creeping softness toward Communism, of which there have been several recent expressions.

Consider that Secretary Robert S. McNamara, in his extended report to the Senate Armed Services Committee defending the current stalemate in Vietnam, disdains to refer, even one time, to the North Vietnamese as "the enemy." From which it naturally follows that vis-à-vis the North Vietnamese, we must watch ourselves very carefully, must be careful not to close their ports, not to interfere unduly with their agriculture or commerce. Air strikes against the movement of provisions to South Vietnam, yes—but carefully, oh, so carefully, much as we would be careful to respect, to the extent possible, our neighbor's property even while making use of it to fight a fire on the adjacent lot. The war in South Vietnam, says Mr. McNamara, has to do with assuring "the people of South Vietnam the freedom to choose their own political and economic institutions." Period? If so, of course, we have no business there. It is an inescapable conclusion that we are refusing to impose our will on North Vietnam because we are afraid that to do so would get in the way of the grander policy of convergence.

Anti-Communism, we all know, is unfashionable. SNCC was only a couple of years ahead of the trend when its officers said coolly in 1964 that they knew there were Communists in their organization, so what?

Kingsley Amis, the British novelist, writes bitterly about his disillusion with the left he cherished for so many years. "I might think differently if Mr. Wilson had done what he ought to do and what, after gaining his increased majority last year, I fairly fully expected him to do: boot half a dozen of the Communist M.P.'s out of the Labour Party and threaten the rest with expulsion unless they step into line. And say why.

"Why? For a set of reasons odiously familiar to both sides in this matter: because a Communist's loyalties lie, not with his own country, but with a foreign Power, one that is, both externally and internally, hostile to democracy, and therefore our enemy. To some of us, enemies of our country are worth opposing; others find something positively attractive about them. It is having at last become fully aware of this that has led me finally to break off my lingering love-hate affair with the Left. . . ."

It can't happen here? But it has happened, in a strange sort of a way in the Vietnam war, our bizarre conduct of which may well be viewed by historians not as anti-Communism, but as anti-anti-Communism.

That's the way it's going everywhere. " 'I'm an open Communist,' Don Hamerquist (of Portland, Oregon) said. 'I believe in being open. I'm also a division leader in the Democratic party—I have 24 precincts under my jurisdiction. I assume the party leaders know about it by now.' " Well, John Bailey at least knows about it, because an editor down in Florida saw the clipping from the *Oregon Journal* and asked Bailey for an explanation. It came. Sorry about that, it said, but we can't do anything about it—local government, you know. (You know how much the Democratic Party cares about local government.) Expelling Mr. Hamerquist from the Democratic Party would be like bombing Haiphong. You just don't treat Communists like enemies.

SENATOR FULBRIGHT AT JOHNS HOPKINS

May 14, 1966

Really, it sometimes seems as though Senator William Fulbright is becoming more than flesh and blood can bear. His recent series of lectures at Johns Hopkins University wandered all over the lot, but seemed to arrive home at the conclusion that the United States' role in Vietnam not only is unjustified legally and morally, but is to be understood historically as one of those spasms of aimless military exuberance which are characteristic of great na-

48

tions overgrown in the arrogance of power.

The Senator cited other civilizations similarly addicted, in an effort at historical analogy which left students of history mystified by the strained connections—indeed, mystified at what is beginning to look like personal mania.

Senator Fulbright appears not to be able to think about anything else besides Vietnam, and his statements concerning it are like a fanatic's, growing stronger and stronger, more and more disorderly.

At his final lecture, for instance, he sputtered that "both literally and figuratively, Saigon has become an American brothel." Most of the criticism he has received for that statement zeroes in on the literal applicability of the word.

But it is the figurative applicability of the word that is most astounding. The Senator appears to be saying that Saigon is engaging in a great act of immorality in order to give pleasure to the United States of America. In order to justify this metaphor, it becomes necessary to assert the proposition that Saigon, as headquarters of the movement to resist the Vietcong, is acting immorally. And to assert the proposition that the United States enjoys sending its soldiers there to be killed and its dollars there to be spent by the billions.

Anyone who seriously believes that it is immoral to resist the Communist terrorists or that the United States is such a power as enjoys such hideous experiences as this one in Vietnam, or the other in Korea, has lost his hold on reason.

We must hope, reaching for charitable alternatives, that Senator Fulbright lost his hold on the language and used the term "figuratively" more or less because he was scratching around for an adverb to waltz about with "literally."

Which brings us to the embarrassing contemplation of the Senator's influence as chairman of the Senate Foreign Relations Committee. Senator Barry Goldwater suggested last week that the Senator ought to resign the post on the ground that his position as chairman gives an inflated importance to his pronouncements. But I disagree with Senator Goldwater. Unwelcome though Fulbright's eccentricity is at this point in history when we need —precisely because our engagement to Vietnam is more like a visit to Gethsemane than to Sodom—to steel ourselves to the necessity of duty, it is healthy to hear a voice in the legislature criticize the Chief Executive.

The satellization of Congress by the President of the United States is a long-term danger which Senator Goldwater has frequently remarked, and we need only to consider in order to force ourselves to endure Fulbright that in the future the situation might very well be reversed; might be as it was in the novel by Allen Drury *Advise and Consent,* where the President is the appeaser, and the principal Senator in the Foreign Relations Committee, the exercised patriot. Far better, as I say, to tighten our belts and offer up Senator Fulbright's daily appearances in the newspaper as a small sacrifice in behalf of our boys at the brothel.

It is strange to consider that but for the accident of Senator Fulbright's origin, he might have been serving us as Secretary of State. It is generally accepted that when elected President, John Kennedy first considered Fulbright for Secretary of State but was warned away from him on the ground of his consistent record of opposition to civil rights for Negroes—it is most vividly recalled that Senator Fulbright refused to criticize Governor Orval Faubus when the governor closed down the schools in Little Rock in 1957 and became the principal badman of recent American history. Otherwise, Fulbright would have become Secretary of State. In which event it would have been quite appropriate for Senator Goldwater to call for his dismissal, assuming it had not already been effected by the President.

Under the circumstance, there is no alternative to coexistence. Though, at least we are free, as individual citizens, under the First, Fifth, and Fourteenth Amendments, to turn off our hearing aids when the Senator opens his mouth and, on those few occasions when he closes it, to look out at the heavens and rejoice at the momentary composure of the universe.

DEMOCRACY, LATIN AMERICAN STYLE

Mexico City, July 9, 1964

It is an offense in Mexico not to vote. I mean if they catch you not voting, they can fine you, and besides, there is great moral disgrace attached to the delinquency, because, as the official broadcasts keep reminding you, the vote is a high and precious privilege, and good citizenship requires that you exercise that privilege. It is all very impressive, and Mexico has earned a reputation as the most democratic and stable of Latin American nations. She is certainly democratic if the test is how many of her citizens vote. And she is certainly stable, because the same political party wins every election. Never, ever, fails.

Not, understand, that other political parties are illegal, as, for instance, in Spain. They are perfectly legal; only there is a sort of general understanding, on the part of all who exercise power of any sort in Mexico, that no opposition party ever, under any circumstances, get anywhere. Here and there a harangue by the opposition is all very well, but nothing serious, you know—nothing that might stand in the way of the ruling party, the Partido Revolucionario Institucional (PRI). The new President, by the way, is Gustavo Díaz Ordaz. As is almost always the case with a President-elect, he had only a minor reputation before the party elders decided to tap him, back in the fall. That is true of almost every potential candidate because politically this is a heliocentric society (pretty much as its getting to be in the United States, where increasingly, we are all, public figures and private, mere epigoni who by some act of cosmic favor are permitted to orbit, at a respectful distance, about the Presidential sun).

This, of course, poses a problem when the time comes for the sun to set, which, in Mexico, is every six years. It is a dimly held dogma of the Mexican Revolution of 1910 that no President may serve more than a single term, and as for this, there is no nonsense—there have been no FDR's in recent Mexican history, who contrived successfully to set aside tradition. And so when the new sun is designated, the entire country is harnessed to the effort of popularizing, not to say apotheosizing, the new re-

51

deemer's name, so much so that all Mexico seemed to have been transformed into a clumsy way of spelling Díaz Ordaz. His name appears across the podiums of policemen who direct traffic and across the mountain peaks; nothing, but nothing, on which a placard can be hung or a motto painted is overlooked. One has the feeling that only the clouds in the sky, which declined to spell out Díaz Ordaz, are antidemocratic. So that by election Sunday he had become, as I once noted observing the election of Mr. Ordaz's predecessor, the best-known thing in Mexico this side of Coca-Cola.

During the three days immediately preceding the election, no one is allowed to electioneer; the idea is to build up great suspense over who will win the exciting contest. I doubt if 1 Mexican in 100 could name the Harold Stassens who ran against Díaz Ordaz; no matter, what we have here is democratic theater, and what matters is to go through the motions. To give the drama a spiritual dimension, bars are closed down tight—not merely on the day of the election, as is the general practice, but on the day *before* the election. "Why?" a visitor asked thirstily. "Because it is important," said the concierge gravely, "that one's political judgment be not disturbed by a hangover."

Mexico's is truly a managed economy, probably as near a socialized state as exists in this hemisphere, short of Bolivia. The government hand is everywhere, yet the economic inertia of the age carries the country forward, sort of. Mexico has not regained the economic preeminence among Latin American countries that it had in 1910, at the beginning of all those revolutions that so tied up the country and led, finally, to the hegemony of PRI. But it inches forward, sometimes seems almost raring to go; only at such moments it must register its enthusiasm in triplicate before blasting off, by which time its energy is often dissipated.

"For three hundred years," the guides tell you at the museum, "we were enslaved by the Spaniards." The visitor forbears asking for how many hundred years before that the people were enslaved by the Aztecs or from meditating on how many hundred years of servitude lie ahead of them to the successors of Montezuma, Cortes, Juárez, Porfirio Díaz—to the buttoned-down bureaucrats whom the people are given the freedom to reelect every six years.

QUIET: CONSPIRACY AT WORK

January 6, 1963

It is very unfashionable nowadays to believe that conspiracies can accomplish anything at all, and it is widely charged that to suggest that a conspiracy might account for any American reversal whatsoever is un-American, and worse, unsophisticated. Awhile ago General MacArthur's chief of staff wrote a book charging that the reason why the Red Chinese ventured to descend south of the Yalu was that they found out from their spies in Washington that orders had gone out to General MacArthur that he must not under any circumstances bomb the Manchurian bases. The critics jumped all over the poor author, pooh-poohing such melodramatic political speculation. And, of course, the fuss over Robert Welch of the John Birch Society is to a very considerable extent based on Mr. Welch's fascination with the conspiracy as the operative agent of our decline and fall.

I happen to believe that if there were not a single Communist spy in America, we'd still be losing the cold war—because the classrooms of Harvard are simply no substitute for the playing fields of Eton. And where our statesmen go to school, they drink deeply in liberalism, and liberalism makes for the worst and most ineffective foreign policy in the history of diplomacy.

But I have a very great respect for the accomplishments of professional conspirators. Great respect, for instance, for the Fuchs-Rosenberg apparatus, which succeeded in whisking off the secrets of our atom bomb to the Soviet Union, enabling our enemies to detonate a bomb in 1949, six years before our military planners had anticipated, thus rocking our entire strategic thought. I have respect for the accomplishments of Martin and Mitchell, who eloped to Moscow, surfacing just after our U-2 plane was apprehended, and respect for the theory, held widely in Washington, that the boys arrived in Moscow with the full details of our U-2 operation, on the basis of which the

Russians were able to knock down Powers' plane and alter diplomatic history. Do you remember Israel Beer? He was the state of Israel's "Barney" Baruch, friend and confidant of everyone in the government, especial friend of Ben-Gurion. What do you know? Two years ago he was arrested; it transpired he had been a Soviet spy for years. It is conjectured that Beer informed Russia that Israel was on the point of invading Suez in 1956, whereupon Khrushchev felt free to send the tanks to crush the Budapest rioters. Had he not the assurance of the great international distraction to be caused imminently by the invasion of Suez, he would not have had the nerve to march on Budapest, and the revolution might have succeeded.

And it isn't just Martin Dies, Joe McCarthy, and Robert Welch who talk about conspiracies. The liberal hero Thomas Jefferson waged his campaign in 1800 on the charge that the opposition was conspiring to undermine the American Revolution and introduce a monarchy. The liberal hero Andrew Jackson charged that the Bank of the United States was engaged in a vast plot to subvert republican government. Abraham Lincoln in 1858 went around the country insisting that there was a conspiracy embracing two Presidents, a Chief Justice of the Supreme Court, and the Senator from Illinois (the famous Four Horsemen—"Stephen, Franklin, Roger, and James") to spread slavery, not only to the free territories, but to the free states. Many of the bloody shirt elections after the Civil War were fought on the premise that there was a plot to undo the results of the war and restore slavery. As a matter of fact, the first party to hold a national convention was the Anti-Masonic Party, which charged that the Masons were in a conspiracy to assassinate all their enemies.

Conspiracy talk, in a word, may be naïve and may be deplorable, but it is hard to find anything that is more authentically American.

As in so many situations, the truth lies somewhere in between. I tend to fear that the pendulum is going not too far in the direction of Robert Welch, but too far in the direction of total nonchalance about the fact that (a) conspiracies do exist and (b) that they do accomplish great purposes. At this very moment, thousands (not hundreds, thousands) of men are receiving training on how best to take advantage of your weaknesses and mine and Mr. Johnson's. And some of these men, conspiring with others, will affect the battle lines of the future, and always they will cackle at the foggy, foggy superstitions of our dogged intellectualizers, that conspiracies —assuming, sniff, that they exist—don't, sniff, accomplish anything very much.

WE WANT OUR POLITICIANS
TO BE HYPOCRITES

October 17, 1964

A few weeks ago at Hershey, Pennsylvania, a candidate for the Presidency of the United States was made to say something which the general public viewed as recantation, pure and simple. To declare that Senator Goldwater was made to say something he does not believe is more than this admirer of the Senator is willing to do. What the Senator did say—and this is as far as anyone is entitled to go—is something that runs contrary to his stated opinions as expressed over the years. His remarks about civil rights and the UN were merely conciliatory; with respect to Social Security, however, they were clearly submissive. It is quite possible that by the time he came to the "Unity Conference" at Hershey, he recognized mechanical difficulties of a disqualifying sort in his previous position and that he has therefore come to believe that the Social Security program, even as it operates on a compulsory basis, is a good thing. He may, upon reflection, have become convinced, let us say, by the arguments of Nelson Rockefeller, or William Scranton, or the late Elizabeth Gurley Flynn, that the program, otherwise conducted, would fall to pieces. Maybe he himself came to that conclusion. And then again maybe he was persuaded by his advisers that you cannot at one and the same time campaign for President of the United States and against Social Security. The point is that strong public pressure was on him to make that declaration at Hershey, pressure that took no account of the relevance of his view on Social Security to his fitness to serve as President of the United States. American

55

politics is evolving into a religion (talk about the dangers of escalation!), a far thing from the practice of the science, or even the art, of government. And, accordingly, people are demanding that their spokesmen act, not merely as administrators or leaders, but as priests and votaries of the political dogmas and liturgy that are in fashion.

Let me illustrate. Suppose Senator Goldwater had said at Hershey something like this: "Ladies and gentlemen. I have never opposed Social Security *as such.* I have never argued for its abolition. I have said what I believe—namely, that any government program that *requires* the participation of all citizens in certain categories is an imperfect one, precisely because it requires some people to do something they need not and would rather not do. It is perfectly reasonable to require all citizens not to do certain things (not to kill, rob, rape, for instance) and even to *do* certain things (aid the country in time of crisis; go to school; stop at a red light). But a *free* country is constantly concerned not to require of its members that they should do something which it is unnecessary for them to do in order to provide for the safety of others. And I have become convinced that it is not *necessary* to require Mary Jones or Nelson Rockefeller to join the Social Security system if they choose not to do so and are prepared to subscribe to other programs, privately organized, for looking after their old age.

"What, if you elect me President, will I do respecting the current Social Security program? The answer is that I cannot and will not do anything at all. I am asking you to elect me President, not to elect me as a substitute for Congress, turning over to me the right to pass whatever laws happen to appeal to me. I acknowledge that the overwhelming majority of the American people are convinced that *any* contraction of the Social Security law is undesirable. I would, as President, respect your wishes, while disagreeing with your conclusions. I would urge modification only if a sufficient demand for it were to build up. Until then the Social Security law is as safe from me as from Kwame Nkrumah.

"Now, I know you would like me to say that I heartily endorse the Social Security program as it is written. But I am not going to say that. I *don't* approve of any law that is unnecessarily coercive. I assume you want me to speak out. I have just done so."

Nothing doing. What the people wanted is what is known in religious terminology as internal assent. "The people"—I am here assuming that there is solidarity on the issue—are demanding an explicit affirmation of belief in an article (Social Security) of a political creed (state welfarism). The exaction of that homage amounts, in fact, to a tyrannization of the conscience. It is ironic that the tendency, in our progressively secular culture, is to go further than the individual was asked to go during the Late Middle Ages, when most Western governments were blunt theocracies. In the thirteenth century Thomas Aquinas was preaching the supremacy of the conscience. The individual's prime obligation, said St. Thomas, is to the dictates of his own conscience—"the will is evil when it is at variance [even] with erring reason." A man dutiful to his church has the obligation to listen to the church's established moral leaders, patiently and attentively. But if they then fail to convince him, he must not surrender his conscience; he must not *do* something he believes wrong.

How curious it is—or maybe this is exactly what we should have expected—that in the modern community, in which we so greatly stress the division between church and state, we should find ourselves easing into the habit of requiring a pseudoreligious adherence to the articles and bylaws of the day. The zeal for conformity is so great that we tend to distrust any man who disagrees with us on any point in our secularist little catechisms, and never mind whether that disagreement is truly an operative matter of public concern as, truly, the question whether Senator Goldwater agrees with the Social Security program is not, any more than it is relevant to the voters whether he believes in the Assumption of the Blessed Virgin Mary. But ours is an increasingly inquisitorial cast of mind. Our colleges and universities, although they are always coming out noisily against formal loyalty oaths, are busily engaged in brewing their own conformity. And so is it in the opinion-making network. The Establishment's witches stir away at those great vats of dogma, which are ladled out to the alter boys and communicants as essence of liberalism, and anyone who declines to drink the stuff down is as suspicious as that furtive little fellow next door whom

57

yesterday we were denouncing to the Inquisitor because he hadn't attended church on the Feast of St. Bonaventure.
. . .

They suffer from it, to be sure, on the other side of the political fence, too. We have conformities within conformities and many of them are mutually exclusive. A few years ago President Eisenhower appointed a New Jersey judge to fill a vacancy in the Supreme Court. It was during the heyday of McCarthyism, and it was well known among his friends that William Brennan despised Senator McCarthy and all his works, which he had on one public occasion likened to the rebirth of "Salem witch hunts" and denounced as "barbaric." However, as a witness against Brennan before the Judiciary Committee, the Senator was in a position to slow things down not a little bit, though it was never supposed he could block the appointment. The nation's liberals watched anxiously to see how William Brennan would behave at the committee hearing. Senator McCarthy strode in, and Mr. Brennan crumpled. "Not only do I approve" of the Senate investigations of the Communist conspiracy, he said, "but I can think of no more vital function than searching out subversives." What about the witch-hunt-barbarism talk? "A little orator's license," said the postulant Justice meekly. One would have thought he was being called to the Supreme Court from the Americanism Commission of the American Legion. "Joe McCarthy destroyed the character of Supreme Court Justice William J. Brennan yesterday, or anyway, presided at its suicide," commented the liberal columnist Murray Kempton.

Sir Arnold Lunn, the distinguished English essayist, once said, in reply to an effusive toastmaster who had remarked on Sir Arnold's great political courage, that courage is something you display when you take a position that might end you up hanging from a gibbet, rotting in jail, or on the receiving end of an economic boycott, and nothing he had ever said, Sir Arnold maintained, stood to bring down upon him any one of those three ends; hence, he insisted, he had not really earned his badge of courage. William Brennan, if he were really risking a seat on the Supreme Court, might understandably have declined to assert his manhood in Senator McCarthy's presence. But even knowing he would not lose out, he uttered the pieties of the situation, a dutiful acolyte at a black mass, and for some reason the McCarthyite community felt good about it. Even though nobody believed a word he said.

Once again a scene in a Senate chamber, and another distinguished liberal, whose appointment as Undersecretary of State is being considered. "Governor Bowles," said Senator Sparkman, "do you believe that we should at this time recognize Red China?" "I do not believe we should," said Governor Bowles and, evidently deciding to kiss the bull square on the nose, added, *"and have said so on many occasions."* As with Senator Goldwater, one must give Mr. Bowles the benefit of the doubt. On the other hand, Chester Bowles had very clearly and very ardently proposed the *de facto* recognition of Red China in 1960, before two separate forums. We should be prepared to assume he had changed his mind. We have no alternative than to assume he was under fearful pressure to say what he said.

Now, what is most beastly about it all, as I hinted in the episode involving William Brennan, is that the people who administer the pressure actually take pleasure in turning our politicians into hypocrites. It is a form of bullying and a truly sadistic form because as a rule no functional purpose is achieved. It is one thing when a bully constrains a weaker boy to do errands for him; at least he manages to get the errands done. It is something else again merely to torture the boy for the sake of it. There was no point at all in getting Brennan to say in effect that he was pro-McCarthy; no point at all in pretending that Chester Bowles has always been against the recognition of Red China— or that Senator Goldwater has abandoned all objections to the coercive planks in our welfarist programs. Here were cases of humiliation pure and simple. Goldwater could not, as we have seen, abrogate the Social Security Law, William Brennan didn't have the power to eliminate McCarthyism, and Chester Bowles didn't have the power to admit Red China. The argument can always be made that people elevated to power are thereupon poised to use their influence toward mischievous ends, that therefore it *does* accomplish something to force them to put on the public record views which are congruent with the majority of the time and place. Yes, that argument can be made. It is an argument that says in effect that you can get so you can really trust a politician by simply corrupting his spirit, and I say that is not a plausible lesson for this Sunday or for any other. At the Republican Governors' Conference in Cleveland, several prominent politicians went around saying in effect that they could only trust Mr. Goldwater if he would desert his principles. "Thus Governor Romney of Michigan," commented columnist James Wechsler, "a dedicated Mormon, broke his long standing rule of non-participation in politics on Sunday to say in effect that he would reconcile himself to a Goldwater candidacy if he could wrest the assurance that Goldwater did not believe what he was saying.

"One can only remark," Mr. Wechsler concluded, "that a man to whom Sunday has so much religious meaning might have at least waited until Monday to demand that Goldwater repudiate conscience and conviction [in order] to wrap up the Michigan delegation."

The essential difficulty lies, I do believe, in the apotheosis of the majority, begun a couple of hundred years ago by a little cult of democratist ideologues, grown in our time into a raging universal obsession. We are so concerned to flatter the majority that we lose sight of how very often it is necessary, in order to preserve freedom for the minority, let alone for the individual, to face that majority down.

In the recent past there have been only two conspicuous dissenters in the Senate (I do not count Senator Morse; professional mavericks do not figure here). They are Senator William Fulbright and Senator Barry Goldwater; each with formidable minority support. Senator Goldwater has got away with it by steadily increasing his following. The most interesting non-political aspect of his startling nomination is the postoperative adhesions that are caused when a minority suddenly blurts out its claim for majority recognition. Look how sharp the pressures then become to blur the image of the dissenter! The engines of conformity are powerful. Conformity to the popular view is always a drag upon a person's reason and emotion and even his conscience, and it is good, up to a point, that it should be so, inasmuch as people have decided to live together rather than apart. A society that seduces the conscience by sweet reason is one thing, but ours is developing into a society that harpoons the conscience and tows it right into the maws of the mother vessel, there to be macerated and stuffed into a faceless can.

The enemies of the human spirit are outpacing even the population explosion, and it becomes harder and harder to fight them down. It is so much easier to succumb, and there are so many formulas for doing so gracefully, and the great conscience shriver is the wink on Univac's face on election night. We have come a long distance from the way of Hilaire Belloc when he ran for Parliament, to the way of John F. Kennedy when he ran for the Presidency of the United States. In the terms I speak of, we have unprogressed. In 1960 John F. Kennedy pleaded with his fellow Christians, of Protestant denomination, not to take seriously the fact that he was by "accident of birth" a Roman Catholic. Hilaire Belloc was asked by a lady, while answering questions from a platform in 1906, whether it was true that he was a "papist." "Madam," he roared out his answer at the top of his voice, reaching into his pocket and drawing out a rosary, "do you see these BEADS? I say them every MORNING as soon as I get UP, and every NIGHT before I go to BED. And if YOU object to THAT, Madam, I can only PRAY to God that He will spare me the IGNOMINY of representing YOU in Parliament!" Belloc won, and achieved something more than his own election.

THE DETERIORATION CONTINUES

November 10, 1966

New York City is a continuing textbook. An unfolding, unending classic in political and moral duplicity. The cynicism is so overpopulated that occasionally, even in this enormous city, it runs into itself—as, for instance, on the day before Election Day in the New York *Times,* where on a right-hand page a couple of dozen advertising agencies breast-beat themselves over the enormities of a previous advertisement opposing the Civilian Review Board, and on the left-hand page, the defenders of the

Civilian Review Board publish an advertisement so chock-full of cant, nonsense, and hysteria as to qualify for *Mad* magazine.

One likes to think that, sitting on a high stool out of sight of the mighty, there is a clerkish, poker-faced layout clerk who woke up smiling inside at what he had committed. Alas, it is likelier that no one noticed the irony— that defenders of the review board were deploring on one page the kind of thing that other defenders of the review board were, cheek by jowl, committing on the other page.

The opponents of the Civilian Review Board (which was abolished by the voters on Election Day) came up, in the closing hours of the campaign, with a melodramatic reason for opposing the amendment to abolish the board: It contained a "sleeper clause." Listen: "If you abolish the board, New York will move towards totalitarianism and the destruction of the basic principles of democratic government." Those who want to abolish the board are linked with "the forces of fear and hatred." "There have been people and groups that have been condemned and tortured because decent free people shut their eyes and let themselves be overcome by fear. That's what's happening in New York."

Now who said that? The Minutemen? Gerald L. K. Smith? Savonarola? No, it was none other than New York City's Mr. Clean, the honorable John Vliet Lindsay, who a year ago became mayor by persuading some people that otherwise they would be herded into concentration camps, and the rest that that was a responsible way to make politics. A reporter following Mayor Lindsay's dilations on the sleeper clause apparently couldn't stand it any longer and asked the mayor whether he was "talking about Nazi Germany." Pressed thus to be specific, the Mayor retreated into Spenglerian generality. "I'm talking about history and nations in general."

Senator Javits, not to be outdone in demagogy, announced that if the review board were defeated, it would "give the force of reaction an impetus in this country which it has never been given." And elaborated: "You will destroy the powers of the Mayor and the Commissioner of Investigation [to investigate the police] and you will destroy a hope for stability in the city. And there will be the destruction of basic principles of democratic government."

One does wonder, sometimes, about the principles of democratic government.

The opponents of the review board sought to revert to the *status quo ante*. If the so-called sleeper clause is going to have the effect of permitting freedom to perish from this earth, then one wonders why it wasn't noticed by the city's corporation counsel in the course of the dissections he performed on it during the spring and summer. Or by the courts that patiently but firmly overruled the corporation counsel's objections to the issue's being put on the ballot (none of them based on the sleeper clause). If there is a sleeper clause, it necessarily follows that the corporation counsel is asleep. And for that matter, so also were asleep the judges who okayed the thing, if in fact the proposal is as outrageous as Messrs. Lindsay and Javits suggest—or for that matter one-hundredth as outrageous.

But in New York, it is good politics (a) to exaggerate (b) to object to exaggeration, and then, of course, (c) to exaggerate the exaggeration. Candidate Rockefeller said that Candidate O'Connor's opposition to Rockefeller's dope addict program meant there would be a higher crime rate. "If you want a higher crime rate, vote for O'Connor," the Rock said. Gleefully O'Connor's people republished the generality as final proof of the irresponsibility of Rockefeller. Whereupon Rockefeller people said that it was proof of the irresponsibility of the O'Connor people to allege that Rockefeller could have said something irresponsible about O'Connor. Get it?

If so, you should run for office.

RIP, THE FOURTH LITTLE INDIAN

May 11, 1967

There is an oh-so interesting post-mortem discussion going on on the question: Who killed the New York *World Journal Tribune?* What is particularly interesting is that everyone playing the game seems to be agreed on the rules—namely, that if the murderer is identified—the evidence is overwhelming, of course, that the labor unions did it, all by themselves—he is not under any circumstances to be restrained.

Yes, there has been the usual sighing about labor union excesses, and the deep-throated New York *Times* clapped a little doom on the general subject. But not one newspaper, not even the peppery *Daily News,* ventured to suggest that what is needed is legislation to keep such a thing from happening elsewhere in the country.

If New York City cannot afford a second afternoon newspaper for which there was a market of 700,000 people every day willing to pay ten cents per copy, then the economic situation for newspapers is very dim indeed, and we should take seriously the dark vaticinations of the union leaders. These gentlemen, having choked the goose to death, suddenly start talking in Spenglerian accents about long-term ebbs and tides, the idea being, of course, to distract from what they had done, which was to have killed off a gigantic newspaper struggling to survive as the single survivor of three antecedent newspapers—by posing impossible demands.

The figures are well known, but let us sound them again in mourning. The defunct newspaper was employing 500 people it did not need. It was forbidden to use those employees it desired to use to do the jobs that management desired to be done—for fear of trespassing on union seniority. The paper was losing an average of $700,000 per month. And then the typesetters' union concluded an agreement with the New York *Daily News,* whose terms, applied to the *World Journal Tribune,* would have added $10,000,000 to the deficit over the next three years. Had enough?

There was yet another factor. Under the proposed new contract, the unions intended to negotiate a 300 percent increase in severance pay. In order to launch the existing amalgamated paper, it had been necessary for the parent corporations to pay $1,000,000 in severance pay to employees let go. Management reasoned that whatever the arguments for trying to hold on a few more months by, say, killing the Sunday edition and hoping for an increase in advertising, they were clearly overwhelmed by the prospect of having to pay three times the current severance rate if the paper faltered.

The result is known acutely to the many employees of

the paper who will find it difficult to get work for which they have been trained and acutely also to a considerable portion of the reading population of New York, which is without the afternoon paper of their choice. Everyone is angry with the labor unions, even as they were angry with the union that caused all New York to go to work on foot eighteen months ago when the buses and the subways were stopped. But as was then the case, so now no one is proposing remedial legislation.

Well, I will. Extensive revisions of the basic labor law are greatly overdue. Among those revisions that would have figured for the benefit of the community in the recent situation: (1) no corporation which can be shown to have lost money during the average of the preceding few years should be required to bargain collectively, which means that management would have been free to negotiate directly with individual employees; and (2) no labor union contract should deprive management of the right to institute cost-saving practices and machinery, which means that management would have been free to automate, trim its staff and overhead, without consulting the union. Remember that the alternative is what we now have: unemployment and no newspaper.

THE TWENTY-FOURTH AMENDMENT

February 18, 1964

Do you solemnly swear to defend and uphold the Constitution of the United States against its enemies, foreign and domestic? Yes, of course, you do, and so do I, but every now and then where the law is involved, the question arises of internal assent. I do not give mine to the Twenty-fourth Amendment (which specifies that no poll taxes will be levied in a federal election) and take the opportunity, quickly before history completely transfigures that amendment into revealed truth, to attempt to say why.

The amendment in question is an advance on the proposition that everyone should vote, and I do not believe that everyone should vote. Any such statement begets the responsibility to state an acceptable alternative, and mine is this: Everyone should have the right to vote whose record or accomplishments more or less suggest that he attaches an importance to the vote that goes beyond his immediate self-interests.

I do not doubt that such are the qualifications of the majority of the voters. But it needs to be emphasized that the act of voting, in a highly centralized society, has less and less to do with what you desire to protect yourself against than with what you desire other people to do to protect or enhance you. If the government is depriving you of your right to free speech, or of your right to practice your religion, or of your right to your own property, the vote exercised exclusively in your own behalf is infinitely understandable, infinitely commendable. But as our society vests more and more power in the federal government, the average vote has more and more to do with the regulation of people's lives.

Consider the field of social welfarism. A vote on a typical issue, involving federal aid to education, federal aid to the aged, federal aid to the poor, federal aid to the underprivileged, has to do with yourself primarily in the sense that you are being asked to decide what the government should instruct others to do in respect to yourself. Now the idea that you may vote to tell others what to do is perfectly traditional and natural in any society in which, after all, your own identity and freedom are substantially defined by what other people let you do or do to you. But now we have passed from a society in which the main purpose of the laws was to guard you against the aggressions of others (those who would in the absence of laws murder you, steal from you, enslave you) and entered into a welfarist society. In such a society, it seems to me, the man who casts his vote should be encouraged, by whatever mechanical means are at the society's disposal, to weigh the consequences of his vote.

And here is why I regret any step that tends to routinize the vote, to distract from the solemnity of the ritual; why all routine, ceremonial impediments to voting, inasmuch as they have the effect of turning the attention of the voter to the awesomeness of the ritual he is about to perform, are welcome; why I believe in potholing, rather than broadening, the highway to the voting booth. I should never want to see the situation where the lack of money kept any man from voting—but lack of money for poll taxes affected very few people. I'd have preferred to see laws waiving the poll tax, where hardship could be proved.

But instead, we went to that sacred citadel, the Constitution of the United States, and jerry-rigged a hyperdemocratic abutment upon it that, in my judgment, damages the architecture, tilting us further along in the direction of a thoughtless democracy in which people are increasingly encouraged to vote for the sake of voting. The states are still permitted to maintain literacy requirements. When will *they* go? The argument for their abolition can be made, has in fact been made, and one supposes it is only a matter of time until the hyperdemocratists will marshal the arguments for their constitutional proscription. The next step, of course, will be to deplore the undemocratic inconveniences involved in going all the way to the public booth to cast the vote. At that point, undoubtedly, AT&T will come to the rescue, and we will contrive a system by which we can all vote over the telephone.

THE MOON *AND* BUST?

June 1, 1963

Nobody, but nobody, seems to have any idea, however vague, what our moon man project is going to end up costing the United States, and those stolid Congressmen who have undertaken bravely to find out meet universally disappointment and rage. Partly it is ignorance of the unknown; partly it is the fault of the federal budgeteers, who have elevated fiscal mystification to a science. The estimates I have seen ranged from $20 to $75 billion, repeat billion, as America's capital investment in landing a man on the moon.

The result has been to cause some to wonder whether the project is worth it. Worth what? Frequently the moon project is compared to the heavy investment Ferdinand and Isabella put into the original voyage of Columbus. But the analogy will not stand hard scrutiny. Their Catholic Majesties were primarily motivated not by the spirit of scientific inquiry, but by the prospect of commercial advantage, and although Columbus did not pioneer any easy road to the riches of India and China, he did, by what the scientists call serendipity, uncover other riches, which handsomely repaid the curiosity and venturesomeness of the Spanish Crown.

But it is nowhere suggested that the moon project proposes a commercial exploitation of the galaxies. Even if the first astronaut discovered that the moon was made of solid gold and jewels, like the Emerald City of Oz, we could not hope to retrieve even a noticeable part of our original investment by lugging back bullion a quarter of a million miles in spaceships. All the gold that was ever mined in the New World would not pay for one year's agitation over the moon flight.

Defense, then? If we have to spend $70 billion to protect this country from its enemies, clearly we shall spend it, and spend it with relative lightheartedness. But on this point the scientists are disturbingly vague, and our leaders positively unintelligible. They speak to us, convincingly, of the necessity of space platforms and the like, from which to meet any threat the Communists might launch against us. But—examine their arguments—you detect a self-serving vagueness when such questions are posed as: "Do you need to reach the moon in order to develop orbiting spaceships which would be sufficient to meet the needs of the national defense?" Spaceships we must have, but the estimated cost of having them, vague though it is, falls way below the cost of launching a moon man. If there is a sublime military justification in the moon project, based on somebody's exalted vision, then let the prophet step forward and share the revelation with the people. I suspect that our leaders do not know what the justification is, though they are prepared to encourage the superstition that something, something we know not of, will develop out of the voyage which will justify, in terms of self-defense, the enormous sacrifices necessary to its realization.

The time has come for cautious leaders of the opposition to raise two points. The first, and the one that needs to be raised with utmost caution, is this: If it will cost many billion dollars to reach the moon, it is relatively safe to say that the Soviet Union will not reach it. Whatever are the advantages they have over us as the result of perfected techniques in dispatching heavy objects into space, these cannot possibly mean an economy for them so substantial as to make the effort economically painless for them. If it costs us $50 billion, they couldn't do it for $5. Under the circumstances, a sober estimate of the Soviet Union's economic resources would justify our strategists in assuming, with an educated confidence, that the Soviet Union is not going to hurry to get to the moon—not if it's going to cost them *that* much money.

And then we need to explore the extent to which the administration, as the most public-relations conscious administration in the history of this country, is driven to the goal of reaching the moon by the impulse to score a great victory in international public relations. We suffered, granted, from the initiative of Sputnik. We are determined, said President Kennedy at a recent press conference, not to permit the Soviet Union to take a fresh lead in interstellar acrobatics. But what lies beneath the reasoning of Mr. Kennedy is the superstitious reliance on unrealized achievements as the means through which to propagandize successfully for the West; vast efforts to be the first to penetrate the unknown—quick, before the other fellow does it—so as to avoid doing public relations battle on the basis of our present accomplishments. But we do not need galactic bombast to prove to the people of the world that ours is a superior society to the Soviet Union's; we could, had we the imagination to do so, prove that point again and again, profoundly and convincingly, if we could only free ourselves from the inferiority complex to which we have been enslaved for years. One riot in Birmingham, Alabama, having to do with the acquisition of rights for Negroes which are not enjoyed by the top elite of a Communist state, and we fall back abashed before the judgment of the men who sent in tanks to Budapest to run over students who would have been happy to have one-half the rights enjoyed by sweatshop Negro workers in the industrial South.

I grant, and am humble before, the mysterious promptings of the historical imperative: the desire to get there for no other reason than that to get there appears now to be physically conceivable. But subsidizing with billions of dollars that gleam in the eye of the adventurer, which drove Magellan around the world, Edison to electricity's lair, Admiral Byrd to the North Pole, is no substitute for successfully thinking through the basic psychological problem which America, the great self-lacerator, suffers

69

from—which is national uncertainty. Let's say it flatly, because we know it is true: that anything they, a slave society, can do, we can do better; that merely because they *seem* to be engaged in a Stakhanovite effort to reach the moon does not mean that we must accept the challenge they pose in their own terms. I doubt, for the reasons I have given, that the Russians are planning to land on the moon any day now, but if they are, and if they reach there, can't we say, with composure, at that crowded session of the United Nations: Very well, you have reached the moon, but meanwhile, here in America we have been trying, however clumsily, to spread freedom and justice.

III. The Politician at Work

A RELAXING VIEW OF RONALD REAGAN

November 28, 1967

In this here neck of the woods there is some uneasiness in the air, and the reason why is Ronald Reagan. Here is how the nightmare goes. Romney does so-so in New Hampshire, not well enough to give him a solid lead, not poorly enough to dispose of him once and for all and leave time to build up another liberal. Nixon does poorly, maybe not so poorly as to make him withdraw either, but poorly enough to prevent the bandwagon's forming. On to Wisconsin. Same sort of thing. Then in Oregon and Nebraska Reagan supporters submit his name, and without campaigning Reagan wins decisively. On to the convention. A bitter fight, but once again the liberals are disunited. George Romney has had a divine visitation telling him to stay in the fight, and he does: through the first or second ballots, fracturing the liberals. And—big difference from 1964—somehow the disparagement of the Reagan forces hasn't had the desirable effect of weakening the Republican Party so as to guarantee, at least, its ultimate defeat in November. Add to that the ecumenical goo that Ronald Reagan is so good at extruding—why you would think, sometimes, that Senator Kuchel was his best friend. So Reagan gets nominated, and then we all rush off to our artillery pieces, aim, pull the triggers, and—typical nightmare—nothing happens, so that, smiling that confounding smile of his, he rides his horse right onto the front lawn of the White House, dismounts, hands the reins over to the benumbed editor of the

Washington *Post,* and proceeds to the throne, whence he judges over us all.

The nightmare peters out at this point, for one thing because it never is absolutely clear just how a political conservative is actually going to succeed in destroying the country—it is better for nightmares to end with such details unspecified (a haunted house should never be entered—no bad can come of it). Presumably, that which he would do which is undesirable is a projection of what he has done that is undesirable in California. And concerning what he has done in California, there is thoroughly mystifying disagreement in many quarters.

There is the opinion, for instance, of Hale Champion. Mr. Champion, who is now uncoiling at Harvard at what has been called the Center for the Advancement of the Kennedy Family, served Governor "Pat" Brown as state finance director (one thinks of serving President Kubitschek of Brazil as budget balancer). Mr. Champion undeniably earned a period of repose in the groves of the academe or even of a sanatorium. He suggested an appropriate structure for the criticism of the Reagan administration in *West* magazine (April 23), in which he commented on the new governor's first 100 days. Governor Reagan, said Mr. Champion, (a) is "in deepening trouble with the legislature and with the public"; (b) has a "completely negative and destructive attitude [toward] higher education"; (c) has "accomplished" almost nothing "except the dismissal of Clark Kerr"; (d) is likely to be swamped by "the future consequences of [his] failure to work out solutions to problems"; and (e) is esthetically offensive, as witness "the loose bundle of social and moral pronouncements that constitute the governor's vague, historically inaccurate, philosophically sloppy, and verbally undistinguished inaugural address."

From this criticism we all were to infer that Mr. Reagan is quite as bad as it was feared by the most fearful that he would be. Well, perhaps not *quite* as bad as some of Governor Brown's campaign rhetoric predicted. After all, at one point in the campaign, Governor Brown, addressing a Negro child in a widely played television spot, reminded the boy that Ronald Reagan was an actor and that it was an actor who had shot Abraham Lincoln—a sorites that Mr. Champion did not, at the time, identify as philosophically sloppy or even verbally undistinguished. On the other hand, Mr. Champion is in a position to point out that Reagan hasn't had the opportunity to assassinate Abraham Lincoln, and how can we know that, given the opportunity, he would not seize it?

But then, having prepared ourselves to think about Mr. Reagan the way Mr. Champion thinks about him, one is confused by the contradictory analyses of another very liberal critic of Mr. Reagan, Andrew Kopkind, who has kept in very close touch with Reagan over the years and disapproves of him every bit as much as Mr. Champion—but for different reasons. He thinks that Mr. Reagan is a phony—that he isn't really conservative at all, just talks that way. Whereas Mr. Champion warned that precisely Mr. Reagan's difficulty is his genuine commitment to his atavistic ideas (a "surprising number of state employees, educators and members of mental health organizations . . . didn't really believe he meant what he said in the years before 1966"), Kopkind quotes an anonymous observer as remarking that "Reagan plays Pat Brown better than Pat Brown." "Reagan," he begins his recent analysis, "is selling out. . . . He rationalizes his own position by calling himself a pragmatist and may even believe that he is working from the inside. But he is out for himself alone." Once again he finds a useful anonymous observer to quote: "There are three big phonies in politics in this state—Sam Yorty, Max Rafferty, and Ronald Reagan."

Granted, there are people on the right who also believe that Reagan has sold out. California has a state senator, John G. Schmitz, who is a member of the John Birch Society, and *he* says that Reagan is "a tragic end to the brightest hope on the American political scene today. Many of the best of our citizens may never again be willing to trust the word of a seeker or holder of high political office." On the other hand, there have been no complaints from the conservative Californians who helped finance the Reagan movement and who would presumably feel most deeply the weals of ideological infidelity—no complaints from Henry Salvatori, Holmes Tuttle, William Knowland. Moreover, they contend, and Mr. Kopkind would go along, that if the election were held again tomorrow, Reagan would win against Brown as triumphantly

(1,000,000 votes) as he did last November.

All this is very confusing to non-Californians. There are the liberals (*e.g.,* Champion) who say he has done the state irreparable damage—and liberals (*e.g.,* Kopkind) who say that he has, as a matter of fact, administered a stoutly liberal government. How can you cause irreparable damage—in the liberal view of things—by taking militantly liberal action? There are those (*e.g.,* Champion) who say he is losing popularity and those (*e.g.,* Kopkind) who say he is gaining popularity. Some say he is true to his conservative faith; others that he isn't. Some that he is sincere, that's his trouble; others that he is insincere, that that is his trouble. The Birchers (*e.g.,* Schmitz) who are greatly disillusioned, and the conservatives (*e.g.,* Salvatori) who are by and large elated.

What's he like personally? Ask Evans and Novak: "Naturally aloof. The thing Reagan needs to do [they quote an unnamed "Republican leader"] is to ask the legislators over to his house to play poker and drink some booze. But that's not going to happen any time soon." Fascinating. But—oops—*Time* magazine quotes Assembly Republican Caucus Chairman Don Mulford: "I don't think there is a single legislator who doesn't like Governor Reagan as an individual." *Time* commented on Reagan's "success" at the end of his first session, which he accomplished "by holding frequent meetings with the lawmakers, infect[ing] them with his straightforward, purposeful approach." Champion insisted on the diminishing prestige. Now William S. White observes that "no one who has recently been in California with eyes and ears open can doubt that Reagan is going from strength to strength. By every ordinary measurement he is both a popular and an effective state executive."

As far as the outer world can see, there have been three significant confrontations between California and Reaganism. They had to do with (1) education, (2) mental health, and (3) taxes.

The first was in two parts. There was to begin with, the firing of Clark Kerr. In fact, Reagan's role in the dismissal of Kerr while it could be held to have been psychologically critical, was insubstantial. It is true that the regents, execution-bound, addressed the freshly inaugurated governor at the regents' meeting in January and

74

said to him: If it would be greatly embarrassing to you for us to proceed with the business at hand—which is to ask Clark Kerr for his resignation—we are willing to put off doing so for a few months. Reagan's answer was: Don't mind me, go right ahead, and God bless you. What happened then is instructive. In the first place, Reagan's siding with the majority of the regents, who after all had been named as such by his celebratedly liberal predecessors Brown, Knight, and Warren, ended him up carrying the onus of the entire majority. Thus, Mr. Champion, relaxing in the scholarly detachment of Harvard University, refers to Mr. Reagan's having "accomplished" the "dismissal of Clark Kerr." In fact, Reagan did vote for Kerr's dismissal. If he had voted against Kerr's dismissal, Kerr would nevertheless have been fired (the vote was 14 to 8)—unless one assumes that Reagan controlled the marginal votes, which why should one assume it considering that only a single voter directly owed his status as a voter to the governor? Never mind, Reagan was widely held to be responsible.

And second, one learns ever more about the powers of the Educational Establishment, and they are, of course, formidable. The rule of thumb is: Never disagree with the educators; never give them less than anything they want; and never act other than as a postulant at their shrine. It is all neatly put by Professor James Q. Wilson of Harvard University, who wrote recently a "Guide to Reagan Country" for the academically chic *Commentary* magazine in which he ventured a number of observations not entirely congenial to orthodox anti-Reaganism, and thought to protect himself winsomely by acknowledging: "I do not intend here to write an apology for Reagan; even if I thought like that, which I don't, I would never write it down anywhere my colleagues at Harvard might read it." No indeed: academic freedom is very broad-minded, but it stops short of defending the position of Ronald Reagan. Stops short, that is, of defending the indefensible.

It is a perfectly reasonable criticism of Ronald Reagan that he does not entirely understand the influence of the Academic Establishment. Not very many politicians do, and it is not enough merely to tell them that that influence exists. Barry Goldwater was scandalously late in harnessing what academic support was available to him for the asking. Richard Nixon's cheering squad always sounded rather like William Yandell Elliott, plus the deans of the schools of business administration of Midwestern Baptist colleges. Actually, there is a great deal of potential support available to a right-bent public figure, but he must know how to discharge the correct vibrations to shake it out, and Governor Reagan didn't know how to do that in January, 1967, and does not know—and here is his most baffling dereliction of the moment—how to do so even now. It isn't really all that difficult. The supporters, as I say are there: One has only to meditate on the silent vote against Clark Kerr among the chancellors of the individual university campuses in California, who for years have deeply resented his importunate ways, and there are the others who recoil against the anti-intellectualist spirit of the Berkeley disorders and even against the antipersonalist impulses of macroeducation.

But those folk need to be approached in just the right way, and it may be the single lesson—he gives signs of mastering almost all the others—that Governor Reagan has not learned. So that when Reagan simultaneously voted with the majority to dismiss Kerr and came out (via a subordinate who spoke out ahead of schedule) in favor of uniform reductions (10 percent) in state spending and in favor of charging tuition at the University of California and the state colleges, all the educators felt the tug of class solidarity that Karl Marx, Eugene Debs, and James Hoffa never succeeded in eliciting from the proletarian classes. It was a field day for the professors and the students, who delightedly burned their governor in effigy. The canny and brilliant Jesse Unruh, lord of all he diminishingly surveys in the evenly divided state assembly, quickly took his advantage. Only months before, because he had seen the necessity to deplore the excesses at the Berkeley campus, he too, had been burned in effigy; but now, in gratitude for his scornful resistance of the governor's position that students should contribute to the cost of their own education, the placardists bore signs: JESSE SAVES. The speaker was vastly amused and vastly instructed: He knows, he knows, the strength of the Harvard vote.

And then Governor Reagan made probably the principal verbal *faux pas* of his career, a remark to the effect that the state of California has no business "subsidizing intellectual curiosity." The difference, Mark Twain reminded us, between the right word and almost the right word "is the difference between lightning and lightning-bug." Intellectual curiosity is a very good thing; intellectual frivolity is not. When asked to document his case against educational excesses Governor Reagan brightly observed that he did not see why the state should need to support courses in "how to burn the governor in effigy." An amusing response, the kind of riposte that an Adlai Stevenson or a John F. Kennedy would make with pleasure and profit. But Ronald Reagan needs to remember that he is a Republican and a conservative and does not have the ordinary man's license to exaggerate. In fact, industrious reporters discovered, the course in question was being offered by an organization adjacent to the state university, which teaches the theory of nonviolent resistance, and though to be sure the university was extending credit to students who took the course, it was technically untrue to say that the taxpayers were spending money to finance the burning of their governor in effigy. Just a little research would have armed the governor with copious examples of the abuse of education. It can be maintained (and is, by some people) that all life is an education, in which case, as a matter of logic, one automatically loses any argument to the effect that training in this or that is a waste of money. But Reagan could have split the university community and got going a very useful debate by asking whether in fact all the gentlemen and scholars in the university system were prepared to defend the notion that courses in home economics and fly fishing and hotel hygiene and life adjustment are a part of the life of the mind, to the advancement of which the voters of California are dedicated.

And then, too, Reagan should raise the question: Granted the infinite desirability of more and more education, what are the practical limits that even an idealistic community should observe? During the past decade, enrollment in California state colleges is up 397 percent, operating costs are up 260 percent, capital expenditures are up 260 percent—whereas population and hence the ability to pay are up only 39 percent. Question: How much further? Here is a very serious question, which Governor Reagan has an excellent opportunity to probe.

77

The society would be ideal in which everyone with a velleity to become a doctor of philosophy could proceed to stroll through the years of his early manhood in order to become one, at no expense to himself. But—as Professor Ernest van den Haag of New York University tartly pointed out a few years ago—isn't it a fact that the figures show that professors will earn more money than plumbers and taxi drivers and that, therefore, to tax plumbers and taxi drivers to subsidize the education of professors is a form of regressive taxation, and therefore antiliberal, by a definition with which both Mr. Champion *and* Mr. Kopkind could agree?

Such questions as these Mr. Reagan has not asked as yet, and, indeed, he has not perfected any line of communication to the academes. Meanwhile, the question rests. The case for the firing of Clark Kerr is at least defensible. Certainly it is true that he'd have been fired irrespective of Reagan's adventitious attendance at the regents' meeting on January 20, 1967, and as regards tuition, the seed has been planted and voters are aware that a public question has been raised. The State of California provides, typically, more than one-half the expenses of the university. The university proposes a budget, the regents examine it, it is submitted to the governor, and he in turn submits it to the legislature. Reagan persuaded the regents this year to spend $20,000,000 of their own reserves, and he vetoed a supplementary appropriation proposed by Unruh. And the university emerged from it all with $10,000,000 more than it got the year before—but the percentage rise was reduced. And more important heuristic questions have been raised—questions which should have been raised before; questions which properly relate higher state education to the total resources and needs of a community. The exact formulation of the ultimate questions neither Governor Reagan nor anyone else is ever likely to come up with. But Reagan has naysayed the superstition that any spending in the name of higher education ought (a) to be approved of and (b) to be exempt from public scrutiny. And that, perverse though it may sound, is a contribution to public education.

Concerning mental health, it was widely disseminated that Reagan's superficiality caused him to ignore the

78

salient point. True, the inpatient population had been reduced from 34,000 to 20,000, and true, the state budget for the maintenance of the mentally ill had not been reduced at all. Why not, asked Reagan, reduce it *pro tanto*? Because, his critics leaped, the fact of the diminution of inpatients is testimony to the effectiveness of the entire working force of the mental hospitals, and precisely the wrong thing to do under the circumstances is to reduce their total firing power. Reagan countered that that was supposititious, that he was quite prepared to reverse his recommendations in the event of a decline in the rate of the cured.

Sounds reasonable, one would suppose. But the point, of course, is that economies are never easily effected and just about never effected when the emotional instrument at the disposal of the spenders is, no less, the mentally ill. Take the incidence of stricken mothers-in-law, and multiply it by the prospect of their repatriation, and you have an idea of the size of the political problem. If President Eisenhower was unsuccessful, even during his relatively brief period of militant frugality, in eliminating the Rural Electrification Agency because of the lobbies available to agitate for its survival, one can imagine the difficulties in paring the mental health agencies of a single state of the nation. So Reagan yielded. Actually he had no reasonable alternative than to do so. But again he had made a public point. And as in the case of education, the point would yield dividends, or should at any rate, when the time comes, as routinely it always has, to augment the budget for mental health. Reagan's position is after all distinguishable from the position that says that the state should ignore their mentally ill. It is a position that says: if modern psychiatric advances, *e.g.*, through the use of tranquilizers, permit a diminution of the problem, even as the Salk vaccine has diminished the problem of polio, oughtn't the states to adjust their budgets accordingly?

And then, of course, the big question of the budget. It is a matter of universal hilarity. The most economy-minded governor since the inauguration of J. Bracken Lee as governor of Utah in 1953 forwards to the legislature the highest budget in state history! Loud guffaws. Not utterly wholesome guffaws, to be sure. Nelson Rockefeller, who at least noticed, though he did not precisely run against, the extravagances of his predecessor Averell Harriman as governor of New York, also proceeded to submit a higher budget than that of the Democratic Mr. Harriman. But in Rockefeller's case, that was considered an act of statesmanship, or at least it was considered such by the same kind of people who have reacted so ardently against Ronald Reagan.

Reagan's reasoning can, of course, be made to sound disingenuous. He claims to have discovered only *after* achieving office the programmed deficit of Governor Pat Brown. Casper Weinberger, chairman of Reagan's Little Hoover Commission, likes to tell the story: "Hale Champion, outgoing director of the department of finance, cheerfully walked into the conference room, greeted [us] affably, and announced that while there would be a surplus available on June 30, 1967 (when the last of Governor Brown's eight fiscal years ended), there was going to be a problem starting in January, 1968.

"The department's best estimates showed, he said, that there would be a cash-flow shortage in January, February, and March of 1968 amounting to $740,000,000. Champion added that approximately $340,000,000 could be borrowed from other state funds, leaving the state's bank accounts short by $400,000,000, of the amount needed to write checks covering the state's daily bills during those months. When the new tax monies came in April, 1968, most of the cash-flow problems would be behind us, added Champion, but, of course there would be quite a big deficit by June, 1968, if present rates of revenue and expenditure continued. In fact, the deficit by then would probably amount to over $350,000,000.

"After a moment's silence," Mr. Weinberger recalls, "somebody asked, 'Hale, what would you have done about this if you had been reelected?' 'Well,' he answered with a slow smile, 'we've been telling you Republicans we needed withholding and more taxes, but you've always defeated them.' "

"We knew there would be a deficit during the campaign," Reagan reminisced. "But we didn't know how large it would be. Accountants told us there simply wasn't any way of ascertaining how much. Brown kept borrowing all over the place. The civil service people said there was a bare chance we could make it without raising taxes. As we got closer to the election, it began to look as though there wasn't any chance. I said during the campaign that there would have to be new taxes. The Constitution requires that you submit a budget right after you take office. I did. But the research hadn't been completed. And soon it became clear that even if we could effect $250,000,000 in economies, there wasn't a chance for a balanced budget. We just didn't know the extent of the problem. We had no way of knowing that Brown was spending most of the contingency funds. I've now recommended that in the future, independent auditing firms be given a crack at the figures, so that how the state stands financially can be a part of the public knowledge."

He paused to wave back cheerfully at four college types, who had pulled their sedan alongside, driving 55 mph in tandem with the state trooper who was chauffering the governor and exactly observing the speed limit. A honey-blonde leaned, smiling, out of the open window, hoisting a cardboard square hastily improvised from a grocery box or whatever when the party spotted the governor's license plates. Scrawled on it with lipstick was NO TUITION! Reagan laughed as the collegiates pulled away. "The faculties are mostly responsible for that," he said. "They tell you one thing, and then they tell the press another." He gave examples. "The no-tuition bit is a local superstition. Even Brown said years before the election that tuition was 'inevitable.' Did they jump him? But it'll take time. Right now the point is to save money where we can. I'm a *good* person for people to trust their money with. I'm a good *manager,* and I'll treat their money as though it were mine. When we suggested 10 percent across the board, we knew some departments would have to expand, though others could trim back even more than 10 percent. We won't make 10 percent, but we will make about 8½ percent. And remember, that's 8½ percent of the spending we have control over. Two-thirds of the spending in California is fixed by the constitution or by statute, and we can't do anything about it. It's bad enough to try to make economies when you need the help of a legislature that's controlled by the opposition party. We can't very well tackle the Constitution at the same time. But what we're doing will take hold. What makes me mad
81

is obstructionism that's clearly intended to screw up your program. For instance, I said no more new hiring. If one department needs another secretary, pull her from the department where there are surplus secretaries. So some of the civil service people got together, and when you need a secretary for the most urgent job, they tell you sorry, there isn't one available in the whole goddam state of California. You know there is, of course; but it's a problem of locating her, and that takes time, takes time to canvass the departments and identify those that have the excess people, and there are plenty around. It isn't any different from what you would expect. Why should the bureaucracy behave any different from the way I always said it did—protectively toward its own authority and vested interests? A governor can't do everything; he hasn't got that much authority, and maybe he shouldn't have that authority. I have only a psychological authority, because the politicians know that the people are with me, that they see a lot of waste, and they resent the taxes and the inflation, and that they'll support me. There are lots of things I just can't do, at least not for a while. Take judicial reform. You know how many judges Brown appointed as lame ducks? Four hundred! I must be the only governor in the U.S. who can't fix a parking ticket. But in time there will be vacancies, and I'm trying to reform the system; but Unruh hasn't let the bill out of committee. You've got to be patient, and you've got to make a start. I'll be around for a while."

So the budget went finally to the legislature, a $5-billion budget, 8 percent higher than his predecessor's. (By contrast, Rockefeller's first budget was 11 percent higher than *his* predecessor's.) But, Reagan explained, the increase was almost entirely on account of Brown's commitments, plus the annual increase in California's population (2½ percent in 1966). Assuming you merely want to stand still, you have to raise the budget 8 percent to cover inflation, plus immigration. Reagan needed to cover the deficits of Pat Brown—and did so, raising the budget only the requisite 8 percent. Up went the income tax, the sales tax, and the so-called sin taxes. And on the issue of withholding, he was against it because, he said, "taxes ought to be out in the open. They should hurt, so that people know the price of what they're getting." Jesse Unruh was as determined that taxes should be painlessly withheld drop by drop as Reagan was that they should be collected in one painful annual extraction. Reagan held out; Unruh held out. But, finally, on July 28 the legislature approved within less than 1 percent the figure Reagan asked for and without the withholding tax. "All in all," Jesse Unruh, obviously taking another look at Reagan, concluded, "he did very well."

The critics of Ronald Reagan are fond of quoting from his autobiography, *Where's the Rest of Me?* It is an unfortunate book, not at all for what it says, which is wholesome and intelligent, but for the way it is said. There is no doubting that it is primarily responsible for the insiders' assumption that the governor is a hopeless cornball. The opening passage of the book (it is Mr. Kopkind's favorite) is, well, disastrous. "The story begins with the close-up of a bottom. My face was blue . . . my bottom was red . . . and my father claimed afterward that he was white. . . . Ever since . . . I have been particularly fond of the colors that were exhibited—red, white, and blue."

I suspend the narrative in order to allow a minute for derision.

Now the fact of the matter is that the book was coauthored, and coauthored "autobiographies" are, as a general rule, the stylistic work of the other guy. It is too bad that Mr. Reagan did not go further and publish it as an as-told-to book, which is undoubtedly how the book was actually produced. Because the fact of the matter is that Reagan is not that way. "John Jones," I observed recently to him about a controversial public figure, "has the face of a bank teller." "Bank teller, hell, he has the face of the neighborhood child molester." One cannot be as banal as (a) and as mordant as (b), and the circumstances clearly argue that the second, not the first, is the real-life Ronald Reagan. "Stand in front of the asparagus counter today," he told a political gathering, "and you discover that it's cheaper to eat money." That kind of crack, Made in America, unmakable anywhere else, is a pretty big industry in California. But—good. And homemade. "Keeping up with Governor Brown's promises," he said during the campaign, "is like reading

83

Playboy magazine while your wife turns the pages." Good. Very good. And they come effortlessly. They are a function of his vision. The perspectives are very good; the mind very quick.

I met him seven or eight years ago. He was to introduce me at a lecture that night at Beverly Hills. He arrived at the school auditorium to find consternation. The house was full and the crowd impatient, but the microphone was dead; the student who was to have shown up at the control room above the balcony to turn on the current hadn't. Reagan quickly took over. He instructed an assistant to call the principal and see if he could get a key. He then bounded onto the stage and shouted as loud as he could to make himself heard. In a very few minutes the audience was greatly enjoying itself. Then word came to him: no answer at the principal's telephone. Reagan went off-stage and looked out the window. There was a ledge, a foot wide, two stories above the street level, running along the side of the window back to the locked control room. Hollywoodwise, he climbed out on the ledge and side-stepped carefully, arms stretched out to help him balance, until he had gone the long way to the window, which he broke open with his elbow, lifting it open from the inside and jumping into the darkness. In a moment the lights were on, the amplifying knobs turned up, the speaker introduced.

During those days he was busy delivering his own speech. *The* speech, it came to be called—probably the most frequently uttered since William Jennings Bryan's on the golden crucifixion. All over the land, to hundreds of audiences, a deft and rollicking indictment of overweening government. And then the speech became the most galvanizing fund raiser in political history. He televised it during the Goldwater campaign for a statewide showing in California. "And then, an hour before it was scheduled to go on, word came from Goldwater's headquarters to hold it—the boys at HQ had heard it rumored that it was 'too extreme.' I remember I went to the nearest pay booth, just by a gas station, and called Goldwater. There were only minutes to go. Luckily, he was on the ground. I reached him in Arizona. 'Barry,' I said, 'I don't have time to tell you everything that's in that speech, but you can take it from me, buddy, there isn't a kooky line in it.' Goldwater said: 'I'll take your word for it,' and I called the studio in the nick of time."

If Goldwater hadn't been at the other end of the telephone, Reagan would not have become governor. Because the speech was an incomparable success, statewide and subsequently nationwide. (It is said to have elicited almost $5,000,000 in dollar-bill contributions.) It was on account of that speech that the Reagan-for-governor talk began.

I saw him during a long evening a few weeks after Goldwater's defeat, when the Reagan movement was just beginning to stir. We talked about the national calamity for the conservative movement and how it bore on his own situation. He was then quite positive that the Republican Party of California would not want him, especially not in the aftermath of so definitive a loss. But, he said, he wasn't going to say anything Sherman-esque. He talked about the problems of California. The discussion was in generalities, very different from a second conversation a year later, in December, 1965, on the eve of the year when he would run. The change was striking. He knew a great deal about specific problems of California. But he had grown, too, in other ways. I remember being especially impressed when, looking out over the city from the elevation of Pacific Palisades, he remarked: "You know, it's probable that the cost of eliminating the smog is a cost the people who want the smog to be eliminated aren't, when it comes to it, willing to pay."

Still later, on a half-dozen occasions, I noticed the ongoing improvement in his personal style, particularly in his handling of the press. Last June in Omaha, after a press conference before his speech to the Young Republicans, the New York *Times* correspondent impulsively blurted out to a young correspondent he hardly knew: "I've never seen anything like it. I've been covering them since Truman. There isn't anybody who can touch Reagan." It's something people are going to have to get used to as long as Reagan's star is on the ascendancy. "To those unfamiliar with Reagan's big-league savvy," *Newsweek*, pained, dutifully pointed out last May after observing Ronald Reagan and Bobby Kennedy in a joint appearance answering student questions on Vietnam, "the ease with which [Reagan] fielded questions about Vietnam may come as a revelation. . . . Political rookie Reagan left old campaigner Kennedy blinking when the sessions ended."

I mean, it is more than flesh and blood can bear. Reagan, the moderately successful actor, the man ignorant of foreign affairs, outwitting Bobby *Kennedy* in a political contest. It's the kind of thing that brings on those nightmares.

Richard Nixon was in the room. Who, someone asked, would the Republican Party consider eligible in 1968? Nixon gave the usual names—and added Ronald Reagan's. I objected. It strikes me, I said, as inconceivable. "Why?" Nixon asked. "Suppose he makes a very good record as governor of California?" (This was in December, just after Reagan's election.) Because, I said, he is very simply an implausible President. Anyone would be whose career was in Hollywood. People won't get used to the notion of a former actor being President. People are very stuffy about Presidential candidates. Remember what Raymond Moley said when someone asked him how to account for Kefauver's beating Adlai Stevenson in the Minnesota primary in 1956: "Did *you* ever tell a joke in Minneapolis?"

And then—I added, carried away by my conviction—how does one go about being a good governor in an age when the major moves are, after all, up to the federal government? Who last—I asked Nixon—can we remember, whose record as governor propelled him to the first ranks of the Presidential hopefuls?

Dewey, Nixon ventured—then corrected himself: Dewey became famous as a prosecutor, not as governor. Rockefeller was projected by the fact of being a Rockefeller, being personally able, being wealthy, and being governor of New York, not because New York had become a model state under his administration.

During the next year California will spend, as we all know, $5 billion. During the next year the federal government will spend approximately $140 billion. Well over 17 billion of these dollars will be spent in California. But more important, it is the federal government that will decide how many California boys are drafted into the Army, how much inflation there is going to be, how far the monopoly labor unions can go, whether there will be any praying in the schools, whether Californians can sell their property as they choose, where the main highways will come from and where they will go, how the water flowing in from nature is to be allocated, how large Social Security payments will be. Are there interstices within which, nowadays, a governor can move, sufficiently to keep himself in focus and establish his special competence?

Reagan clearly thinks so. After all, he has brought almost everyone's attention to the problems of California, even to some of California's problems over which, as in the matter of tuition, he has no control. Always there is *some* room. "To live," Whittaker Chambers wrote, "is to maneuver. The choices of maneuver are now visibly narrow. [But] a conservatism that cannot find room in its folds for the actualities is a conservatism that is not a political force, or even a twitch: it has become a literary whimsy. Those who remain in the world, if they will not surrender on its terms, must maneuver within its terms."

The knowledge of that is what causes Mr. Kopkind to call Reagan a hypocrite, a phony. Brings the Birch senator to consider him an impostor. Brings George Wallace to call him a lightweight. What did they expect? That Governor Reagan would padlock the state treasury and give speeches on the Liberty amendment? They say that his accomplishments are few, that it is only the rhetoric that is conservative. But the rhetoric is the principal thing. It precedes all action. All thoughtful action. Reagan's rhetoric is that of someone who is profoundly committed, *mutatis mutandis,* to the ancient ways. His perspectives are essentially undoubting. Mr. Kopkind has recently written that the United States' venture in Vietnam is "the most barbaric imperialistic war of this century." If that is so, there are phonies in America by the scores of millions. Reagan would never get the Kopkind vote; Reagan is more inscrutable to Kopkind than the Aztec calendar. For the Kopkinds, America itself is inscrutable. Reagan is indisputably a part of America. And he may become a part of American history.

THE VERY, VERY HONORABLE
LYNDEN O. PINDLING

August 24, 1967

The Honorable Lynden O. Pindling is the Negro Premier of the Bahamas and a great tease. A couple of weeks ago he gave a speech at Freeport, on Grand Bahama Island, at which he got a standing ovation from the most nervous agglomeration of businessmen since the financial elders of Havana met to hear the economic policies of the fledgling Premier Fidel Castro in January, 1959.

At stake was, roughly, $100,000,000. That is the value of the improvements that have been lavished on Grand Bahama Island during the past four years by the G. B. Development Company, which, having got through the Nassau government and then through the Crown the so-called Hawksbill Creek Act back in 1955, began its undertaking of transforming 214 square miles of flat and uninteresting island into a paradise for business. Imagine: no taxation of corporate or personal profits before 1990. No land taxes. Freedom from customs duties. Freedom from immigration restrictions.

Venture capital poured in, and the rise in the economy was spectacular. To everyone's surprise, it was not only business that came, but tourists (330,000 last year). In 1963 there were 33 hotel rooms on the island. Now there are 2,400, and that number will double just around the corner.

But then it began to look as though politics would gradually transmute the reverie into nightmare. The Bahamas have been governed since time immemorial by the so-called Bay Street Boys, the white plutocrats who took over bit by bit from the Crown, as English responsibilities diminished in the general retreat from colonialism. Then the opposition uncovered fetid odors surrounding the enactment of Hawksbill. Nassau's Sir Stafford Sands, who has now gone to Spain to, ah, retire, turns out to have got a $1,000,000 law fee for his egregious services in connection with the passage of the Hawksbill Creek Act.

Now I was always under the impression that all lawyers

get at least $1,000,000 a year, including the soldier-scholar who will read these lines before you are permitted to. But Sir Stafford's million clams became a very heated campaign issue, and a royal commission was impounded to look into the entire "Freeport Situation" and is even now taking testimony from the principals. But meanwhile the rumors went out that Premier Pindling, who as head of the Progressive Liberal Party routed the Bay Street Boys at the election last January 10, was going to announce dramatically at Freeport at the big banquet to commemorate the beginning of a $20,000,000 waterway, that Hawksbill would be repealed, even if it meant a complete break with the Crown.

He began his talk (delivered without notes) by commemorating the four most important dates in Bahamian history: 1492 when the islands were discovered by Columbus; 1834 when the English emancipated the slaves; 1967 when his government was elected to office—and 1955, when the Hawksbill Creek Act was passed. The audience went mad, mad with delight.

He certainly does not intend to kill the golden goose, he said; he intends to encourage private enterprise to proceed with the miraculous development of Grand Bahama. And he does really wish that all those rumors would cease. Why did nobody ask him about those rumors? "Mr. President"—he turned to face the dinner chairman—"let me say to you, sir, that my telephone number is 22805. The name is spelled P-i-n-d-l-i-n-g. If you can't get me on the telephone, a telegram will do, and if you just send it to Pindling, Nassau, it will get to me." And then, a little punctilio concerning the implicit indebtedness of Bahamians to Americans: "I can see no reason why from this day forth a new and vibrant partnership cannot be forged between those of you who have visited us with your enterprising talents, because it seems to us that we have something that we can teach each other. We need to learn your enterprising techniques, and we need to teach you how not to commit suicide, something we don't believe in." *Touché*.

There was irony, drama, humor in the occasion. And there was the reiteration of the oldest lesson—namely, that the best way to combat poverty is to relieve an area of the exactions of the political incubus. In a few words, Premier Pindling did more to endorse practical means for helping the poor than all the eggheads and the Marxists who in recent years have cluck-clucked about the Caribbean and Latin America to no effect.

IV. The Politician at Play

BARRY GOLDWATER VISITS
THE GRAND CANYON

February, 1967

Be-Nun-I-Ken, Arizona. The bell rang, and Senator Goldwater kept right on talking to his visitor but automatically slid his chair back. That way, when Mrs. Goldwater or the butler opens the door, whoever it is who rang won't have a clear view of Goldwater sitting behind his desk. By his sliding back 3 feet, the line of vision is cut off, and all that the man at the door can see is a desk top—from which 24,000 letters were dictated last year alone. It happens all day long. Strangers. They find out where he lives, drive right into his driveway, take pictures of the house and the swimming pool, and often ring the bell to chat with Goldwater or to ask him to pose for a picture.

Goldwater is the friendliest man in the history of the world, so that when he has work to do or is conversing with someone, he simply slides the chair back, secure. The other day he neglected to do so, assuming that the ring at the door, at seven in the morning, could be only the milkman or Western Union. It was a large lady with a large camera, who whinnied with delight on spotting the Republican Presidential candidate of 1964. Could she take a picture of him? Yes, he said politely, but would she mind terribly waiting just a minute until he put on a bathrobe?

You drive to the hotel or to the airport, and everyone waves at him. They are unawed, because he has always been a part of the city—the most approachable part of the city which, when he was born there, had only 10,000 inhabitants and one big general store called Goldwaters.

The visitors, along with his daughter and granddaughter, crowd into his twin-engined Bonanza, which cruises at 230 mph. He is taking them to see the Grand Canyon, and soon the plane is off the ground and climbing to 7,500 feet. At the copilot's seat is a tiny little woman who looks a hundred years old, but that is an impression you get primarily from her venerable condescension to the complex gauges and buttons and valves and instruments. She is an old friend, has been flying thirty years, and the insurance company likes to have a copilot along when the pilot is over fifty.

Along the way—the Grand Canyon is 250 miles north of Phoenix—the visitors are shown everything. The youngest extinct volcano, where recently, under the influence of strong spirits, some local jokesters sneaked up at midnight and lit a couple of logs and practically caused a mass evacuation of the valley. There, to the east, is where the Tewkesburys and Grahams feuded for so many years, a bloodier feud by far than anything that ever happened in Kentucky. It was the cattlemen against the sheepherders, and one victim was tied up and eaten to death by wild dogs, so the story goes—there are Vietcong in our own history. . . .

On the left, in the bright sun, there is Jerome, a ghost town, freshly discovered by artists who are moving in. Over there a dead mine. Goldwater's uncle was asked to stake it to $10,000 fifty years ago, but said he didn't have the cash and wouldn't borrow it. Before they were through they had taken $40,000,000 in gold and $100,000,000 in copper out of it.

Over there is where Goldwater once crash-landed an Ercoup. Bits and pieces of the airplane are still cherished by the Hopis as amulets and as eternal proof that flying over their territory is forbidden by their earth god, a reverence for whom prevents them even now from permitting wells to be drilled, so that they have to go 3 miles for water.

To the northwest, archeologists have found traces of life dating back before the beginning of Christendom, indicating that the population of northern Arizona was once as great as it is now, when they are charging thousands of dollars per acre. He points out all the archeological strata. "One day I hope to go back to college and get my degree, and it will be in geology."

We are getting close, and he radios ahead that he should be landing "in about seven minutes." But there is no airport in sight, and the visitor challenges his capricious estimate. He accepts the challenge and sets the stopwatch going. Six minutes and forty-five seconds later we are within 100 feet of the runway. He slows down the plane to stretch out those fifteen seconds, but Miss Ruth on the right sees what he is up to and calls his game. "You want to reach the field or stall?" she says sternly. "Shut up, Ruth. Your job is to tell me when we're on the ground," he says gruffly, unconvincingly. She smiles, and we touch down at exactly seven minutes, without even setting off the stall warning indicator. He turns, triumphant, to his visitor.

Oh, yes, he was recently in Saigon and Bangkok, and he has, later in the day, to meet with the governor and the Congressmen and political leaders, and plan his lectures, do some writing, and return a thousand telephone calls. But he has shown why he is concerned to fight political—and military—wars, so that he can enjoy what he truly enjoys: his country, its people, the desert, the rocks, the reservations, the history, his grandchildren, his friends.

JOHN CHAFEE GOES TO THE RACES

Newport, Rhode Island, September 16, 1967

The contenders were, of course, *Intrepid*, which is the American boat, and *Dame Pattie*. ("How do you pronounce Pattie," I asked the governor, "as in Patty Berg or as in Pat*ee*?" "I don't know," said Governor John H. Chafee, whose candor is the phenomenon of Rhode Island politics, "but we'd better assume it's plain Patty." It would not do to assume otherwise in the absence of specific knowledge. Might sound affected. Governor Chafee is *not* affected.)

Dame Pattie is a gesture of Australian affection for the ingratiating wife of Sir Robert Menzies, who was Prime Minister roughly forever. His wife is as beloved over there as Eleanor Roosevelt was here, and much less controversial. There is no higher compliment than to have a challenger named after you, and considering the pride with which the name was bestowed, the disappointment will be the keener if, as is now expected, the race becomes a rout. An unchivalrous spectacle, the American *Intrepid* running away from the hotly pursuing lady.

There were 500 boats to watch, and several dozen Coast Guard cutters, destroyers, helicopters, to keep the spectators out of the way of the contending boats, which the Coast Guard did rather too officiously at times, as though the spectators were peeping Toms. Which isn't the case, of course. Without public interest in the event, you don't get all Australia up at three in the morning listening to the radio to see if they have finally got hold of the most inaccessible trophy in the sports world, and you don't get Americans putting up $1,000,000 or so of non-tax-exempt money to build yet another boat, season after season, which will shave a whisker off the speed of last season's winner. One helicopter descended menacingly on the little 39-foot Pacemaker owned and operated by a friend of the governor. "We can go out on a destroyer if you like," he had written me. "But there are disadvantages, you have to make a lot of small talk to a lot of people, and there is no booze." (The governor drank hot tea on the cold, sunny, breezy afternoon.) The Coast Guard bellowed through a loudspeaker that our boat should retreat to a point behind the destroyers a mile away, which seemed unreasonable inasmuch as there were another 20 boats between ours and the racers', and the half dozen of us aboard the Pacemaker knew lots more about how far to stay away from racing boats than helicopter pilots do.

"We'll settle this for good and all," said the skipper, leaving the wheel for a moment in the lurching seas to unfurl the official ensign of the governor of Rhode Island. Spotting this, the soft-spoken governor cracked out an order: "No," and the operation was immobilized. But always a democrat, he finally succumbed to the consensus—so long as his captivating wife is among the majority—that it was quite proper to fly it; after all, we were sailing in Rhode Island waters. ("But I'm *embarrassed*," he said, mocking a little-boy voice.)

And he *was* unhappy about it. He is known as a

gregarious man, who greatly likes all kinds of people; he had that reputation even back at Yale, which he entered with John Lindsay just before the war. As a campaigner, his forte has always been personal contact and total accessibility. He knows there are usufructs of office and accepts them. But he does not like to rely on them or get into the habit of relying on them and this quality of personal modesty, alongside a toughness which causes bureaucrats and chiselers, if not helicopter pilots, to give him a wide berth, has made him the most popular figure in Rhode Island and a political super phenomenon (he won reelection last year by getting 64 percent of the vote, and did this in a state whose Democrats outnumber Republicans by 3 to 1). On the national scene, Chafee is pulling for Governor Romney. Officially. And unofficially, too. By officially, I mean because people who back Romney are, most of them, backing a force—much as one might say that one is officially for decency. For alas, John Chafee is a modern Republican.

Intrepid was pulling farther and farther away. The radio commentator didn't much know how to keep the gab going, so he tuned in at frequent intervals on a local savant who knows all about sailing, and he was reduced to scolding the spectator fleet for getting in the way of the contenders. The next day *Dame Pattie*'s skipper complained not at all, and one was left with the impression that the spectator fleet had, after all, got in the way of the boat that carried the savant and his microphone; John Chafee was greatly amused. And when the winning boat came over the finish line, his enthusiasm was genuine, and he waved his affection and esteem at the crew and did so without reproach from a single helicopter.

We motored back to Wakefield, and he talked politics, professionally, inquisitively. What would George Wallace accomplish? (Not much, he thinks. When it gets to actually voting for a President, people straighten up. Martin Luther King would do better than Wallace.) How will Richard Nixon do in the primaries? (Chafee is for Romney, remember.) When will John Lindsay make a national bid—"I thought you were pretty tough on Lindsay in that column on his walking the streets." "Did you?" I replied.

And then, in the quiet anchorage, the state trooper waited to drive him home, and we walked up the slip, lugging our gear, and he chatted on: "Somebody wrote me, 'Between you and LBJ, I find myself headed for the Republican Party.' I don't know whether that's a compliment or not."

"It is," I assured him.

V. The Communist Question

ON INVITING A COMMUNIST SPEAKER TO YALE

October 22, 1963

In the fall of 1962, the Yale Political Union invited Gus Hall, secretary of the Communist Party of the United States, to address it later in the season. The speaker scheduled at the meeting immediately preceding Gus Hall was myself. I wrote to the PU to say that I declined to appear as one speaker in the same series that included a Communist Party functionary. However, I said, if the invitation to Mr. Hall were reissued as contingent upon the vote of the PU at the end of an evening's discussion on the question "Resolved, That a Communist functionary should not be invited to speak at Yale," then I would appear—to defend the negative of the resolution. My terms were accepted, and the debate was held. The negative carried the house, and the invitation to Gus Hall was withdrawn.

Last spring, Dr. John Meng addressed a letter to his faculty. Dr. Meng is the president of Hunter College, a political scientist by training, and a man well known for his liberal views. "Ladies and gentlemen," he wrote, and I quote the letter almost in its entirety, "a properly chartered student organization . . . complying with all the requirements established by the Faculty Council and by the Office of the Dean of Students . . . has organized a series of . . . forums under the general title 'Out of the Mainstream.' The first two of these forums, scheduled for April 11 and May 2, are to be addressed by George Lincoln Rockwell, self-styled Commander of the American

97

Nazi Party, and by Gus Hall, General Secretary of the Communist Party, U.S.A. . . . Student sentiment on the . . . campus with regard to the propriety of these invitations is sharply divided. . . . Students on both sides of the controversy agree in expressing detestation for the doctrines professed by the . . . two invited speakers. What the students are arguing about is whether they have properly assumed the responsibility which is theirs as a result of the freedom accorded them by the College. . . . Those of us who remember the Second World War, the horrors of Nazism, and the cruelties of Communism on the march tend to forget that these memories are not a part of the mental equipment of most of our present student body. Their knowledge of those events is largely knowledge transmitted by an older generation or through the medium of historical accounts. It is not surprising that many of them should evince some intellectual interest in listening to a living, avowed Nazi or to an openly-dedicated Communist speaking in the American idiom.

"This situation affords the teaching staff of the College an opportunity to manifest true understanding of the intellectual curiosity of some of our students and at the same time to drive home to these students with more than ordinary effectiveness the lessons so many of us learned through harsh experience about the meaning of democracy and the individual responsibilities which it entails.

"Certainly none of us welcomes the presence on our campus of these disciples of discord. Neither does any one of us wish to foster the spread of the iniquitous teachings. . . . I am completely confident that neither the staff nor the students of Hunter College will permit the foul mouthings of a pipsqueak Hitler, or the delusive dialectic of a Khrushchev in kneepants to persuade them to abandon their intellectual integrity. To accord these undistinguished visitors anything more demonstrative than a shudder of polite disgust would be to attribute to their presence a totally fictitious importance.

"Those of you," Dr. Meng concluded, "who prefer love to hate, beauty to bestiality, and freedom to bondage may join with others of us among the staff and students of the College in attending the Passover Assembly at Park Avenue . . . at the time [the Führer and the Commissar are] scheduled to speak in the Bronx."

Dr. Meng thus expressed himself, movingly, on what he understands to be the moral question involved in inviting a Nazi or a Communist to speak on a college campus: To do so, he is saying, is to put curiosity above other values, communicating a kind of callousness, a sense of aloofness from the suffering caused, and still being caused, by those who practice their ideologies on whole peoples all over the world. But moving though his words are, they seem not to be at the center of Dr. Meng's analysis, which is, as it should be in any deliberation of this nature, intellectual and analytical, rather than emotional. What Dr. Meng is saying to his faculty is this: Those who issued these invitations are undergraduates. They do not know what Nazism was and do not, apparently, know what Communism is. Therefore, they deem it necessary to their intellectual experience to hear out a Nazi and a Communist in—as he puts it—the American idiom. But Dr. Meng, by declining to examine more closely the unarticulated premises of this summary, yielded that point which I most earnestly cherish and wish to stress, even beyond the moral or, if you wish, the human point.

Dr. Meng says in his remarks governing the forthcoming appearances of both the Nazi and the Communist speakers—he never distinguishes between the two—that the students of Hunter have not experienced Communism, more specifically, that they have not heard a defense of Communism in the American idiom, delivered by a Communist. Conceivably, Dr. Meng himself and many members of his faculty have never heard a live Communist defend Communism or a live Nazi defend Nazism, but, he implies, it is not *necessary* that they should have this experience in order to permit them to know what they need to know as educated and responsible members of the academic and civil communities. He did not say to the faculty: Those of you who have not heard a Communist should make it a point to attend this lecture, to fill out an otherwise uncompleted educational experience. He speaks on the assumption that the faculty know quite well enough what is the Communist position and how it sounds articulated in the American idiom, that, by implication, the ends of education are not served by listening to a Communist who comes on campus to speak, but rather —but rather what?

What *is* served, other than extrinsic points? An affirmation of the students' administrative right to invite whomsoever they please to address them? But Dr. Meng does not challenge that right, assuming it to be a right, any more than the authorities of Yale University: It was never in question. What then? What does one come to know, that one did not know, on listening to an American Communist speak?

Nothing, presumably, that one did not know before, if one is ready to participate in a political union, concerning either Marxist analysis or Communist rhetoric. It is inconceivable, Dr. Meng would presumably say, that a thirty-minute address by an official of the Communist Party would add to an understanding of the theory or nature or strategy of the Communist Party. Every official of the Communist Party ruthlessly observes the discipline of his calling, and over four decades when has it ever been reported that a Communist official, addressing a college gathering or any other non-Communist gathering, said something unexpected? When last did an official of the party speaking to a college audience let himself improvise, speak ad libitum, vouchsafing us, for even one instant, a sunburst, illuminating the dark mysteries of the Communist pathology? Communists do sometimes speak their minds, but never to bourgeois gatherings: Here they are on duty, fighting men on the march; they come to recapitulate their dogmas, to press their drive to coopt the moral slogans of the West, and to practice the science of confusion. Not that they succeed in confusing; they seek rather self-legitimization. They do not confuse the proletariat, for heaven's sake, in whose name their own slogans are forged; they are hardly likely to confuse an audience of college students. They are not likely, in Dr. Meng's phrase, to "persuade [the students] to abandon their intellectual integrity."

Might they, then, these Communist speakers, contribute as much factual or even human knowledge about the current Communist program, about Communist apologetics, as a single copy of the *Worker?* Less, by far, one would think, considering that the average issue of the *Worker,* which takes no more than thirty minutes to read, covers a wider range of issues, giving the Communist view of the day on everything from Cuba to Ross Barnett to the New

York Giants and does so, moreover, without that encumbering self-consciousness which is the greatest barrier to human communication—though the difference in the version one gets from Gus Hall at Yale and Gus Hall in the *Worker* is even there not great enough in and of itself to justify a professional political curiosity about the disparity between the two renditions. And if it were, that curiosity is easily gratified by reading the *Worker,* where Mr. Hall's speeches to the college audiences are often printed, in full.

Is this enough of an argument, one might ask? That an individual's views are well known and that it is known that he adheres to these rigidly? No, that argument is not sufficient. If it alone were relevant, it might be used by the protectionists among you to shield the Political Union from, say, a typical spokesman for the Democratic or the Republican parties, on the grounds that their lines of argument are at any given moment predictable and that, therefore, the chances of hearing something new, something fresh, are, if not as much against you as in the case of the Communist, nearly enough against you to permit you to argue analogically against their appearance.

The argument broadens here in many directions, and one needs to draw a breath deeply, for to go from here to there, we must tread on highly delicate ground, step right over one of the most highly cherished dogmas of the modern age—namely, the notion that all ideas are created equal, that it is the responsibility of academic freedom to guard the gates of epistemological relativism. Even so, the reason why a Democratic bore might be acceptable while a Communist bore would not is not emotional, but intellectual. Fiercely though the archetypal Democrat or Republican will resist the opportunity to respond to the challenge of public debate as a human being, rather than as an automaton, in his heart and mind, calcified though they may have become out of long and unthinking and unquestioning service to his party, there is at the root a disposition to think of himself as a member of our community, possessed of a point of view which is held by the community at large to be, within the widest limits of toleration, reasonable. Some views are unreasonable and tolerable. Some views are unreasonable and intolerable, especially insofar as they are systemic, rather than merely personal. The Democrat and the Republican will regularly exaggerate in behalf of their causes; sometimes they will consciously lie; they will feign concern, where none is felt; they will decry the manners and morals of the opposition, knowing well that their own manners and morals are indistinguishable—but they remain, flesh and blood and heart, a part of America; they are as they are because American politics is as American politics is, and until we reform it, that is how they will continue to be, the men whom our institutions have nurtured.

The Communist has, of course, renounced our institutions, which is perhaps all right, but he has done something very much more: He has renounced the bond—whatever it is; but fragile though it is, it is there, make no mistake about it—that holds together Republicans and Democrats, socialists and Manchesterians, syndicalists and elitists, pacifists and warmongers, civil libertarians and McCarthyites, Townsendites and Coughlinites, Southerners, Westerners, Easterners, Northerners. The Communist has renounced the bond explicitly and intentionally—renunciation in the first degree—and for the duration of that renunciation he cannot speak to us, and we cannot speak to him, because however deep we reach, we cannot find a common vocabulary; we can no more collaborate with him to further the common understanding than Anne Frank could have collaborated with Goebbels in a dialogue on race relations. Until that trance is broken, formal communication is impossible, for he speaks to us in a language whose utter unrelation to reality rules out any possibility of meaningful discourse. There is no idiom available to us for simultaneous usage. Certainly the American idiom will not do. We all abuse the instruments of discourse, but we seek, under the massive rococo superstructure of point and counterpoint, to say things to each other that come truly out of our minds and our hearts, because we feel that in deeply significant ways, we are related by that highly elastic, but not infinitely elastic, bond, that binds us to each other.

Such a man, then, whose explicit message we know beforehand, which message he must deliver undeviatingly, cannot communicate to us orally anything of *political* interest, the subject with which the Political Union properly interests itself. He is a fit object of curiosity for students of certain other subjects than politics. A Communist might with good reason be called on to address serious students of sociology, seeking some accidental insight into the social causes that might have led a man to ideological mania, or to serious students of psychology who seek to examine the reflexes of a man who, for the sake of his truth, will utter and defend every necessary untruth, every necessary depravity. The courtroom at Tel Aviv was crowded with professors of the specialized social sciences, but they were not men who would have invited Adolf Eichmann to their college to defend the regime of Adolf Hitler.

The Communists are of concern to nonspecialists, I am trying to say, *primarily as human beings* suffering from the most exotic and the most mortal illness of our times, that mania of ideology, which in one of its excrescences in our time, while you were living, blithely stoked the ovens of Germany with Jewish flesh; which, without the quiver a normal man feels on running over a dog, committed millions to death by starvation in the very breadbasket of Soviet Russia; which, driven by ideological lust, this very day commits dozens of millions of Chinese to death in pursuit of a lunatic delusion in China. The servants of these ideologies are dislodged from the human situation and yet—

And yet they are human beings themselves, for no one has the power formally to renounce his membership in the human race. And it is over their plight as human beings that we must, it strikes me, pause, for that is the problem supremely that you face, above all others—certainly above the political problem, it being conceded that you are immune to seductive passes at your intellectual and moral integrity and that the words, the wooden words, are words you knew before.

That problem is human. What will you do when Gus Hall, the human being, comes here to defend the cause of what you know ahead of time to be the cause of organized inhumanity? Will you show that "shudder of polite disgust"? Is this a new social skill we need to cultivate, in our time—a part of the social equipment endowed upon us in virtue of our great good fortune as recipients of a Hunter or Yale education? Did *your* son learn at his college how to give off a shudder of polite disgust?

Or will you applaud him when he is introduced? Yes, there will be applause—in recognition of his courage in facing a hostile audience. But the applause will be confused—will it not?—because you know very well that objective courage is not necessarily admirable. The man who threw acid in the face of Victor Riesel in the middle of Times Square was courageous, as was Khrushchev when he ordered the tanks to run over your courageous counterparts in Budapest. Is it not likely that among those of you who applaud there will be those who are in fact applauding their own courage in applauding a real live apologist for human atrocity? But the applause is likely to be of that special metallic quality, no matter how frenetic it sounds, which issues uniquely out of that ambiguity that comes out of your unpossessed souls. Some of you may feel the obligation to externalize your knowledge that *you* know he is here to defend the indefensible. You may jeer him, as he has been jeered by those who wrestle for their livelihood with their hands, who especially despise him because he claims to speak for them; some of you may treat him with that terrible coldness that is the sign of the intellectual foreknowledge that you cannot, at your level of attainment, take seriously the man who speaks and works for a kingdom which it is the very purpose of your education to know to despise. Why then bring him here, if no purpose can be served and if it can only result that you will humiliate yourselves and him? Because you are *willing* to humiliate yourselves in order to humiliate him?

Fight him, fight the tyrants everywhere but do not ask them to your quarters, merely to spit on them, and do not ask them to your quarters if you cannot spit on them. To do the one is to ambush a human being as one might a rabid dog; to do the other is to ambush oneself, to force oneself, in disregard of those who have *died* trying to make the point, to break faith with humanity.

WHO ARE THE NEW PRO-COMMUNISTS?

January 27, 1967

Only a few years ago one could hope to identify the pro-Communists by such simple measurements as the number of officially classified Communist-front organizations they longed to or, better still, by observing them before a congressional committee pleading the Fifth Amendment to the question: Are you now or have you ever been a member of the Communist Party? In the former case it was possible for the rational man to reason: Look, if John Jones took sides time and time again with organizations the single common denominator of whose programs is to back the Communists against the United States—well, said a reasonable man could infer from such activity pro-communist ideological inclinations. Then, of course, the others—the Fifth Amendment types—were even easier to spot. They refused to answer the question on the ground that they knew that someone, in most cases a planted FBI agent, knew them to be enrolled members of the Communist Party, and they dared not risk a perjury rap.

Subtle changes are taking place. Sure, there are still Communist fronts—*e.g.*, the Fair Play for Cuba Committee, which seduced naïfs like James Baldwin and Norman Mailer into membership. But the new pro-Communist is not nowadays necessarily a Communist-front joiner. He is too cool for that kind of thing, though he does not disdain occasionally to identify himself with apparently pro-communist organizations. The new pro-Communist is less that he is because he is a conscious Marxist—the kind of man Alger Hiss was, who sought to serve the Communist Party by performing explicit assignments in its behalf. He is rather an attitudinal pro-Communist, moved less by Marxist convictions than by a positive animosity toward the West. The hatred of the West and its ways is stronger, in his case, than his older brother's positive faith in the Communist vision.

Begin by exclusions. Professors Arthur Schlesinger and Hans Morgenthau are by now outspoken critics of the Vietnam war. Are they for that reason pro-Communist? Clearly not. Columnist Joseph Alsop insists that their opposition to the war is based on a near-vulgar ignorance of the Asian situation. That, in fact, is only a partial explanation. They oppose the war on account of complicated attachments—some of them political, some of them theoretical. And this much at least can safely be said about Messrs. Schlesinger and Morgenthau, that no matter how adamantly they insist, as one of their reasons for opposing the war, that it is plainly unprofitable and unwin-

nable, no matter the resultant blow to their intellectu
pride, they would be pleased and happy if, in fact, the w
turned out to be successful for the West, in the sense, sa
that the Korean war turned out to be successful. The cri
Richard Rovere—to take a kindred example—rail
against President Eisenhower's resolution in defendi
Quemoy and Matsu, but when Eisenhower's policy su
ceeded, he had the grace to rejoice in its having done
and to meditate publicly on his own panicky misrecko
ing.

But then there are the others. You probably know
least one. The man whose attachment to the propositi
that we are wrong for fighting in Vietnam has translated
into a desire to see his views confirmed by the maximu
shedding of American blood. The man who, having sa
we cannot win in Vietnam, rejoices at any evidences th
we are losing in Vietnam. He might be an isolated ty
whose commitment is only as regards Vietnam. But the
are the others whose attachments do not stop at Vietna
I have someone in mind.

He is someone whose hostility to the West is not limit
to its role in Vietnam. It is a total hostility, manifest in I
attitudes everywhere. To him the issue of the morni
newspaper which carried the news of the total breakdo
of the Western position would be absolutely ideal. Such
paper would bring to his breakfast table the news that 1
American planes had been shot down over North Vietna
the day before; that the North Koreans had renewed th
aggressions into South Korea; that the Communists ha
scored enormous gains in the Indian elections; that Ju
Bosch and João Goulart had counterrevolutionized th
way into power in the Dominican Republic and Braz
that the OAS had decided to rescind its boycott agai
Cuba; that the Communist vote in West Germany had t
bled; that the Lumumba-ites had recaptured control
central Africa; that Rusk was booed in India and Ho C
Minh cheered there; that Alger Hiss was exonerated and
Edgar Hoover indicted for perjury; that Bertra
Russell's war crimes tribunal had captured the symp
thetic attention of the West; that the Pope had announc
that modern research proves that Christ was a my
ological allegory; that T. S. Eliot's last will and testame

isclosed that his defense of Christianity was an elaborate
terary hoax.

The man I have in mind would be supremely happy on
hat eventful morning. He is pro-Communist in effect. No
oubt if he should have to end up living within the con-
trictions of the Communist system, he would chafe, lack-
ng as he is in any self-abnegating faith in the Communist
deal. But meanwhile, he would be a happy man, happy
hat external events are bringing down the curtain on the
ld bourgeois, Judeo-Christian world. He is the new ef-
ective pro-Communist. But he is difficult to fingerprint.

TO RUSSIA WITH LOVE?

October 13, 1966

It is the thesis of the romantics that among the highest
olls we are paying in Vietnam is the loss of the con-
idence of the Russians, the loss of a great historical op-
ortunity to strike a *détente* with the Soviet Union and
narch hand in hand with her toward the happy horizons
f time. No doubt because he is aware of that criticism,
he President in his address last week to the newspaper
ditorial writers stressed and restressed his desire for hap-
ier relations with the Soviet Union, and there is talk of
ven more cultural exchange, of even more trade, of
dopting the consular treaty the Soviet Union cov-
ts—anything at all to persuade the Soviet Union of our
ood intentions.

One wonders what it is that "good" intentions are and
vhy it is that we feel the need to court the respect of the
Soviet government. A "good" intention, as far as the So-
iet world is concerned, is a resolution by the United
States not to stand in the way of any Communist enter-
rise anywhere on earth, whether military as in Vietnam,
olonialist as in Cuba, economic as in East Europe, or
olemical as in the New York City *Worker*.

U.S. intentions are, by the Communist vocabulary, at
heir worst when we send American troops physically to
esist a "war of national liberation," and the Soviet press
as never ceased to thunder against us over the issue of
Vietnam. What many American analysts are un-

derestimating is the inverse factor between Soviet rhetoric and Soviet aggressiveness. When she thunders most, she tends to agitate least. Because, from time to time, she has come up against Western resolution: as in Greece after the war and, subsequently, in Korea, in the Formosan Strait, in Berlin, and in Cuba. Good intentions, by the Western definition, are, or should be, to show a mailed fist whenever and wherever the Soviet Union coils to strike a salient.

And anyway, as Lord Chesterfield wrote to his son about sex, the posture is ridiculous. That we should worry about what the Soviet Union thinks of us is more than the humblest self-pride can bear. A few weeks ago I had a telephone call from the assistant to Louis Lomax, the prominent Negro writer and commentator on the West Coast, asking me whether I would consent to debate with Mr. Lomax at the University of Moscow. Debate with him about what? I asked. Civil rights, he said. Whose civil rights, I pressed, the Negroes'—or the Russians'?

The conversation terminated as though I had announced membership in the Ku Klux Klan, but I promised to write directly to Mr. Lomax and did so, expressing myself as baffled that two Americans should appear before a group of political slaves and humbly beg their favor and toleration for the condition of civil rights in the United States today.

Now if the debate were to be on the topic "How Should the United States Deal with the Soviet Union, a Liberal and a Conservative View of United States Responsibility to World Freedom," I said to Mr. Lomax, that would be different, and I would be glad to engage in such a debate before the students of the University of Moscow. I never heard again from Mr. L., though it may be that the adverse decision was not his, but Moscow's. Soviet authorities are about as anxious to sponsor a discussion of Soviet freedom before Soviet students as missionaries in the Congo would be to sponsor a lecture to the local gentry on the delights of human flesh.

It may be that in the years ahead we shall combine with Russia, for some purpose or other; after all, we did just that a quarter of a century ago. The historian John Lukacs has said sweepingly that the most significant datum of the first half of the twentieth century is that the United States was an English-speaking country and that the most significant datum of the second half of the twentieth century will prove to be that the Russians have white skins. Maybe such cultural and ethnic affinities as these will in due course transcend the sundering philosophical differences.

But if so, why not wait and let it happen and, meanwhile, hang on to right reason by informing the Soviet Union that her solidarity with the Communist imperialists of Southeast Asia reminds us once again of her bloody past and her bloody commitments and that, at least for the duration of the Vietnam war, they can take their consuls and their ballet and go jump in the lake? Maybe Mr. Lomax would be willing to act as emissary.

ON DEAD-RED

November 10, 1962

Many arguments are nowadays posed, and opinions influenced, by gaudy references to the extent of the devastation that would ensue upon a thermonuclear exchange in a third world war. I have heard lecturer after lecturer describe in macrocosmic terms, almost as if they took pleasure in describing all that gore, the meaning for the United States of a thermonuclear attack on us by, say, 100 ten-megaton Russian missiles. I can hear the words of a man who spoke last week: "at least a hundred million deaths . . . starvation and contamination for most of the rest of the population . . . reduction of our economy to a primitive level." I shall spare you more, especially the description of the physical appearance of an incinerated child in Hiroshima. There are few things more gruesome.

Still I ask: What actually is the relevance of all that talk (which is used primarily by pacifists and collaborators and those who plead for disarmament at any price)? We know the meaning of violent death intuitively, do we not? Even so we are committed, as individuals, as a nation, and as a civilization, to the proposition that death is the price one must be *prepared* to pay to oppose certain kinds of threats. Granted, if there were a war today, there would be more deaths—far more deaths—than were caused by yesterday's war. But what is the meaning of that statistic to the individual dead man? None. He knows not whether he died alone or in the company of 100,000,000 others. What is the meaning of it for the survivor? None that goes beyond that abysmal grief of personal loss, experienced well before the nuclear age by, for instance, the frontiersman's wife whose husband and children were massacred by the Indians. An individual human being can sustain only so much grief, and then bereavement becomes redundant. If my wife, son, mother, brothers, and sisters are killed, I have little capacity left to grieve over the loss of my college roommate's uncle. What, then, is the meaning of that statistic for civilization? Civilization has no feelings and knows not pain. It is we, the dead and the survivors, who feel the loss or advancement of civilization. And here we come to the nub of the question.

What we are asked by those who devote their energies to describing the effects of nuclear war to consider then, when you analyze it, is less human suffering than the loss to humankind of so many of those things that lived on and on even when generation after generation of human beings died: the intangible things—the sense of community and of nationhood—and the tangible things—the cathedral at Chartres, the museum at the Prado, the White House, the Vatican, the Bodleian Library. It is, I think, more the sense of these losses than the concern for human life which hard analysis betrays as lying beneath the unreasoned hysteria of many of our contemporaries, and indeed, when we contemplate shattering, say, the stained-glass windows of Chartres, we know that unlike the extinction of human life, we contemplate extinguishing something which, because it was not afflicted with mortality, might otherwise have gone on and on, to refresh and console the people, right through empires risen and fallen, barbarians repulsed or submitted to, the appearance and disappearance of the one-hundredth French Republic.

And yet that is a pagan's analysis. Because human life, even though it cannot last beyond a few score years, is more valuable than all the perdurable treasures of the earth.

It is necessary, when we listen to a Norman Cousins or a Steve Allen or a Sidney Lens or a Bertrand Russell or a Kenneth Tynan going on and on about the horrors and scale of nuclear death, to force ourselves to face explicitly

hat we know intuitively. And that is this: If it is right
1at a single man is prepared to die for a just cause, it is
rguably right that an entire civilization be prepared to die
or a just cause. In contemporary terms it can scarcely be
isputed that if ever a cause was just, this one is, for the
nemy combines the ruthlessness and savagery of Genghis
.han with the fiendish scientific efficiency of an IBM ma-
hine. As we have seen, the collective bereavement is not
1ore than the sum of individual bereavements and cannot,
1erefore, in human terms, outweigh in quality or in in-
:nsity the pain that has always been felt, throughout the
istory of the world, by individuals who did not place
1ese arguments, so as to escape the net of those facile lit-
e clichés which reduce complex issues to disjunctive
ngles. Better Dead than Red is an inaccurate statement
f the American position, listing, as it does, nonexclusive
lternatives. Properly stated, it is: Better the *chance* of
eing dead, than the certainty of being Red. And if we
ie? We die.

VI. The City, the Races

TWO BOOKS

October 2, 196

Here are two books about urban problems and politic
one of them wonderfully enlightening, the other useful or
ly, I fear, to IBM machines who desire to be mayor—
limited, though not inconsiderable, market. Henry W
Maier is the successful mayor (Democrat) of Milwauke
a vigorous and efficient young man who, whatever h
qualifications to administer the public affairs of an impo
tant city, clearly has none at all as an author. It could b
maintained that *Challenge to the Cities* is in refreshir
contrast with books by the typical modern politician, wh
uses a ghost. One reads the opening pages and conclude
that no ghost could possibly have written such sentence
as Mr. Maier's without incurring permanent unemploy
ment. By the time the reader has gone through the boo
he is not likely soon again to disparage the profession
ghostwriting.

One could more easily forgive His Honor his literar
underdevelopment if he had, in spite of it, succeeded
evolving his vaunted "approach" to a "theory of urba
leadership." He has not done so, unless a collection of i
telligent truisms can be said to add up to a theory, whic
is possible, but a theoretical revelation based upon them
strictly a pseudoevent. Illuminating new theories canno
whatever the pressure at one end, be extruded from emp
old tubes, and it doesn't help at all to design pretentio
schematic chapter titles if all they do is introduce a seri
of clichés.

Mr. Maier doesn't tell us how to deal with people

with politicians or with pressure groups or with the press, beyond informing us that people are human, politicians politically conscious, pressure groups single-minded, the press news-hungry—a venture in tautology excusable in a book only if the author, in his narrative or analysis, disgorges a fresh perspective. There is none of that in this unfortunate book, which does a disservice to what by all accounts is the record of a competent, if tendentious, municipal administration.

It may be that there are graduate students in political science who will learn from the "Philosophy of Local Leadership" with which Mr. Maier, mercifully, ends his book. But that presupposes that there are graduate students in political science who will note and remember such distillations of the mayor of Milwaukee as that "there is a time for a mayor to fight and a time not to fight" or that "the central city mayor survives only when he has the psychological capacity and the resourcefulness to handle at one time three man-eating gorillas of crises and two of the paper tigers that, it seems at times, are thrown upon his back just to test him." That such students undoubtedly exist is hardly consoling, let alone that someday they may decide to write their own books.

By contrast, William Lee Miller's book is a fascinating, readable, provocative, illuminating romp through the recent civic history of New Haven. The author is a professor of social ethics at Yale University, an ordained minister, a former writer for the *Reporter*—a doer-intellectual whose childhood romance with liberal politics has grown into a consuming, but not altogether uncritical, passion. Mr. Miller, it should instantly be noted gratefully, is, notwithstanding his own avid partisanship, an observer capable of an affecting fairness, as when on occasion after occasion he rejects, even if he falls short of scorning, the facile generality that all those who oppose this or that proposal of a civil rights lobby are necessarily racist. Such thinking is not only unfair, says the professor of social ethics, but occlusive.

It is necessary, in order to advance the goals of integration, civil liberties, better housing, and the lot, to understand the exact nature of the opposition. To be sure, the reader is permitted to conclude that the opposition if not racist, tends to irrationality in some cases, moral

113

backwardness in others, a mixture of both in most. Still, as a social taxonomist of generous disposition, Mr. Miller urges that liberal militants resist the temptation to a kind of reverse yahooism, whose attitude toward conservative dissent is roughly comparable to the xenophobia and racism of the lapidary demons of American society. The reader infers that he learned this respect, if not for dissenting opinion, at least for those who express it, as a direct result of having served over the past three years as alderman of the Fifteenth Ward of the city of New Haven. It is an experience which has greatly benefited him and will greatly benefit anyone who gives himself the pleasure of reading this sprightly and informative chronicle.

The book is in a sense a celebration of the tenure of Richard Lee as mayor of New Haven. Mr. Lee has other bards; indeed he is probably more written about than any mayor in the United States since La Guardia, but he has none nearly as Homeric as Mr. Miller, who in dramatic perspective gives him personal credit for the major urban accomplishment of our time, the rebuilding of New Haven.

The objective accomplishments of Mr. Lee are rather widely known. They consist, if one reaches for a theatrical formulation, in nothing less than the reconstitution of a moribund city. He has managed this feat by a combination of skills, the greatest of which (talk about an approach to the theory of government!) has been the ultimate development of the science of extracting money from outside the community you live in for the benefit of the community you live in. Extracting money from the state, from the foundations, from, principally, of course, the federal government, in order to subsidize, in Mr. Lee's case, his profuse ambitions for his beloved city of New Haven. Mr. Miller gleefully records, for instance, that exactly ten minutes after Mayor Lee received from the hands of Lyndon Johnson one of those fountain pens with which the President signed into law one of those urban renewal acts, the mayor materialized at the office of the relevant federal bursar and put in for New Haven's share.

If one lived in New Haven, one would find it difficult to be other than enormously enthusiastic about and everlastingly grateful to a mayor so enterprising. The figures

114

show, for instance, that New Haven has in recent years sucked in 438 federal dollars per capita, during a period when New York took in 31. Such prodigies of public money mulcting are quite understandably a matter of enormous civic pride in New Haven. Citizens of other cities may be less enthusiastic and may be excused for reasoning that the federal dollar that ends up in New Haven is a federal dollar that doesn't end up in their own city—always assuming that the available supply of federal dollars is somehow limited, a datum, which, if pressed, could just possibly interrupt Mr. Miller's reverie about New Haven, which may be why he doesn't bring it up.

If Mr. Miller's figures are correct, then it would follow that to do to other cities of comparable or greater magnitude as has been done to New Haven (a formulation which Mr. Miller, as a professor of ethics, would have difficulty arguing with) would require the expenditure of the impressive sum of $146 billion. Nowhere in this exuberant book does he pause over vulgar macrocosmic details of this sort.

One result of Mr. Miller's neglect of the general problem is that some of his readers may be tempted to conclude that, in the last analysis, Mayor Lee has proved nothing much more than that $500,000,000 can go a long way in refurbishing a city of 150,000 people. And perhaps to go on to wonder whether, as our dependency on the federal government grows and grows and grows, it is possible that that elusive new theory of municipal politics reduces to the relative leverage a given municipality can exercise on the federal Treasury. The trouble with everybody's getting behind that theory is that, assuming the federal government's resources are finite, civic enterprise becomes something which is accomplished by one municipality at the expense of other municipalities.

Mr. Miller has also concerned himself with civil rights, and his book is an invaluable account of the kind of thing that happens in a middle-sized city when integrationist and anti-poverty programs are rigorously promulgated. The worst experience was with an experimental busing program, designed to break down *de facto* segregation in a few of the public schools. By Mr. Miller's testimony, New Haven was torn apart by the issue, and although the pro-

115

gram was executed as a result of the indomitability of the school board, only 313 out of 21,000 schoolchildren were affected, and then only temporarily. Temporarily because the construction of new schools finally put an end to it, and one gathers that the neighborhood school principle is back in operation.

Mayor Lee, the politician, apparently spotted a potential nemesis and entered the controversy with a well-balanced tergiversation. He reminded the voters that the experiment was short-term and promised to concede them their most adamant desire, the local election of the school board—provided, however, that the new school board also assume (and relieve Mr. Lee of) the responsibility for raising the money for paying for the operation of the schools.

On the matter of busing, Mr. Miller is a little evasive. Although he backed the busing experiment, he does not seem to regret its termination. And then, later on in the book, in quite another connection, he parenthetically refers to it as a "disaster." On the other hand, he stops short of warning other municipalities entertaining the idea of busing to benefit from New Haven's experience, which leaves it unclear why he used such a word as "disaster" in referring to it, though ordained ministers are given to eschatological usage.

He does, however, intrude his fine pragmatic intelligence to make the point that numbers are greatly important; that if buses are to be used to transship students, they should not be crowded; that if Negro students are to be imported to theretofore all-white schools, they should be a small, rather than a large, minority, the better to accelerate their assimilation, the less to disturb the general atmosphere.

Mr. Miller finally informs us that in his view "economic integration" is the most important future objective of social urban policy. His reasoning is enormously seductive. The reason for poverty, he says (and here he makes an explicit concession to traditional conservative analysis), is not merely material or environmental malnutrition. It is the ethos that is crucial, and the ethos of those who care to rise from poverty and know how to do so is not easily communicable to the despairing poor, however opulent their new, federally subsidized shelters, if the poor are

116

cloistered together outside the earshot of the better adjusted.

What is needed is what he calls—a term one will have to get used to, I suppose—scatteration. A public housing project here, another one there, etc., each of them plopped down in a middle-class neighborhood, the better to expose the beneficiaries to the spirit and folkways of the going community. The idea turns out to be the hottest potato of them all. Indeed, the one paradigmatic venture in scatteration with which Mr. Miller was directly involved aroused such protests as to compel even the Lee administration to abandon it.

The protests from the target communities are based on many factors: the projected decline in property values; the projected contamination of local children by other children with records of vandalism, sexual promiscuity, drug addiction, general ne'er-do-well-ism; the interruption of the prevailing *Gemütlichkeit*. Mr. Miller reasons that the fears, material and spiritual, are exaggerated. He adds that, whatever the residual inconveniences, here is the only practical way to break the poverty-cycle, and that to break it is not merely a humanitarian concern (one must worry about one's impoverished neighbor), but also a practical concern (one must hope someday to be done paying one's impoverished neighbor's bills).

I tend to agree with Mr. Miller, agreeing as I do that the ethos is nine-tenths of the problem, though I think he owes us another book addressed to the problem of how to maintain the potency of the ethos in those communities into which the unfortunate are to be introduced. If we progressively deprive the community of those usufructs of liberty and civilization which contribute to the vitality of the ethos, if we deprive the people of self-government by removing their authority to rule themselves, if we deprive them of private property by steeper and steeper taxation, if we impair the sense of community by introducing antibodies, if we disfigure the personality of the community by constant tampering, if we integrate at the expense of educating, isn't it likely that something will happen worth worrying about?

And mustn't the social planner, whether the alderman of the Fifteenth Ward of New Haven or the President of the United States, reflect on the problem and proceed with

117

his grand designs a little more apprehensively than Mr. Miller has shown himself disposed to do in this otherwise conscientious, revealing and rewarding book?

DR. KING PROPOSES
MASSIVE CIVIL DISOBEDIENCE

August 19, 1967

Now Dr. Martin Luther King proposes massive "dislocations." Not violent dislocations, understand. Just "massive civil disobedience," like blocking plant gates, highways, government operations, sit-ins in federal buildings, that kind of thing. But not violent, repeat. The man reporting to work at his factory is not expected to press his way through Dr. King's human wall, nor the wife driving her car to pick up her child at school to trample the toes of the *satyagrahi*. No violence, just a national convulsion.

Actually, Dr. King can't bring it off. He has lost much of his following: "Last summer in Chicago," Andrew Kopkind remarks in a review (*New York Review of Books*) of Dr. King's recent book *Where Do We Go from Here?* "he was booed at a mass meeting, and later, as he lay in bed unsleeping, he understood why."

Why? Because the dream that he kept preaching had not come. The Freedom Now that he sang from coast to coast had not been realized. "The Movement," Mr. Kopkind observes, "is dead: The Revolution is unborn. The streets are bloody and ablaze, but it is difficult to see why, and impossible to know for what end. . . . If it is any comfort, liberalism proves hardly more effective than fascism."

The civil rights movement as such is, of course, transformed. The realization has dawned that all those legislative enactments calculated to produce equality before the law were not enough to reify the heavenly kingdom. Indeed and perversely, it sometimes seemed as if the greater the effort to integrate, to dispense welfare, the less that was accomplished.

"Jerome Cavanaugh of Detroit," Mr. Kopkind continues, "is the most 'progressive' mayor in the country; his battleground is bloodier than Sam Yorty's was. At least we know now that even if all Martin Luther King's programs were enacted, and all Jerome Cavanaugh's reforms were adopted, and the Great Society as it is described materialized before our very eyes, there would still be the guerrillas."

Understand, Mr. Kopkind is of the school that cannot bring itself to criticize the guerrillas. The dissatisfaction with King is that he does not recognize the essential cynicism of the American system. Mr. Kopkind's frame of reference in contemporary affairs is best suggested by his reference to the Vietnam war as "the most barbaric imperialistic war of this century" (for which of course America is to blame). He is simply one more observer who welcomes the general chaos because it could bring down the American system, and that is the goal for which they most devoutly wish.

What specifically does Dr. King want? In his book he asks for a guaranteed annual income, which is not so different from the radical but attractive proposal of Dr. Milton Friedman for a negative income tax. He wants: more Negroes elected as officials (since the book's appearance, the state of Mississippi has munificently obliged); better schools (who doesn't?); more jobs (the unemployment rate is reassuringly low); and protection of everyone's rights.

But the point is, as Mr. Kopkind rightly intuits, that if all this were realized, there would still be the guerrillas, to use the phrase he so obviously relishes, even if he came later than others to appreciating why they developed.

James Baldwin said in June, 1963: "Martin Luther King is a great man, but he has come to the end of his rope." And on that occasion, conservatives also discerned the same thing. "It is a tragic matter" (I wrote, commenting on Baldwin's book *The Fire Next Time*), "tragedy here defined as an irresistible force moving on a collision course towards an immovable body. What Baldwin has asked for is nothing less than the evanescence of color. So long as the eyes remark the difference between black and white, existential differences, of greater or lesser consequence, but of meaning just the same, will exist. The job at hand is not to try to obliterate differences which only autohypnotic color blindness could achieve, but to stimulate man's capacity for love and his toleration,

119

understanding, and respect for other, different people."

Such a program will not likely be accelerated by any new, desperate exhortation to chaos. Nor should it. Repression is an unpleasant instrument, but it is absolutely necessary for civilizations that believe in order and human rights. I wish to God Hitler and Lenin had been repressed. And word should be gently got through to the nonviolent avengers that in the unlikely event that they succeed in mobilizing their legions, they will be most efficiently, indeed most zestfully, repressed. In the name, quite properly, of social justice.

STAUGHTON LYND ON THE REBELLION

September 14, 1967

Staughton Lynd of Yale University is assistant professor of radicalism, in pursuit of a firsthand knowledge of which, you will remember, he went off to Hanoi a while ago and mooed his solidarity with the Communists there, returning to Yale to display proudly all the new hair on his revolutionary chest. Since then he was granted a leave of absence by Yale.

Meanwhile, Lynd continues busy polemicizing and most recently has advanced solemnly the doctrine (in the New York *Times Sunday Magazine,* on September 10, 1967) that the kind of thing we have seen in Detroit and Newark and Los Angeles is really okay, that it is the kind of activity sanctioned implicitly by John Locke, Thomas Jefferson, Abraham Lincoln, and Norman Vincent Peale. The thing of it is (he explains), what is happening is not "riots"—they are vulgar and unjustified—but "rebellions." And everybody acknowledges that rebellions are okay when positive law clashes with transcendent law; otherwise you get Eichmann, see?

The notion that there is a right to rebellion ultimately rests on one of two grounds—the first sociological, the second moral. Concerning the first ground, Professor Lynd acknowledges that the theorists of revolution, *e.g.,* Locke, insisted that rebellions were indefensible except insofar as the revolutionists in fact spoke for the majority of the people. Clearly Stokely Carmichael and H. Rap Brown do not speak for the majority of the American Negroes, let alone e majority of the American people. Mr. Lynd gets round this difficulty by saying that the Carmichaels do peak (that is not true) for the majority in the ghetto reas and that it is sovereignty over these areas that the lack rioters, or rather revolutionists, hanker for.

The defect in the argument is obvious to anyone who meditates on the doctrine of majority rule. If there is a ght to revolution by the local unit against the larger unit, nen who is to decide what is the feasible size of the evolutionary unit? Certainly by those standards the South as correct during the Civil War. But why not also the mish, who by their lights are oppressed by the majority? r, for that matter, the solidly Republican Orange County f California, which is oppressed by a Democratic administration?

The moral argument is no more usable. If anyone is entitled to revolutionize against a government whose policies re "immoral," then, of course, the question arises: Who ill decide what is moral and what is not? When Thomas efferson drafted the Declaration of Independence, he appealed to the "decent opinion of mankind" to justify him, nd such civilized men as Edmund Burke found in that eclaration sufficient grounds to justify revolution.

Are there civilized men who see justification in the evolution of Carmichael and Brown? No, there are only ne perverts—the Lynds. And what is most perverse in rofessor Lynd's essay is that he seeks to enlist believers the Carmichael revolution among the ranks, not of nose who are rebelliously dissatisfied with the plight of ne Negro in America, but from the ranks of those who ppose the Vietnam war.

Thus, Mr. Lynd slyly introduces the Port Huron statement of 1962 by the Students for a Democratic Society as some way affirming the riots in Detroit and Newark. ut the Port Huron statement deals mostly with the ecessity of abandoning deterrence as an instrument of inrnational policy blah blah blah, and says not a word out the necessity of encouraging rioting Carmichaelites shoot policemen so as to expedite the acquisition of col- television sets.

Apart from the sociological and the moral arguments, ere remains the much more palpable argument of power. dmund Burke argued the rightness of the American

cause. But he never went so far as to argue that Kir
George did not have the right to resist the rebellion of tl
Colonies. Who then will go so far as to argue that tl
United States, whose principal domestic concern over tl
past decade has been with means of helping the Negro
reach full civic and educational parity, has no right
treat the rioters, if indeed they succeed in classifying ther
selves as revolutionaries, as revolutionaries?

In other words, if Mr. Lynd should win his intellectu
argument, then does it not follow that the responsibility
the United States government would be, not to jail tl
Browns and Carmichaels for a month or two, which is tl
kind of thing that is now in prospect for them, but to li
them up and shoot them quite dead or put them in conce
tration camps, the way we shot and imprisoned the revol
tionists during the Civil War? One would think, in oth
words, that Mr. Lynd's line of reasoning would strike hi
as strategically unprofitable. Fortunately for him, it is n
likely to be taken seriously.

THE END OF MARTIN LUTHER KING

April 9, 19(

It is curious and melancholy that hours after the dea
of the Reverend Martin Luther King, and 100,000 wor
after the doleful announcement of his murder, not
single commentator on radio or television has mention
what one would suppose is a critical datum—namely, th
Mr. King was an ordained minister in the Christian fai
and that those who believe that the ministry is other th
merely symbolic servitude to God must hope and pray th
he is today happier than he was yesterday, united with I
Maker, with the angels and the saints, with the proph(
whose words of inspiration he quoted with such telling (
fect in his hot pursuit of a secular millenarianism.

Those who take seriously Dr. King's calling are oblig
above all to comment on this aspect of his martyrdom a
to rejoice in the divine warranty that eyes have
seen—nor have ears heard of—the glories that God I
prepared for those who love Him.

No, it is the secular aspects of his death that obsess

ery well then, let us in his memory make a few observa-
ions:

1. Whatever his virtues and whatever his faults, he
id not deserve assassination. There are the special
ew—one thinks of Joan of Arc—whose career dictates,
s a matter of theatrical necessity, a violent end, early in
fe. Dr. King was not of that cast. His virtues were con-
iderable, most notably his extraordinary capacity to
nspire. But although the dream he dreamed appeared to
many Americans, particularly the black militants, but not
xcluding many orthodox liberals, less and less useful
freedom now, in the sense he understood it, *was* a dream,
mischievously deceptive), it simply wasn't ever required
hat in order to reify that vision, he should surrender his
wn life. In that sense his martyrdom was simply not
useful. Because it is plainly impossible that on account of
his death, things are going to change. The martyrdom he
eemed sometimes almost to be seeking may commend
him to history and to God, but not likely to Scarsdale,
New York, which has never credited the charge that the
white community of America conspires to ensure the
wretchedness of the brothers of Martin Luther King.

2. And concerning his weaknesses, it would take a
lunatic (his murderer has not at this point been apprehended, but he is sure to be one) to reason that Dr.
King's faults justified a private assassination. The theory
to which most of us subscribe is that there is no vice so
hideous as to justify private murder. Even so, we tend
emotionally to waive that categorical imperative every
now and then. If someone had shot down Adolf Eichmann
n a motel, the chances are that our deploring of the
assassin's means would have been ritualistic. The only
people who were genuinely annoyed by Jack Ruby's
assassination of Lee Harvey Oswald were those who
maintained a fastidious interest in the survival of Oswald,
or the sake of the record.

Dr. King's faults—and they most surely existed—were
ar from the category of the faults of those whose
assassination is more or less tolerated, as we all of us
more or less tolerated the assassination of George Lincoln
Rockwell. Those faults were a terribly mistaken judgment—above all. A year ago he accused the United

123

States of committing crimes equal in horror to those com mitted by the Nazis in Germany. One could only gasp a the profanation. Ten days ago in his penultimate speech delivered at the Washington Cathedral, he accused th United States of waging a war as indefensible as any wa committed during the twentieth century. Several years ag on the way back from Stockholm where he received th Nobel Peace Prize, he conspicuously declined to criticiz the Gbenye movement in the northern Congo, which wa even then engaged in slaughtering, as brutally as Dr. Kin was slaughtered, his brothers in Christ. But for suc transgressions in logic and in judgment, one does n receive the death sentence.

3. The sickening observation of the commentators i therefore particularly inapposite. The commentator (most of them) said: How can we now defend nonvio lence? Surely the answer is: more perfervidly than eve before. It was—need we remark—violence that killed D King. Should we therefore abandon nonviolence?

Those who mourn Dr. King because they were his clos est followers should meditate the implications of the dee of the wild man who killed him. That deed should bring t mind not (for God's sake!) the irrelevance of non violence, but the sternest necessity of reaffirming non violence. An aspect of nonviolence is subjugation to th law.

The last public speech of Martin Luther King describe his intentions of violating the law in Memphis, where a injunction had been handed down against the resumptio of a march which only a week ago had resulted in th death of one human being and the wounding of fif others.

Dr. King's flouting of the law does not justify the flou ing by others of the law, but it is a terrifying thought tha most likely, the cretin who leveled his rifle at the head Martin Luther King may have absorbed the talk, so fre ly available, about the supremacy of the individu conscience, such talk as Martin Luther King, God rest h troubled and compassionate soul, had so widely and so i discriminately made.

July 20, 1967

What happened at Newark? You would think we would all know for sure. After all, there are (at the last count) 1,300 persons arrested, so that there are plenty of people around to interrogate. How will the typical interrogation go? Here is how most of our moralizers hope it will go:

MAGISTRATE: Mr. Jones, why did you burn down the corner delicatessen store?

A: Because of my sense of despair.

M: Why do you feel a sense of despair, Mr. Jones?

A: Because my people have been persecuted for 400 years.

M: But you do realize that there are laws against burning down delicatessen stores? Especially when the manager and his wife are still inside the store?

A: Laws schmaws. Have you never heard of civil disobedience? Have you never heard of Martin Luther King? Have you never heard of the dialectic of violence?

M: What are you talking about, Jones?

A: Just this, whitey. You and all the other judges and all the lawyers and the reformers and the whole bloody white power structure aren't doing enough for the people your profit-seeking great-granddaddies uprooted from their native hearths, and it is only fitting under the circumstances that we should protest by whatever means are at our disposal. An editorial writer for the New York *Times* makes an acute historical analogy between what we did at Newark and what you people did at the Boston Tea Party: "Calmer people were so aghast"—after the Boston riot—"that they suggested that the ministers and rabble-rousing patriots who incited this riotous act become turnspits in the kitchens of the English nobility." In the twenty-first century they'll be building monuments to the heroes of Watts, and Buffalo, and Cincinnati—and Newark.

M: But surely you realize that the effect of what you did is likely to be exactly the opposite of what you desire? White hearts will harden against you?

A: Hearts schmartz. The point about rioting is precisely that it works. The Reverend Fred Shuttleworth, a very holy man and the principal assistant to Martin Luther King, said about a new park being built in the riot area of Cincinnati, "A lot of people think they got that because of the rioting, and I think they are right. Nonviolence didn't get it."

M: But you can't go around breaking laws you disapprove of.

A: And you can't go around exploiting races you disapprove of.

M: I sentence you to thirty days, suspended sentence.

A: Remember, judge it'll be *the* fire next time. We let you off easy this time.

M: I appreciate that, Mr. Jones. Thanks very much.

But, of course, it won't be that way. There is probably only one Stokely Carmichael out of a thousand rioters. Governor Hughes of New Jersey is a liberal prominently identified with the civil rights movement, and after observing the riot for seventy-two hours, he arrived at a conclusion.

"It was plain and simple crime and not a civil rights protest," Governor Hughes said. At other moments he called it, rather loosely, an "insurrection," a "rebellion," in which case it was surely among the most futile and chaotic rebellions ever recorded. There was no hope of coming to power. There was no prospect of a radically altered relationship, save possibly for the worse. There were no concrete objectives listed, not even a new park or swimming pool.

It is rumored—it is nothing more than a rumor—that the proximate irritations were the failure of the mayor to appoint a Negro member to the school board and the displacement of a number of Negro families by a public building—which, if it had not been built in the ghetto would perhaps have caused as much resentment. But nobody knows for sure.

At another point, the governor said that economic misery was the root cause of the riot, and it is true that the unemployed in Newark are at double the national rate—yet that only makes for 8 to 9 percent. Was there a master choreographer? Stokely? The Communist Party? No, though the governor does believe that some of the ioters were from out of town and that some of the snipers were expert marksmen, practiced in evasive tactics.

What fueled the riot was, of course, a raging disease of he spirit, which is unrelated to statistical abstracts having o do with unemployment and economic opportunity. It is he anarchic passion to smash, the phrase of Herbert Agar s he surveyed the wreckage of Europe under Communism and Fascism during the thirties. The spirit has got o be contained, and the National Guard can accomplish only so much. The Shuttleworths and the Kings and the New York *Times*' need to return to philosophical bedrock and do a little hard labor on history and morality and the causes of the rise of civilizations and of the fall of civilizations.

ARE THE RIOTERS RACISTS?

July 29, 1967

Add to the judgment of Governor Richard J. Hughes of New Jersey that the riots are unrelated to civil rights the judgment of Mayor Jerome P. Cavanaugh of Detroit, also a Democrat, of Governor George Romney of Michigan, a Republican, and of Governor Ronald Reagan of California, ditto. It is easy enough to see what these gentlemen mean. A man who breaks into a store to hijack himself a case of whiskey can hardly be said to be engaged in the advancement of colored people. And it is certainly true that most of those who are roaming the streets like drunken janissaries pillaging and razing our cities are not engaged in the forwarding of any certified ideals.

Even so the riots are, in a critical sense, related to civil rights broadly understood—*i.e.*, they are politically motivated. The point is that those who have succeeded in transforming local disturbances into wholesale insurrections seem to have been motivated by racial animosities which rise, or are said to rise, from a concern for the distribution of power.

Most obviously, there is H. Rap Brown, successor to tokely Carmichael (who is nowadays in Havana giving he Communists a postgraduate course on the art of evolution). Mr. Brown lectured on Tuesday in Cambridge, Maryland, and urged his listeners to "burn this town down. . . . Don't tear down your own stuff," he cautioned. "When you tear down the white man, brother you are hitting him in the money. Don't love him to death. Shoot him to death. . . . You better get yourselves some guns. . . . This town is ready to explode." And explode it promptly did—though ironically it was the Negro section of town that was demolished, not the white section.

The volunteer firemen declined to move their fire engines into streets manned by snipers acting on Mr. Brown's injunction to shoot whitey to death, the position of the voluntary firemen being that they had volunteered for fire duty, not combat duty. Here, in other words, was a pretty clear case of civil rights involvement, if one is still prepared to think of Mr. Brown and SNCC as related to civil rights.

Elsewhere, for instance in Newark, there was the critical role of the snipers to consider. *Life* magazine reported an extraordinary interview held with several of the snipers during mid-fighting. These were no more routine looters than Danton and Robespierre were routine executioners. They calmly explained that their purpose in sniping was not to kill the police (you may have noticed that in fact very few policemen were killed) but rather to exacerbate the situation so as to hone the revolutionary spirit and, while at it, to permit an effective redistribution of goods. How else, one sniper asked, can you get color TV into the hands of those who do not have it? (An interesting note for the International Revolutionary Bulletin Board: Man is born free, but everywhere he is without color TV.)

Once again, these gentlemen are related to the civil rights movement, even as Malcolm X and the Black Muslims are related to the civil rights movement, however much it can be said that they perverted that movement. In other words, a hard taxonomic look at the riots places them other than in the category of wanton crime. They are racist and political in character, even if most of the participants can be said to have been moved only by a concern for free liquor and color TV. How many of those who stormed the Bastille or the Winter Palace were true idealists? Yet no one doubts that those assaults were revolutionary in their final meaning, even if pantie raiding was the spirit of the mob.

In short, if one subtracts from the situation those who were motivated by malevolent racism, you have pretty well defused the riots, which without the snipers document nothing very much more than the tiresome commonplaces that there are reserves of anarchy in all of us and that demagogy, especially if armed by a righteous rhetoric, can bring those reserves to violent life.

Well, the FBI has now issued a bulletin on riot control for use by local police forces, and we can assume that the FBI will penetrate the racist organizations and abort some of the riots planned for the future. But there is work for the moralizers to do, and in order to speak effectively, they will have to speak the truth. The truth is that some of the civil rights rhetoric of recent years has provided the phony justifications for violence which the Carmichaels and the Shuttleworths and, yes, some of our principal journalists have leaned on in explaining the disasters they are partly responsible for creating.

THE RIOTS AND VIETNAM

August 10, 1967

There is a shift in the making—a shift in public opinion on the question of Vietnam—and in a strange way it relates to the Negro problem, or rather is being made to relate to the Negro problem. There are signs everywhere—and from very important people.

The most significant, in my judgment, is the recent declaration of Bishop Fulton J. Sheen that we should unilaterally pull out of Vietnam. Bishop Sheen is neither senile nor loose-minded. His anti-Communism is unalloyed, and his knowledge of the strategic realities is unsentimental. I put off for another day an analysis of the bishop's reasoning; for the present purposes it is significant to note merely that he has taken that position and that he is an enormously influential priest.

Moreover, a priest who is grimly engaged at the moment, as Bishop of Rochester, in attempting a substantive reconciliation between the Negro and white people in that tense city. Notwithstanding his great urbanity and learning, he is at heart an evangelist, and he is asking for nothing less than reconciliation, between white and Negro, but also between white and yellow.

At this point, the mind sets out doggedly in search of a nexus. Is there one between the Negro problem and the Vietnam war? The effort is being made to find one, and we can trust to the ingenuity of the politician to discover one.

During the weekend Senator Robert Kennedy went on a paralogistic spree. The occasion was a Democratic fund-raising dinner in San Francisco, the immediate purpose of which was to show the great big biceps of Speaker Jesse Unruh, who was recently worsted at the OK Corral by the deft gunmanship of Ronald Reagan. Senator Kennedy got his usual running ovation. But it was interrupted by a special ovation when he called on the American people to note the "monstrous disproportion of anyone willing to spend billions for the freedom of others while denying it to our own people." That is one of those political effusions which are the highest testimony to the moral and intellectual emptiness of the political idiom.

The costliest riot in United States history took place a few weeks ago in Detroit, whose Democratic mayor, a longtime hero of the National Association for the Advancement of Colored People, can hardly be said to have conspired against the freedom of the Negro people. But the Senator was just warming up: "We cannot allow involvement in the name of independence and democracy in Vietnam to interfere with democracy for our own people." Another burst of applause, more testimony to nonthought. Who is asking that democracy for the Negroes be put off until the end of the Vietnam war? Lyndon Johnson? Ronald Reagan? Abigail Van Buren?

And then the old blackmail: "We must reject the counsel of those willing to pass laws against violence while refusing to eliminate rats." It's sentences like that one that discredit the democratic process. Sentences like that one, plus the applause they receive.

But the outline emerges. Somehow our commitment in Vietnam is the cause of the riots in the United States. Get it? Remember it: The one-two will be very prominent in the rhetoric to come. There is to begin with the sick-at-heartness over the Vietnam war of which Bishop Sheen's manifesto is the expression. Then there is the dazed American attitude toward the riots—why? why? why?

130

There are politicians around who think they can supply a visible answer.

NO WONDER THEY GET AWAY WITH IT

January 27, 1963

If you think the 10,000,000 New Yorkers who are without newspapers now for going on seven weeks are teeming with resentment or that the tens of millions inconvenienced by the dock strikes are a lit fuse making their way slowly but surely toward explosion, you are quite wrong. We are inconvenienced, hurt economically, annoyed, even angry, sort of. But there is all the difference in the world between a passive and a purposive resentment. The former doesn't ever get very much done. The latter can move mountains—which is about what it's going to take if we ever hope to teach the labor union leaders that they cannot hold up entire communities for their particular ends. What they are now doing in the East to individual entrepreneurs, to actors, to delicatessen owners, to waiters, schoolteachers, journalists—everybody—is not morally different from robbing a bank. In both cases they are taking the savings of innocent people, against whom they have no claim of damage whatsoever.

In talking about "public resentment," we usually have in mind such major matters of public moment as summit conferences, coast-to-coast strikes, genocidal warfare, that kind of thing. There is little enough resentment against macrocosmic assaults on the human order. Why? I profoundly believe that it takes a lot of practice to become a moral slob and that if there is anything the American people are diligently engaged in acquiring; it is that skill, that indifference to things minor, which carries over to things major. We simply don't complain about little things, and so a part of our nervous system becomes inert—the part that should always be tingling and on edge if we are to escape totalitarianization by those who exercise great power.

I hasten to add I am among the worst offenders. I tend to complain only in print; in my personal life I am about like a vegetable, except when some silly little things happen to arouse me. Are you the same? What happened to you today for which there is no rational excuse? And what did

131

you do about it? Have you traveled on airplanes recently? A week ago, halfway between New York and Minneapolis on a jet airplane, a couple of the engines acted up. They began firing like an acetylene torch. Then they would lurch drunkenly toward a complete stall, then *zoom,* they would fire again, at what felt like 10,000 rpm. Not a word of explanation from the captain or copilot. After twenty minutes or so, during which the apocalyptic cycle was repeated at least five times, I finally summoned first my courage, then the stewardess, and asked: "Would you mind telling me what is the probable cause of my imminent death?" She replied airily that there was apparently something wrong with the engines, nothing serious, and would I like another cup of coffee? I asked her whether or not the passengers might express their preferences on whether to crash in Ohio or in Illinois, preferring the former, having just finished reading an article comparing the death taxes in the two states. She smiled prettily and beamed off—not, I suspect, to relay my last choice to the captain.

Two days later, on another airplane, we set off at 5 P.M. for a six-hour flight, and at 5:10 my dinner tray was plunked in front of me. Why, I asked, must I eat at 5 if I could just as well eat at 7 or 8? The stewardess had to radio headquarters to receive permission to delay my meal. One airline adamantly refuses to serve you what they are pleased to call an "alcoholic beverage" before dinner, on the ground that the president of the airline wants to shield women and children from exposure to the corrupting sight of whiskey—though it is all right for them to be corrupted if they travel first class. Would you believe it, grown men and women put up with this imposition on the individual's right to decide for himself whether he wants a drink before dinner—the least you can do to distract your mind from your affront against the laws of nature by sitting in a 100-foot-long bullet zooming across the atmosphere at 600 miles per hour? Malcolm Muggeridge, the British humorist and critic, got so angry with BOAC recently when it refused, for some arbitrary reason, to give him a drink, that when time came to land in London, he retaliated by refusing to fasten his seat belt. (That night he dreamed he was up for sentencing at Old Bailey, and the judge, reaching up for a suitable penalty, meted out twenty years of hard labor on Anthony Eden's memoirs.)

I do not rail against the heavenly virtue of meekness. Most of the earth's trials one must bear with the submissiveness of a Christian martyr. There is simply nothing to be done, for instance, about adolescents, the weather, Presidential platitudes, or the New York *Times*. But unless we cultivate the spirit to complain against affronts on the dignity or rationality of mankind, we encourage a spiritual torpor which makes the power-hungry go positively wild with lust. I sometimes have the impression the only thing anyone complains about any more is my sweet-tempered column. More power to my critics. If they will practice up on how to complain, maybe they'll learn to complain purposefully against the appeasement of Communists abroad and, at home, our policy of creeping surrender to monopoly labor unions and to omnipotent government.

Start with the little things. Don't become a grouch. But don't let them push you around. If absolutely necessary, refuse to fasten your seat belt.

THE LITTLE CLOUDS

August 1, 1967

Headline: S.N.C.C. HEAD ADVISES NEGROES IN WASHINGTON TO GET GUNS/BURNING CAPITAL URGED, IF NEEDED/BROWN DENOUNCES JOHNSON AND RACIAL LEADERS WHO ASKED END TO VIOLENCE.

And in the body of the story, an account of the previous day's speech by H. Rap Brown, chairman of the Student Nonviolent [*sic*] Coordinating Committee. Mr. Brown said all the things the headlines said he said. "Get you some guns," he said to his "perspiring, cheering" audience. If necessary, "burn this town down." If necessary to accomplish integration? Not at all. Integration is the last thing Mr. Brown has in mind. "You have to tell the [white] man if you come into my community you are going to come in with the intent of dying or you don't come in at all."

More cheers. "I say there should be more shooting than looting, so if you loot, loot a gun store." Was he really urging murder? Yes, he really was.

"You've got to decide for yourself if you kill your enemy
133

because that is an individual decision. But the white man is your enemy. You got to destroy your enemy."

Anybody in particular? Well, even the unlikeliest target is suitable. "If you give me a gun and tell me to shoot my enemy, I might shoot Lady Bird," said the "affable but angry rights leader," as he was characterized in an adjacent headline by the New York *Times*—Mr. Rap Brown.

Now the affable gentleman in question is free on $10,000 bail, on the charge of having instigated a riot in the city of Cambridge, Maryland. There is a corpus delicti—an entirely ravaged section of town where Mr. Brown's soul brothers used to live. Needless to say, the $10,000 bail was instantly raised, and needless to say, the American Civil Liberties Union and other fastidious organizations will defend the release of Mr. Brown on bail and will, no doubt, file an *amicus curiae* brief at his trial urging the unconstitutionality of the Maryland law under which he has been indicted. Perhaps two or three years from now the Supreme Court will hear the case and judiciously weigh the pros and cons of putting Mr. Brown away somewhere, where he isn't likely to shoot Lady Bird.

What happened to the doctrine of clear and present danger? It was, as everyone used to know, enunciated by Justice Oliver Wendell Holmes as relevant to determining when a society is entitled to assert its rights over those of the individual. It seems perfectly plain that there is a clear and present danger that bloodshed and property damage will follow in the wake of the affable rights leader Mr. Brown and abundant testimony that exactly those followed him in Cambridge, Maryland.

Why doesn't the judge instantly raise the bond on Brown to, say, $10,000,000, just to reach for a round figure with an imperative ring to it? Mr. Brown's lawyers (and how they would flock to him in our suicidally bent community!) could then argue as they liked, giving the other side the right to argue the continuing relevance of the clear and present danger doctrine. But meanwhile, Mr. Brown would be in jail, not out lecturing in—

Episcopal churches, be it noted. The speech about shooting people was delivered from the pulpit of St. Stephen and the Incarnation Episcopal Church, in northwest Washington, under the sponsorship of the Reverend William Wendt, the rector of the church, and with the specific sanction of the Right Reverend Paul Moore, Jr., the Episcopal Suffragan Bishop of Washington.

"The church is a great place for all things," said Dr. Wendt, who perhaps will stage a black mass on St. Stephen's altar next week, to drive his point home. When big live bishops and ministers invite bloodthirsty genocides to preach murder and hatred and the destruction of the capital city within earshot of the halls of government, you have the scenario for a new account of the decline of civilization.

A thousand miles away Mr. Brown's predecessor as head of SNCC, Stokely Carmichael, was also on a speaking platform, shared with Fidel Castro, who was preaching the holy cause of hate-Americanism before a half a million cheering Cubans. The call is for lots of Vietnams in the United States and in Latin America, so that "Our America" might be saved from the United States white imperialists. "It is therefore logical to anticipate that the new revolutionists will eventually seek collaboration with discontented minority extremists in the U.S.A. and Canada, whatever their ideology," commented C. L. Sulzberger. "Clouds now on the horizon are each no larger than a child's hand, but several clouds are already there and more lie in the offing."

We are a very big and very powerful country, but we are nothing at all unless we assert our desire to survive, and that desire requires the reassertion of the doctrine of *salus populi*. A few more references by distinguished newspapers to the murderous Brown as a "rights leader," a few more fawning invitations to him to speak from a church of God, and the enemies of the United States will be entitled to believe that those little clouds no larger than a child's hand will soon engulf this country.

FUN WEEKEND

November 30, 1967

It was a fun weekend in New York City. One twenty-two-year-old student, strolling along the West Side, was accosted by three Negro youths. Did he have a cigarette? Sorry, he hadn't, so they stabbed him to death. A seventy-eight-year-old man was beaten up in his apartment on the

135

East Side, just in case anyone believes that crime in Fun City is asymmetrical. And in the Bronx a husband was tied down while a visitor sodomized his wife, then burglarized the apartment, and left, whistling no doubt. The husband, his bonds untied, rushed out with a shotgun and bagged the asssailant, subsequently discovered by the police who followed the trail of blood.

A cabdriver, age twenty-two, was killed by three young men. And then a plainclothesman spotted, early in the morning, a sixty-year-old man, running hard after an Amazonian lady, wearing only his undershorts. She had broken into his apartment, all 175 pounds of her, rifled his wallet of $8, threatened him with a knife, and he was now running after her. The policeman took charge, arrested the lady, and then escorted the gentleman home. On reaching his apartment building, some loitering young men made cracks about his seminudity, and the plainclothesman explained who he was and why the gentleman was wearing only shorts. The youths fell upon the policeman and beat him up. But they did not kill him. The quality of mercy is not absent from Fun City; indeed, there are those who maintain that it is more fun to maim than to kill.

Not everybody takes that position—New York is very diverse, one of its charms. I have a friend who has always kept his seven-year-old automobile in a garage just west of Ninth Avenue, in midtown Manhattan. He will not return his car to the garage after dark, nowadays, because to do so means that he is exposed to a half block's walk to Ninth Avenue, where he must stand and hail a taxi. It is necessary for non-New Yorkers to understand that it isn't safe to walk a half block in search of a taxi on the West Side of New York.

My friend, who is unprepared to die, has heard a most bizarre report which might have been the inventive work of Robert Louis Stevenson or Conan Doyle, only in this case its provenance is apparently the police. It appears that there is an extremely exclusive club of young Negroes in New York City whose membership is limited to those who have killed a white man. The signature of the club killing is said to be the preliminary question: Do you have a ciga-rette? And the rules are that if the passerby is carrying cigarettes and makes them available, he is spared. If the passerby happens to be a nonsmoker—well, you can't win

136

them all. The FBI turns the whole thing into statistics. In the first six months of this year, compared to the same period during 1966, murder is up 26 percent, rape 14 percent, robbery 92 percent, aggravated assault 36 percent, burglary 49 percent, larceny 15 percent, auto theft 23 percent. And all this, to use the figure of a local commentator, "despite a police force outnumbering a World War II Army division."

The weekend news also brings a rundown of the prosecutions that followed the rioting last summer. Here and there, the prosecution has been vigorous—*e.g.*, in Atlanta, Georgia, Cambridge, Maryland, and Toledo, Ohio. They are the exceptions. In Detroit during the riots, 7,231 persons were arrested. Of that number, exactly 40 adults are now in jail, most of them on account of previous crimes. A thousand or so will be tried sometime next spring, around Maypole time perhaps. In Boston, after three days of rioting in the Roxbury district, 35 persons were arrested. The total result: 5 persons fined $500 each, and three three-month jail sentences. Really, it is riskier by far to walk a dozen blocks in New York City minding your own business than to participate in a riot, burning, stealing, and killing.

And finally, we have a report from Atlanta discussing the plans of the Reverend Martin Luther King to organize coast-to-coast civil disobedience this spring and summer, which Dr. King described as "a method of dislocating the functioning of a city without destroying life and property." For instance, there will be "camp-ins" at the Capitol. Permanent camp-ins. "We intend to go there and stay," said Dr. King. "I am convinced," he says happily, that "civil disobedience can curtail riots."

It is easy to nag at those who believe that the way to "cure" crime is to "get tough." The answer, of course, is that crime is not cured by punishment, but that crime is curbed by the sequestration of criminals, who ought to be strolling the corridors of Sing Sing, rather than the sidewalks of New York. The other point, of course, is that neither is crime cured by asserting the apostolic right of Martin Luther King to decide which laws are congenial to him and which it is the duty of all of us to disobey. Surely there are others who see the nexus.

137

THE MOYNIHAN PLAN

Daniel P. Moynihan is all the more relevant as one broods over the ruins of Newark. There is now available an entire book dealing with the subject; it is called *The Moynihan Report and the Politics of Controversy*. The thesis of the book is summarized by Mr. Moynihan himself in a special report in *Commentary* magazine, and it is imperative reading for liberals and conservatives alike, to say nothing of those who seek to advance the cause of Negro equality free of the shackles of ideological dogma.

There are piquant aspects to the report. Mr. Moynihan never admits it, but it is well known that it was he, acting at that time as Assistant Secretary of Labor, who composed the famous speech given by President Johnson at Howard University in June, 1965. The President found himself saying that the whole question of Negro equality is answered not merely by successive civil rights enactments, but by the acknowledgment that the family is the crucial unit in social progress, and that statistics show that the dissolution of the Negro family is a progressive phenomenon. In other words, said Mr. Moynihan through the mouth of the President, the Negro family unit must be helped to cohere; else all the formal equalities bestowed by Congress in the numerous civil rights bills become meaningless.

Mr. Moynihan's proposed solution? Federal subsidies for the Negro families. To be sure, something of the sort exists, but the subsidies are not payable to families whose fathers are in residence. In other words, there is a *de facto* cash premium on the separation of father and mother. True, Mr. Moynihan acknowledges, preferential legislation in favor of Negroes was on his mind.

"The moment came when," says Mr. Moynihan, understandably enthused by his own proposals, "as it were, the nation had the resources and the leadership and the will to make a total as against a partial commitment to the cause of Negro equality. It did not do so."

Why? Three things happened. The first, on which Mr. Moyhihan does not, fortunately, dwell—because as an

138

aristocratic polemicist he disdains the association with the current demagogy that begins every argument by stating that our involvement in Vietnam has stopped progress at all other fronts—was the Vietnam war, which Mr. Moynihan sees as having preoccupied Mr. Johnson beginning in the summer of 1965, leaving him little time for other matters.

The second and perhaps most important was the sudden opposition of prominent liberals, especially of Negro liberal intellectuals, who discerned in the argumentation of Mr. Moynihan a "subtle racism" whose effect would be to give aid and comfort to an anti-Negro community always seeking rational justification for its sneaking suspicion that Negroes are an inferior race.

Thus, for instance, Dr. Benjamin F. Payton, a young Negro sociologist and minister associated with the New York Protestant Council, bombed the Moynihan Report and indirectly the Howard speech by identifying its views as the views of a "crypto-racist." The Payton report had the effect of intimidating the Johnson administration, so that when the White House conference convened at which the Moynihan-Johnson proposals were to be considered, the whole business of family subsidies was wiped clean off the agenda, leaving only the clichés, which were duly ratified and duly forgotten.

The third fact that worked against a serious consideration of Mr. Moynihan's proposals was Watts. Moynihan points out shrewdly that until Watts, the civil rights movement "had been the aggrieved, the just, the righteous cause. In the South an old game had been going on with a new rule, imperfectly understood by whites, that the first side to resort to violence—lost. Now in the North the Negroes have resorted to violence, in a wild, destructive explosion that shattered, probably forever"—Mr. Moynihan is an Irishman and is just every now and then given to Gaelic pessimisms—"the image of non-violent suffering."

The point raised by Mr. Moynihan, an adamant liberal, is that hypersensitive egalitarianism can be the worst enemy of frank discussion of how to move toward effective equality. A conservative can easily discern weaknesses in his macrocosmic dispensation, while still endorsing the general idea—namely, that massive efforts to help the Negro must be made not merely in order retroactively to appease white consciences, but in order realistically to help achieve desirable results, to reassure that violence in the great cities is not a necessary part of the future of the American summer.

"THE POLITICS OF STABILITY"

October 28, 1967

The Americans for Democratic Action met over the weekend, and the meeting ended with the usual irritating irrelevancies. It was the same, old, reliable bore, except for the appearance of Daniel P. Moynihan who, although a PT-109 liberal, is saying some of the most interesting things being said these days in public life, most strikingly that the liberals have a good deal to learn from the conservatives, with whom they should, here and there, make common cause.

He called his talk "The Politics of Stability," and its theme was that if the United States were going to survive, somebody had better inquire into the politics of stability, which "are not at first exciting. It is only when we come to see how probably our national life is at stake," he concluded his speech, "that the game acquires a certain interest."

Mr. Moynihan, though a passionate man by nature, tends to shy away from apocalyptical rhetoric. He nevertheless believes that so serious is the crisis that liberals have to decide whether, as the New Left believes, liberalism is about to go up in smoke, ushering in a new ideology, or whether liberalism can tuck away its superstitions and get down to the nitty-gritty of achieving stability and progress. His own feeling, and I concur, is that the single most urgent problem at home is to abort the threatening union between the young Negro revolutionaries, who are few in number, and the class of Negro dispossessed and disenchanted, who number in the millions.

To this end, Mr. Moynihan made a number of electric recommendations, electric at least to those who heard them. "Liberals must somehow overcome the curious condescension which takes the form of sticking up for, and explaining away, anything, however outrageous, which

140

Negroes, individually or collectively, might do." Here is a Magna Carta for American liberals, some of whom—for instance, Harry Golden and Theodore Bikel—could bring themselves to resign from SNCC only when it turned anti-Semitic a few weeks ago, never mind that it was more than a year ago that SNCC brought in Stokely Carmichael as its chairman.

At another level, Moynihan pointed out the difficulties of making progress by reason that anyone who reasons at the tactical expense of the Negroes is going to be denounced as a strategic racist. He gave the example of Dr. James Coleman, who is now getting the treatment because his study reveals that it is less the inferior quality of the schools that is injuring Negro education than the demoralized and anti-intellectual atmosphere of their homes.

And then Moynihan touched on the liberals' addiction to centralization. Get over it, he counseled. "In domestic affairs, we have got to become a great deal more rigorous in the assessment not only of the reality of problems, but the nature of proposed solutions. We have to pay attention to what it is we are good at, and to work from strength. The federal government is good at collecting revenues, and rather bad at disbursing services." And then: "If state and local government is to assume an effective role as an innovative and creative agent, it simply must begin to receive a share of federal revenues on a permanent, ongoing basis. Let us be frank: the original, determining opposition to this proposition has come from liberals, not conservatives in Washington, and we should be ashamed of ourselves." Anything we conservatives can do to help, just holler.

And, then, finally, and courageously, having acknowledged that the mess in the cities and the mess in Vietnam are the doings of liberals in power ("These things may not be our fault, but in a world not overmuch given to nice distinctions in such matters, they surely must be judged by our doing"), he suggested an *entente* not exactly *cordiale* with the conservatives, but at least businesslike.

The liberals, Mr. Moynihan concluded, must "see more clearly that their essential interest is in the stability of the social order, and that given the present threats to that stability, it is necessary to seek out and make much more effective alliances with political conservatives who share

141

that concern, and who recognize that unyielding rigidity is just as much a threat to the continuity of things as is an anarchic desire for change."

There is a great deal, some believe, that Mr. Moynihan has yet to learn in order fully to emancipate himself, but that was as good a day's work as any since Ray Moley took a second look at the New Deal and lammed out of Washington on the first train. The liberal press is constantly garlanding any Republican who shows the courage to follow his conscience athwart ideological presuppositions, as when the opinion press recently flipped over Senator Thruston B. Morton's changing his mind on Vietnam. It will be interesting to see how they treat Patrick Moynihan.

THE APPROACHING END
OF EDGAR H. SMITH, JR.*

November, 1965

It is very difficult, in New Jersey, to arrange to see a prisoner in the death house. The visiting regulations are clearly designed in an age when neither legal hanky-panky, nor a deep social ambivalence concerning capital punishment, nor a Supreme Court that sometimes seems more tortured by punishment than by crime could separately or in combination work to keep a man in the death house almost endlessly. A few months used to be routine, and then the prisoner was executed, or, under special circumstances, the governor would reprieve the sentence. Meanwhile, there were to be very few amenities and practically none at all of a social character. One member of your immediate family may visit you once a month, and you can write home five times a month. The correspondence, in and out, is checked by prison monitors, who are supposed to look out for any signs that you are preparing a jailbreak, but who, inevitably, by their faceless presence on every page, inhibit a prisoner, as also a naturally reserved correspondent. The monitor, whose stool is set up alongside your own, is also there to listen to every word spoken to or by the prisoner.

Several years ago I wrote to a prisoner at the death house, having seen a newspaper clipping which described, among other things, his reading habits, to ask if he would care to receive *National Review,* a journal I edit. The clipping from a New Jersey newspaper reported on a day in the life of Edgar Smith, #34837 D.H., as he is officially designated, then twenty-seven years old. The article mentioned that he used to read *National Review* but no longer

* Reprinted by permission of *Esquire* magazine.

saw it because the chaplain whose copy he used to borrow had been transferred. My letter was returned by the prison authorities, with a form note to the effect that I was not an authorized correspondent of the prisoner. One needs, then, to dig around a bit. I did so, and in due course the prisoner and I exchanged, under a temporary dispensation, one or two letters. "I hope all these problems," he wrote me, "will soon be solved and that the temporary difficulties will not reduce your interest in my case." The temporary difficulties had to do with an attempt by a colleague, Donald Coxe, to visit Smith; we had decided to prepare an article on his extraordinary case. But the application to visit the prisoner was ruled out of the question even for Coxe, who is a lawyer. Judge Arthur O'Dea of Bergen County, who presided at the trial and sentenced Smith to death (he had no alternative; the jury did not recommend mercy), appears to have done his duty vigorously during the subsequent eight years in galloping off to every corner of the legal battleground just in time to shoot down Edgar Smith's latest, most unexpected, most ingenious legal flyer, said No in unambiguous terms. He will not permit, he was quoted as saying, the Edgar Smith case to become another Caryl Chessman case. Besides—the judge didn't say this, but I infer from his behavior that he profoundly believes it—Edgar Smith is, as the jury found, guilty as sin, and the time has come to stop humoring him in the courts of law and get on with the sentence demanded by law.

But after two and one-half years Judge O'Dea relented. He is, one judges, a very good lawyer (and, undoubtedly, a very good man), and he felt he had to authorize one (1) visit when I undertook to think through the problem of financing Smith's final fight to save his life. It was Smith, not I, who detected, in this new role of mine, safe passage around the dragon's lair. In February, 1965, he wrote to tell me that the United States Supreme Court had denied his most recent petition for a retrial. And then, as is characteristic when he has bad news to report—which has been exactly as often as any court of law has ruled on one of his many appeals (a total of seven times in the period I have been in touch with him)—he follows up the gloomy news with a dash of optimism or, less frequently, of good news. *Well, I'm not a total failure. Judge O'Dea has*

144

granted the request for the Court order allowing visitation. The dungeons have been thrown open for your inspection."

I drove around the squat red-stone prison, which casts its gloom over the center of Trenton, looking for the tiny doorway through which visitors are unwelcome, and thought about the problem of the immediately preceding few days. Smith, for the first time in my experience, was furious. Judge O'Dea's permission to visit Smith had been actively opposed by the prison's warden and, one gathers, by a New Jersey newspaperman resentful that another journalist was being permitted, though to be sure not in his professional capacity, into the forbidden area. Two days earlier Smith had written me that the anti-visit forces had made their move. "You won't have any trouble getting in to see me—the Order assures that, but the visit would probably be a waste of your time. Rather than follow the accepted procedure of appealing the Order, someone came up with the bureaucrat's typical back-door approach; they obtained a letter-opinion from a Deputy Attorney General, giving the Order an interpretation which virtually nullifies its effect. This interpretation is that the Order bans any discussion of my case—past, present, and future." In other words, although I was to be permitted to see him, I was not to be permitted to discuss any of the reasons why I was visiting him at a penitentiary, instead of at the home where his mother brought him up, in Ramsay, New Jersey, or at the trailer camp where he lived with his wife and baby in next-door Mahwah at the time the murder was committed. "Bill, I'll tell you right now that Smith has just about had it." I was truly alarmed, after long experience with his pre-ternatural serenity. "I don't think we should give in and allow the Order to be circumvented. You can come down next Friday if you wish, but my opinion is that we should go back to Court. This Deputy Attorney General doesn't have a leg to stand on; I think his interpretation should be appealed. Please, let me know what you think. I'm too burned up right now to write any more." I wired him that I would arrive as scheduled.

I was taken in to see Mr. Edmonds, the assistant to Warden Yeager, who was in conference. Mr. Edmonds asked me whether I knew of the restrictions the attorney general had imposed on my visit, and I said I did. Would I wait just a few moments, to meet Warden Yeager, before going in to see Smith? I would, with pleasure, and attempted to make some appropriate conversation. When was the last execution? A long time ago in January, 1963. When was the first? At the turn of the century. How many men had died on that chair? One hundred sixty. How many men were presently in the death house? Fourteen. Capacity? Eighteen. Where had Bruno Hauptmann, the killer of Lindbergh's baby, stayed? In the came cell, it happens, as Smith's.

Warden Yeager was ready, and I met him and his staff, and we exchanged pleasantries. A big man, tough, duty-minded, but nonetheless friendly. It remained for me to be frisked, and an official took me to a private room and asked me to empty my pockets of anything with metal in it. I did so perfunctorily and he began to move a metal-detecting type instrument down from my head. It reached my chest and let out an angry and sustained beep. He shut it off and asked me to examine my breast pocket. Out came a Scripto pencil, with the little offending aluminum catch. The search went on. Twice more the Frisker (pat. pend., I noticed) caught me *in flagrante,* but finally, after it reached my shoes and found there not a file or even a razor, was moved on and introduced to Captain Malkin, who was to be my companion. We moved to a great partition, and a turnkey opened a door. We stepped into a circular, silolike structure, from which two corridors went out, where the regular prisoners were quartered. It was completely enclosed, and high above it, surrounded by bulletproof glass, is the central communications center of the prison. From there an official will confirm or deny an escort's instructions to the turnkeys, who communicate with the center by walkie-talkie. The central command had to be consulted before we were let out of the silo, at the opposite end from which we had entered it, onto the open compound, to walk 150 yards to the small, isolated, windowless fort-within-a-fort, where the condemned go before stepping conveniently into the far end of the same building, to sit down in the electric chair.

Again, radio control confirmed Captain Malkin's instructions to open the door, and it creaked open, admitting a ray of daylight for the briefest moment, visible to the first three or four of the double-decker cells. Naked light bulbs hung overhead, and three television sets were blaring in the corridor, one for three prisoners, programs by majority vote, stations tuned in by the guards. I was led to the very end of the corridor, to within a few feet of the electric chair, from which I was separated by a metal door. On my right was Edgar H. Smith, Jr., who long since has broken the New Jersey record for the longest stay in the death cell; it is now eleven years since he has seen daylight. I couldn't see him well, because in addition to the steel bars, they roll a steel screen that fits snugly over the entire front of the cell. I found myself wondering why it was necessary to exercise the Frisker on me. It was all I could do to see Smith. I could not have passed him a needle, even assuming Captain Malkin had nodded. I could, however, see clearly the dimensions of his cell, 8 feet long, 8 feet wide, 9 feet high. Every Friday he steps out into the corridor and takes a shower under a naked spigot; once a month he steps out into the corridor for a haircut. I commiserated with him once. "I appreciate your thoughts about my lack of exercise. It isn't all that bad. I walk a lot, like the pussycats in the zoo."

He spoke for an hour—careful, though not overly so, not to touch on "the case," which it was Captain Malkin's duty to see that we didn't. We spoke about future appeals. He explained to me in some detail what his present legal situation was and how he hoped, ultimately, to force the courts to grant him a retrial. I found myself, for the hundredth time, marveling at the discipline of his thought. His voice betrayed a background of football lockers and poolrooms and beer taverns, faintly coarse, utterly inconsistent with his writing style, which is Victorian to the point of prudery. ("Damn!" he wrote on hearing my wife had broken her leg a few weeks earlier. "What bad luck!") He had never finished high school, going instead into the Marines, where he served as a paratrooper and was discharged before his tour of duty was over because of a slight deafness in one ear. He was eleven when his mother and father were divorced and was brought up by his devoted mother and his stepfather. At fourteen, he had got into trouble. A ten-year-old girl complained that he had fooled with her. He denied having done so, and the girl apparently had a querulous record. The judge, generally unconvinced, put young Edgar on probation for three years and never received any further complaint against him. His mother sent him, as a day student, to a Catholic boarding

147

school nearby, which Smith left after two years because the school committed the unpardonable sin of abolishing football, to which, above other things, Smith was committed. He went to a public school but left before his senior year to join the Marines.

On getting out of the service he drifted from job to job, a leading member of the fresh set, taking and leaving jobs every few weeks or months. When he married, he bought a trailer. And when he ran out of money, he sold the trailer's wheels—even though they, as part of the trailer, were derivatively mortgaged. A. D. Nicol, a private investigator from Hackensack who was retained by Smith's mother until her savings were exhausted (he worked thereafter, and continues to work today, almost a dozen years later, free of charge, tirelessly running down leads), could come up only with three people, of the hundreds he interviewed, who thought that Smith, notwithstanding his diffuse impulsiveness, could be capable of an act of violence. Two of the three—a taxi driver, and a station attendant—didn't know him well. The third, Don Hommell, was the man Smith swears he left the girl with on the evening of March 4, 1957, a few minutes before nine at night, twelve hours before she was discovered, 60 feet away, just beyond the profile of the sandpit, her brains splattered about by a 14-pound boulder.

I was listening to an almost forbiddingly technical analysis of his legal situation, and it was a full half hour before I got the gist of it. Smith has become, if not a finished lawyer—that takes experience—an extraordinarily resourceful and ingenious one, whose most recent appeal was described by Judge O'Dea as having been drafted with the "comsummate skill of a seasoned practitioner." For eighteen months Smith had been conducting his own legal defense, filing briefs forty and fifty pages long, which had been typed by a fellow prisoner and submitted to the courts in *forma pauperis*. He had exhausted the philanthropic reserves of a lawyer who had taken his case, unsuccessfully, to the Supreme Court and for a while had submitted to a lawyer designated by the Court. After a few months with him, Smith, dissatisfied, fired him—only to have him refuse to withdraw, leaving Smith in a most unusual state of virtual speechlessness. The lawyer "has flatly refused to retire from my case. He said he would go ahead

148

and argue the appeal on May 18. I will press him to with-draw and make certain he does. Can you imagine a lawyer saying he would not be dismissed? It all adds up to the aroma I detected when he was appointed."

My monitor was getting restless, and I got up to go. We said good-bye and I started down the corridor, when sud-denly my escort drew aside to talk to a guard, leaving me directly opposite the elderly prisoner whose cell is adjacent to Smith's. "Hello, Mr. Buckley," he said (the prisoners know the names of other prisoners' visitors). "Hello," I said, not quite knowing how to take the conversation from there. "Whom did *you* kill?" seemed inappropriate. But so was any talk about the weather, the weather being as far removed from the notice of men living in solitary confine-ment, without windows, as the fluctuations of the stock market. We smiled nervously at each other; Captain Malkin rejoined me. I bade good-bye to Smith's neighbor and walked out. As we went back across the compound toward the fortified silo, Captain Malkin explained that most of the prisoners in the death cell are quickly aban-doned even by their own families. "Edgar's wife used to come regularly for a couple of years. Then she went off, married someone else. She doesn't even write him any more. But his mother never misses." I said good-bye to the warden. "Smith seems quite confident he'll leave here one of these days," I observed chattily. "Well, that's a safe pre-diction," he chuckled. "He'll leave here one way or another."

"I do wish," Smith wrote, "our visit could have been longer, and free of restrictions. Perhaps someday we will be able to sit down and have a long talk, without worrying about any regulations. How about adopting me? You could then be on my regular family visiting list! That would go over big with Judge O'Dea!"

In his opening remarks to the jury on May 15, 1957, Guy Calissi, the skilled chief prosecutor of Bergen County, outlined what the state intended to prove Edgar Smith had done. The state's theory of the case was that Smith had picked up Victoria Zielinski, driven to the sandpit with her, tried to make love to her; that she had become frightened and run away; that he had grabbed a baseball bat, chased after her down the sandpit and onto Fardale Avenue, hit her with the bat, thrown it away, brought her (why?) back to the sandpit, carried her up a mound, and there killed her with a heavy boulder.

It took the prosecutor five days to introduce the evidence to back up the theory. On the afternoon of March 4, 1957, Smith went bowling with two friends, Charles Rockefeller and Joe Gilroy. While bowling, Smith injured his ankle, an injury that was to prove relevant. After the game, Smith asked Gilroy if he could borrow his car to fetch some kerosene for the stove in his trailer home. After lighting the stove, he promised he would rejoin Gilroy and together they would have a few beers.

At 8:20 P.M., Smith arrived at Secors gas station to buy the kerosene. He filled a 5-gallon can, talked to a man whose car was having ignition trouble, and left.

Two witnesses testified that the time was about 8:30.

One hour before Smith left the gas station, the flirtatious Vickie Zielinski had gone out the door of her unsavory (to judge from subsequent divorce testimony) home. She had a test coming up the next morning at Ramsey High School and wanted to prepare for it with her friend Barbara Nixon. Vickie was afraid to walk alone at night, so her younger sister Myrna went with her halfway. (Strange. The younger sister then had to retread, alone, the same path her older sister had feared to take alone.) One hour later, at 8:30, Vickie said good night to Barbara and started walking home. As agreed, Myrna again left her house, at 8:40, to meet her sister halfway and escort her home.

The state introduced at trial the statement Smith had given fourteen hours after being picked up.

He was on his way home with the kerosene—Smith said—when Vickie hailed him. He knew her only casually, but stopped to pick her up. The time was 8:37 or 8:40.

When she got into the car, he said, she asked him not to drive her home by the direct route, because her sister was walking to meet her, and must not be allowed to see her in a car alone with a boy. At her suggestion, Smith said, he drove into a sandpit, a local lovers' lane, about 2 miles away, toward the ends of a loop that reached to within a half mile of Smith's trailer. He parked the car. Vickie was talking to him about school. He lit a cigarette and let her drone on. Suddenly—and, Smith said to the police, without provocation—Vickie announced she was going to walk

150

home by herself and jeered at him, "I'm going to tell my father you're just like the other boys." (There are obvious implausibilities in this story, which become apparent in connection with the contradictory account Smith gave at the trial.)

Smith feared disagreeable consequences, he said, and tried to keep her from getting out of the car. She struggled. He hit her "a good one" with his hand. His memory of ensuing events, he then told the police, failed, but he vaguely remembered running somewhere. Eventually, he climbed back into his car and drove home. He remembered stopping, 100 yards or so from the sandpit, on the road home to his trailer, alongside a Christmas tree he had seen planted some months before, but he wasn't sure why he stopped there or what he did there. (The police searched the area and found Vickie's schoolbooks and wallet.) His right foot felt cold, and he noticed that he had lost his shoe (which had not been laced up, because of an ankle injury).

He reached home. Before entering the trailer, he had removed his pants because he saw that they were blood-stained. He told his wife he had got sick over them and discarded them. He filled the kerosene tank outside the trailer and then attempted, and failed, to light the stove. The night being especially cold (22 degrees), he and his wife decided they would spend the night with her mother in Ridgewood.

He went outdoors to a pay telephone and called Gilroy. (The time of his call was 9:10, Gilroy testified.) Smith told him he had been sick and didn't want to drink beer after all, that he hadn't been able to light the stove, and would therefore take the family to sleep elsewhere. Would Gilroy drive them to Ridgewood? He agreed.

Smith set out alone to pick up Gilroy, having informed his wife they'd be back shortly to drive together to Ridgewood. He went directly to the nearby sandpit to retrieve the lost shoe. He must have left the sandpit by 9:30 at the latest to have arrived at Gilroy's at 9:40. On the way he dumped his bloodied pants—just where, he told the police, he didn't remember. They drove together back to the trailer, picked up his wife and child, and arrived at Ridgewood at 10:15.

Meanwhile, Myrna had walked all the way to the Nixon home, only to learn that Vickie had left on schedule. She and her mother waited up until midnight, then woke Mr. Zielinski. He and a third daughter drove around for two hours looking for Vickie. The next morning they renewed the search. Driving along Fardale Avenue, they saw Vickie's scarf and shoe. Mrs. Zielinski went into the adjacent house to telephone the police. Zielinski walked 100 yards down Fardale Avenue, where the road petered out into the sandpit. He saw there, at the crest of the gravel road close to the spot where Smith's car had been parked, his daughter's bloodstained gloves, lying on the road, but ignored them because, he said, he did not recognize them as belonging to Vickie. He turned and walked back to where the scarf and shoe had been found, by which time the police arrived. He and the policeman walked back to the sandpit. The policeman noticed the gloves, and they continued the search. They discovered the brains 60 feet away, whereupon Zielinski spotted the corpse. He called out to his wife that he had found her.

Vickie, the coroner reported, had been wearing boys' blue jeans. The fly was secure; she was wearing "immaculate" white panties and was *virgo intacta*. Her sweater had been pulled up and her bra yanked down. Small bruises, which the coroner said were tooth marks, were found on her. Cause of death, which was declared to have been instantaneous, was the total crushing of the skull. The coroner, at the trial, fixed the time at midnight March 4, "give or take an hour."

That afternoon Gilroy ran into Donald Hommell, a friend of Vickie's and also of Smith's, at their favorite hangout, Tony's Amoco station. Gilroy told him he was on his way to pick up Smith at his mother-in-law's. Hommell suggested they drive over in his car, rather than Gilroy's. When they arrived, Smith came out with wife and baggage and asked whether "the murdered girl" was Vickie—he said he had heard radio broadcasts reporting the murder (details unspecified) of "Victoria" Zielinski. Hommell said, "Yeah," and, with a wink at Gilroy, "the cops know from the tire tracks the make of the killer's car and are checking all the Mercurys in Bergen County."

Smith, according to Gilroy, paled visibly.

Recalling the incident, Smith subsequently told the police, "That's when it hit me really hard I must have been the one who really did it." He meant by that, he said at the trial, that the initial blow he had given Vickie, he thought, might have caused her, unattended, to bleed to death.

Driving along in Hommell's car, someone (just who is disputed) found a lipstick and passed it to Hommell—who had often dated Vickie—saying, "Maybe this is Vickie's?" Hommell said, "No," and tossed it out the window.

Later that afternoon Gilroy discovered two stains in his car—one on the left front seat, which was later identified as type O blood (Smith's blood is A; Vickie's was O), and one on the right side of the transmission hump which turned out to be kerosene. He recalled that Smith had told him about throwing away his pants because he got sick over them. Recalling that he had paled when Hommell mentioned the tire tracks, Gilroy went to the police.

The police picked Smith up for questioning at 11:30 that same night, shortly after he had gone to sleep. Under prolonged questioning he finally broke down. It was shortly after noon the next day that he gave the police the statement described above. He led the police to the garbage can where he had thrown away his shoes (which were stained with type O blood). He was not at any point during the prolonged questioning advised that he was entitled to the advice of counsel.

His pants were found by the police, though not at the spot he said he had left them, with his socks rolled up. They were found later near his mother's home, the pants spread out conspicuously, the socks stuffed in the pants' pockets. They were stained in the lower leg area with type O blood. Two months later the baseball bat was found—in the woods, 160 feet from where the scarf and shoe and hank of Vickie's hair had been found.

The state depended heavily on Smith's statement —notwithstanding his denial that he had ever bashed a rock against Vickie's head. How could Smith explain it away?

To begin with, he gave it under extreme pressure. One of three judges, in the U.S. Court of Appeals voted to give Smith a retrial in 1963, after reflecting on the circumstances.

"The stark facts [said the judge] are that from 8:00 A.M. on the morning of March 5, 1957, until 3:45 P.M.

153

on March 6, 1957—almost thirty-two hours—the appellant had no sleep with the exception of a couple of hours before he was taken from his bed and placed in custody at 11:30 P.M. on March 5; that he was interrogated in relays by prosecutors and their aides, local police and county detectives, as many as seven being present at one time, all through the night, relieved only by his being taken to various places in freezing weather with only a T-shirt on . . . ; that he was given a light breakfast, stripped, and examined by a doctor and questioned repeatedly until 10:00 A.M. on March 6 when he broke down completely and cried and asked for a Catholic priest. . . ."

Smith subsequently tried to release the priest from his confessional vow and asked that he be sworn and testify to what Smith had said to him. But no one can release a priest from his confessional vow, and the priest declined to take the stand. Smith asked that a truth-serum test be administered. The state agreed, and psychiatrists were brought in. Under the influence of sodium amytal Smith babbled on and answered instantly and unambiguously all the questions he was asked. Although he made statements damaging to himself—yes, he admitted, he had tried to seduce Vickie—he said firmly and repeatedly that he had *not* killed her. The tape, for reasons unknown, was erased, and the psychiatrists' notes were not ruled admissible at the trial.

Smith swore he had, from exhaustion and pressure, invented the entire disjointed story he had given to the police, "not thinking anyone would believe it." Now, at the trial, he gave a very different story. Yes, he had picked Vickie up at 8:30 or 8:40, and yes, she told him not to drive straight home because her sister must not see her in the car alone with a boy. (An implausible story, though it was not contested at the trial. Surely Vickie would get into greater trouble at home by letting Myrna walk all the way to the Nixons and back without Vickie, than by letting her sister see her in a car?) Vickie, he said, told him, on hailing him, that she had something she *must* tell him.

They arrived at the sandpit at about 8:45. Smith now said that Vickie told him that his wife was playing around with another man; that he became enraged, slapped her hard on the face, and told her to walk home. She opened

154

the door of the car, went out and ran down the road. Smith paused a few moments, then started to back out of the pit. But he heard "a commotion" down at the corner, and discerned Vickie returning, accompanied by a man. Smith grabbed a baseball bat from the back seat, to be used if necessary "for protection." When the couple came closer, he saw that Vickie was leaning weakly against Don Hommell, bleeding from a scalp wound. Smith offered to take her to a doctor, and she got into the car. Hommell, in a rage, dragged her from the car across the passenger's seat, and her head fell against Smith's pants. (Her gloves, if they came off at that moment, fell exactly where they were subsequently found.) Hommell, said Smith, was renowned for his violent temper and considered Vickie his girl; so, Smith said, without further argument he drove home.

Later, on his way to pick up Gilroy, Smith continued, he spotted Hommell parked in downtown Ramsey. He pulled up and asked how Vickie was. "Don't worry about her," Hommell said, adding, "If you mention my name or in any way implicate me, I'm going to get your wife and baby." It was because of this threat against his family, Smith told the jury, that he invented the particular story he gave to the police.

Hommell swore he had not seen either Smith or Vickie on the night of the murder. He flatly denied Smith's claim that Vickie had been his girl friend. But under cross-examination he admitted having been out with her on ten different occasions.

Smith's story was roundly denounced at the trial by the prosecutor. If Smith had been scared of Hommell, why, when brought in by the police, had he said, "If you want a fall guy, why don't you get Donald Hommell?"

Smith's defense at trial concentrated less on Smith's own disavowal of his earlier statement to the police than on certain objective difficulties in the prosecutor's case. Outstanding of these was the coroner's evidence. If one is to believe the state's own expert, who fixed the time of death (instantaneous) at midnight—"give or take an hour"—and the evidence that Smith was at the sandpit not later than 9:30 (as regards which there were abundant witnesses), then as a matter of fact he simply could not have killed the girl.

Judge O'Dea, however, held that the exact time of death

was hard to fix and that the jury could, in effect, make up its own mind when the murder happened. Even one hour earlier—10 P.M.—Smith still couldn't have done it. Ought the coroner to have testified that Vickie died at midnight, "give or take three hours"? What are coroners for, if not to be precise? Stomach-content analysis had not been made; otherwise the time of death might have been conclusively established. The jury evidently decided that the doctor (although he had performed hundreds of autopsies) wasn't to be taken literally when, originally, he placed the murder about midnight.

Another difficulty. It was conceded that Smith could not have picked up Vickie before 8:35 at the earliest. It took him a few minutes to drive to the sandpit; just how long is disputed (the distance is 2 miles; it took me seven minutes to drive the distance; the road is tortuous). Smith claims he did not arrive before 8:45 because a bulldozer doing road work temporarily blocked the road. This allegation could have been checked and contradicted by the state. The state did not do so, which means that under the rules of evidence, the burden of proof being the state's, it must be accepted as true.

Smith never deviated from his claim of having arrived home before 9, a claim backed up by his wife. He certainly could not have arrived much later than that, because he telephoned Gilroy's house at 9:10, after removing a pair of pants, putting on another pair, going out to the kerosene tank, climbing up on the fence, filling the tank, and tinkering with the stove. In order to reach the trailer by nine, he had to leave the sandpit by 8:55. The state's charge is, in effect, that in the space of fifteen minutes—8:40 to 8:55—Smith: (1) chatted with Vickie, (2) tried to make love to her, (3) progressed sufficiently far to leave toothmarks on her breast, (4) frightened her, (5) pursued her 334 feet down the road, bad ankle and all, (6) cut her head open with a baseball bat, (7) tossed the bat away a distance of 160 feet, (8) brought her 364 feet back to the sandpit, (9) dragged her up to the top of a mound 60 feet away, and (10) killed her with repeated blows from a heavy boulder. Aside from the extraordinary dispatch with which all this would have had to occur, even if it had been carefully rehearsed by both parties, the question does arise: Doesn't it strain the bounds of credibility that an essentially phlegmatic young man, of nonviolent habits, would so far lose control of himself, in the space of a minute or two, as to murder under such circumstances a fifteen-year-old girl he hardly knew?

Another objective problem not raised at the trial becomes apparent from a close examination of the situation. The blood-soaked scarf and hank of hair were found 360 feet from the body. The hank of hair was small, but large enough to suggest a scalp wound that must have bled profusely. Yet there was no trail of blood from that point back to where the body lay, 360 feet away over frozen ground that was carefully examined by numerous policemen. That means the killer either carried her fastidiously from Fardale Avenue to the sandpit in such fashion as to leave no blood on the road or that she was hauled away in a car. Vickie weighed 120 pounds, Smith 150, so that it is unlikely that he would have elected to carry her that distance. (Remember: he was in no hurry. If he returned to the trailer at 9:30 or 10:30, it would not have made any particular difference to a soul.) He would presumably have used the car. Why were there no blood-stains on the right front seat? Or in the back? Or trunk? Or other than on his pants' legs? And anyway, if he had to run back to fetch the car, just how far can one stretch the distance a man can travel or the number of things he can do in a period of fifteen minutes?

Another item overlooked at the trial was Vickie's clothes, which were shot through with minute bone chips. The killer had to stand very close to her to use a 14-pound boulder so accurately. Small bone chips are highly tenacious. A careful examination of Smith's clothing failed to reveal any bone chips whatsoever.

As regards the state of Vickie's clothing, the state was successful in imposing on the jury a logical fallacy. Vickie's sweater was hauled up and her bra pulled down. But the state insisted that Vickie had run a long way before her initial injury. If Smith had pulled up her sweater in the car, as alleged, 2 or 3 running steps, let alone the 100 steps required to take her to the spot where she was allegedly caught by Smith with a baseball bat, would have been enough to drop a loose cardigan back into position (the buttons of her sweater were still done up). Vickie's disarranged clothing suggests that she struggled with her

157

assailant immediately before she died. The state did not allege any such thing. The timetable, stretched already to the breaking point, hardly permitted a twilight struggle at the top of the mound.

No significance was attached at the trial to the location of the bloodstained gloves, discovered 61 feet from the body. There is no apparent reason for the killer to have taken them off the corpse and placed them on the road. Presumably, then, the blood on the gloves came from Vickie's scalp wound. She must have tried to stanch the flow of blood with the gloves. Smith said at the trial that he saw her returning with Hommell. The point at which Hommell allegedly dragged her from the car is in the immediate vicinity of the point where the gloves were in fact found; the gloves could, as noted, have been yanked off her hands while Hommell was pulling her from the car. If Smith had clobbered Vickie with a baseball bat on Fardale Avenue as alleged, it is unlikely that she would have been in condition to stanch the flow of blood with her gloves. The gloves tend to corroborate Smith's otherwise implausible story.

Smith said he told Hommell during their brief conversation in Ramsey on the night of the murder just where he had discarded his pants. The woman who occupies property across the road from which Smith claimed to have thrown the pants (beside a bridge, halfway between the murder site and the trailer camp) swore at the trial that she had seen Hommell rummaging there the day after the murder. The pants were later found spread out near a well-traveled road, 100 yards away from Smith's mother's house. Did Hommell find them and leave them in the other location, thinking to discredit Smith's story and make sure they would turn up? If the witness was correct (and she identified Hommell in the courtroom), then Smith's story about talking to Hommell on the night of the murder is proved, since Hommell otherwise would have had no reason to be there.

Hommell was absent from the pharmacy where he worked at the time Smith was at the sandpit and was seen by—and acknowledges having seen—Myrna Zielinski driving at "about sixty miles an hour" shortly after nine. Yet Hommell later said he was at Pelzer's Tavern (5 miles away) at 9:15 and that he was seen there by Pelzer or his wife and another member of the Smith set, Charles

158

Rockefeller. After the trial, after Smith had been convicted, Pelzer executed an affidavit to the effect that he had obliged Hommell by testifying he had seen him there at the critical period, that actually Hommell hadn't been there at all. In a subsequent affidavit Pelzer said that Rockefeller was not at the tavern when Hommell said he was, that Rockefeller left at 7:30 that night and did not return.

New Jersey law provides that first-degree murder must be either "premeditated killing" or felony murder. The state tried to get around the question of premeditation by charging Smith with a felony murder. But Judge O'Dea ruled this argument out, on the ground that the condition of Vickie's clothing and her physical condition as disclosed by the autopsy ruled out a hypothesis of attempted rape.

That left only premeditated murder, to justify a first-degree conviction and the electric chair. It is incorrect, in legal terms, to suppose that premeditated murder is the kind of thing only Oswald was guilty of—ordering the rifle months ahead of time, studying the victim's itinerary, and lining up the circumstances for maximum convenience. According to New Jersey law, one can theoretically intend a murder in one second and commit it the next ("no length of time need intervene between formation of the purpose to kill, and its execution"). One crucial distinction appears to be murder as a reflex action: murder in self-defense would be the most obvious case in point. Less obvious, but still generally classified as an unpremeditated murder, is murder in response to provocation by the victim irresistible to the man provoked. The provocation in question must be offensive, rather than defensive. If a gentleman tries to seduce a lady and she declines to go along, that is not a provocation which justifies him in killing her other than at the risk of conviction for a premeditated murder. If, however, the lady suggests the gentleman has been cuckolded, that is a provocative statement, and any lethal reply by the gentleman—in a fit of blind rage—may be classified as murder in the second degree. The jury was not invited to ponder these distinctions. Felony murder having been ruled out, the jury had to know that it was not the case that Smith had been provoked into insane action. Assuming he had actually killed the girl, is it more reasonable that he

159

did so unprovoked than provoked? Murder resulting from a "wrongful act or insult" is a mandatory second-degree murder. Under the law, any doubt as regards the question inures to the benefit of the defendant. In which case the jury could have found him guilty in the second degree, and he would have received a life sentence. They found him guilty of a premeditated murder of Vickie Zielinski, by simply "inferring" intent "from the nature of the mortal blow," after a mere two hours of deliberation on an extraordinarily complex case that had lasted two weeks.

Smith settled down at the death house to initiate a series of appeals, all of which have been unsuccessful—except those that asked for a stay of execution pending the adjudication of the incumbent appeal. The first appeals concentrated on discrepancies uncovered in the evidence given at the trial—for instance, Pelzer's *volte-face* on the question of Hommell's alibi. Denied. Gradually, Smith turned to matters of law, rather than fact. So much so as to dismay some of his friends, a diminishing band, who would have preferred, somehow, to see him devote his long weeks and years in the death cell to constructing a compelling case against the killer—whoever he was. (Early in our correspondence I raised the question. "You say in your letter," he replied, "that I am convinced of my innocence and, under the circumstances, I must have 'a strong case against somebody?' You end this statement with a question mark. I am not sure of your meaning. As for my innocence, it is not matter of 'convincing' myself, I know!!") But Smith turned cool—cool especially on the matter of putting his finger on the killer.

And within a very short period he was left with very few friends. His mother emptied her purse in his behalf and could no longer pay legal or investigative bills. A. D. Nicol, the private eye, was paid $100 a week during the eleven weeks preceding the trial. Convinced of Smith's innocence, he never stopped working for him. Nicol is a middle-aged Scotsman, a prodigious worker addicted to meticulous detail, who drove 4,000 miles merely to interview people who had known Smith. He took the job, as did Smith's trial attorney, believing Smith guilty, but believing also that he was entitled to representation. Within a very short period, they both believed him innocent. Nicol is a diffident man, noncombative in his views. Even so, after the conviction, in a conversation with the prosecutor, he listened to Mr. Calissi say: "I would stake my own life that Edgar Smith is guilty." "I would like to say, with all due respect," Nicol said, "that I would stake mine that he wasn't guilty." His mind has never ceased to turn on the subject. He is by no means convinced that Hommell was the murderer, and as recently as the late spring of 1965, he bared to me his own hypothesis, which the laws of libel prevent my disclosing. He does believe that Smith last saw Vickie with Hommell.

In short order, the dramatis personae disbanded. Smith's wife went West with her new husband and renamed her child. Mrs. Zielinski, Vickie's mother, divorced Zielinski, charging him with unspeakable conduct and brutality toward her and her daughters. Hommell took odd jobs. A year ago he was extradited in Florida, after the American Civil Liberties Union took the complaints of fifteen boys at a Maryland reformatory who charged Hommell with brutal and sadistic treatment of them. Characteristically, Smith gave me that information by sending along a clipping from a New Jersey paper without comment. I replied that the arrest was of considerable interest, even though, in conversations with Nicol, I gathered that he himself was not convinced of Hommell's guilt. "No," Smith replied, advancing one of his measured thoughts, "Nicol did not think Hommell was guilty. Then again, no one ever said he was guilty; the only thing I said was that I left the girl with him. As for Hommell's present troubles, I think they are more interesting than useful. Being entirely realistic about things, I would suppose that the only real value to me of Hommell's difficulties would be if a new trial were granted; then I could very well raise hell on the question of Hommell's credibility as a witness for the prosecution. (Wow! What a great title for a book or a play—*Witness for the Prosecution*. Such imagination!)"

Smith's letters are obstinately optimistic concerning his ultimate vindication—at least legally (he never talks about getting his hands on the killer—or at least not to me). His imperturbability, a word he has come to dislike, I found out after twice using it, is sometimes understandable, sometimes less so. July 26, 1963: "It is my sad task," he began a letter in a style so often arch, "to advise you of the

161

denial of my appeal. The denial came on 24 July [1963] via a 2-1 vote." But quickly the note of optimism. "However, for the first time, a Judge saw things my way." He tried a little later (November 4) to persuade his former wife, through a volunteer attorney out West, to execute an affidavit reconfirming the facts on the record—that the police had pretended to her, on the morning of March 6, that Smith was being detained merely to answer questions concerning another suspect and that, therefore, she did not need to worry, as she was disposed to do, to summon an attorney in his behalf. But his wife now pretended she had never heard of Edgar Smith; before the affidavit could be presented, she invited the attorney, curtly, to leave her house. "The information [from out West], unfortunately was not what I would have liked to have heard. I suppose it's best to be philosophic about my problems, when one gets to the bottom of the ladder the only way to go is up. You can believe"—a rare relapse into melancholy—"I have now reached the bottom." *

And then the rejection by the Supreme Court (February 20). "From what I hear from Washington, Justice Douglas voted to give me a full hearing. Four votes are needed. Apparently Justice Douglas was the only one to see things my way. Bless his liberal heart!!"

And on March 25, when a colleague of mine expressed concern over an execution date fixed for April 27: "Don't worry about that April 27 date, a stay is more or less a formality." And changing the subject quickly to more serious matters: "Do me a favor, will you? Call me something besides Mr. Smith; no one else does except Mr. Buckley. Maybe there's some psychological significance, but I feel uncomfortable when people call me Mr. Smith. I prefer anything else, Ed, Smitty, even Edgar. To what might be called the in-group, I answer most often to Igor."

On July 7th: "I have just learned that the State Supreme Court has rejected my appeal. Again, I am surprised!" Smithese for: I am not surprised. "Perhaps by the time you return from celebrating Barry Goldwater's victory in San Francisco, I will be able to give you a positive statement as to my future plans." On July 13th, his buoyancy was

---

* The former Mrs. Smith has since executed an affidavit tending to confirm the facts as alleged by Edgar Smith.

visibly diminished, though finally it surfaced. "I have received the New Jersey Supreme Court opinion on my last appeal; it is even more abrupt than I had expected it to be. I was surprised by the Court's reliance on inference and supposition—all in the State's favor. I have, in the past, been willing to accept the various Court decisions with a reasonable degree of equanimity; this time I find I am rather unhappy. However, what is done is done."

For a year, he believed that the Supreme Court's decision in *Mapp v. Ohio,* which defined the rules of search and seizure in such a way as to illegalize flatly the means by which the state of New Jersey had got evidence from Smith concerning the baseball bat, the pants, and Vickie's schoolbooks, would be his deliverance. The question was whether the Supreme Court would rule that its decision in *Mapp* should apply retroactively—*i.e.,* that prisoners whose plight was traceable to a violation of these rules should be given a retrial. Smith was jubilantly confident that the Supreme Court would so rule in the spring of 1965 and confident that the New Jersey prosecutor was ignorant that the Supreme Court had accepted two test cases which would require it to come to a decision on the matter.

Nothing doing. June 9: "I would suppose you [have] read that the Supreme Court has held *Mapp* to be non-retroactive. They really surprised everyone this time. It makes my problem somewhat more difficult, but I've managed to survive worse setbacks."

His optimism sometimes has stemmed from his confidence in his own superior knowledge, if not of the law, at least of legal tactics. To his dumb amazement, on one occasion the state missed its deadline for filing a brief in opposition to his own. The rules on the matter are very strict: If no brief in opposition is filed, a court is entitled to take the position that the petitioner's point is unopposed, in which case it is, as a rule, automatically conceded. An entire month went by. "The State filed, without explanation, a reply brief on January 21, one month late. I filed a Motion the same day, calling for rejection of the reply [on the ground of its lateness]. Actually, it might be better in the long run if the reply is accepted. My humble opinion is that the reply is the worst brief I have ever seen."

The Supreme Court, once again, turned him down. February 3: "Throw me a parachute," he wrote me to

Switzerland. "I've been shot down by the Warren Escadrille. The decision came Monday, the 1st." And then, like a composer facing an immense organ console, meditating the harmonic combination best suited for the next desired effect: "It may take a few weeks to determine which way, legally speaking, I will go next. It appears that my best bet will be to hang up my appeal in some manner"—he meant delaying action, for the sake of delay—"in order to give the Supreme Court time to reach its decisions." (He was waiting for the Court to declare itself on the retroactive application of *Mapp*.) "Of course, delaying actions aren't ethical—but, then again, I'm not a lawyer, am I? . . . Perhaps this would be a good time to ask the County Court to correct some of these minor errors in the record. . . ."

By March 1 he had decided on his strategy, which he communicated shortly after, writing that he had secured a court order authorizing me to visit him. "After a month or so of hard work, mostly trying to decipher Earl Warren's [opinions], I'm beginning to see a ray of hope. All I have to do now is to convince one of the lower courts that the Supreme Court means precisely what it says; if I can do that—no mean task—I may wind up visiting you."

On March 17, 1965, almost as if to interrupt Edgar Smith in mid-thought, Judge O'Dea set an execution date—April 28. Smith appealed to the New Jersey Supreme Court to stay the execution, pending his appeal. The New Jersey court delayed. . . . At the last minute, Associate Justice Brennan of the Supreme Court ordered the stay of execution (which Smith sent me, marked "No need to return"). This time he had been visibly shaken.

April 18: "My predicted schedule is a fait accompli. Mr. Justice Brennan ordered the stay of execution on Friday, which is in itself singularly appropriate. I will now sit back and bide my time until the end of the [Supreme Court's] term, the 21st of June. Then, with all the Court's decisions at hand [the Supreme Court makes some of its most important decisions at the end of its term, and was due to rule then on the applicability of *Mapp*], I will be able to file my petition on latest authority. That petition will be acted upon the first Monday in October. If the Court then declines to take jurisdiction, off I go to the District Court. All of which means you can keep aboard your boat, head for Nassau and the Out Islands, and forget about Young

Smith for the next six months."

He did not, as was his habit, sustain the levity:

"Bill, you know as well as anyone that I've never been one to grouse about the manner in which my case has been handled in the courts, but today I'm peeved. Back in 1958, my lawyers tried for two days to get a stay [of execution] from one of the State Courts, but couldn't even get the time of day. Finally, with twenty-four hours to go, they managed to find a Federal Judge to issue a stay and take jurisdiction away from the State Courts. Within an hour, the State Supreme Court and the Attorney-General both issued stays, claiming prior jurisdiction. The Federal Judge released the case to the State, after he had finished chewing out the Attorney-General for, as the Judge put it, 'playing games.' Well, 1965 was nearly a repeat performance.

"After filing in the State Court for a stay, I wrote the Chief Justice three letters, explaining the exigency of my situation and requesting a speedy decision. I waited eleven days for a decision usually made in one day, and then heard a story to the effect that the Court was going to sit on the application until the last possible moment, then deny it. So being prudent where my skin is involved, I wrote to the Court and the Attorney-General, telling them I'd wait three more days before asking the Federal Court to again take jurisdiction. *Mirabile dictu,* I received a decision the following day.

"Frankly, my friend, things were a bit close for a while; I had the suspicion I was batting a sticky wicket. You can bet your best ski boots that the State isn't going to throw any parties for Justice Brennan this month.

" 'Tis time I ceased bending your ear. Will keep you posted, always and endlessly (one hopes)."

Edgar's mother gave me a picture less composed: "At the time I arrived for my visit [with Edgar] he did not know about the stay. It was my pleasure to tell him. He did not believe it was true until it came on the noon news."

Smith doesn't write only about his legal problems. In prison he has read as widely as his prior commitment to the law will permit him. He has taken correspondence courses from several universities, in several fields, and is also an avid television viewer. (" 'Tis time for me to settle back for another evening of TV. Tonight is educational TV

165

night, I watch the one and only *Beverly Hillbillies*. Late at night, eleven to one, I watch Johnny Carson.") He spotted Dwight Macdonald one night, describing himself as a "conservative anarchist." "Our 'conservative anarchist' is a real enigma. Perhaps some Sunday afternoon the Hayden Planetarium could devote a special show to attempting to depict the various seasonal positions of the stars in the liberal galaxy. . . ." He takes a modest pride in his scholarly achievements. December 8, 1963: "I thought you might care to know that I have taken and passed the first of two tests given by Mensa.* They advertise in the classified section of *NR*. I am also carrying a ninety-eight percent average in the Accounting and Economics courses I am taking from Penn State University. I will complete the first semester in about three weeks." And on another occasion, August 20, 1964: "Thought you would be interested in my college grades to date. They are: Accounting 1 and 2, six semester hours, final grade B; Business Organization, three hours, final grade B; European History (Renaissance to Waterloo), four hours, final grade A; Advanced Rhetoric (incomplete), three hours, A average. By the way, for my final exam in Rhetoric, I wrote an essay about BG [Goldwater] and the press." And on January 5, 1965, acknowledging a book I sent him at Christmastime: ". . . I guess I'm something of a nut on World War II. Once I get going with all the maps and things I withdraw from the world for days at a time. By the way, did you know that Kosygin was one of the planners of the industrial move to the East in 1941?"

And sometimes, in his letters, just acute high-spiritedness. "P.S." [July 22, 1964] "I see *National Review* is now listing its zip-code number. A sign of moderation?" September 16: "Yesterday I received *National Review*. Who had the bright idea for that section printed on blue paper? I almost went blind trying to read it. (Don't I have a lot of nerve for one who is receiving a free subscription?)" I replied: "The blue paper was a catastrophe. The printer simply substituted his shade of blue for the blue we had designated. We are flatly refusing to pay them for the supplement, so that I may end up in jail myself. You would, of course, write to me?" And a reply: "My opinion

* The organization of top IQers.

is that you'll have to pay for the blue paper. Being in interstate commerce, you cannot discriminate on the basis of color—including the various shades of blue. If you go to jail, I'll write—provided you maintain a modicum of imperturbability."

I thanked him, last December, for sending my wife the Museum of Modern Art's annual calendar. December 18: "Glad you liked the calendar. I would have liked to have done more, but circumstances made it impossible. Perhaps I'll remember you in my will, and leave you my collection of *National Geographic* maps." I thought I saw a wayward trace of bitter-sadness here, and tried to move fast to cope with it, and lead it back to where it normally slumbered. "Thank you for promising to remember me in your will [I replied]. Since I am ten years older than you and engage in activities far more perilous than yours, with perhaps a single exception, I should think it highly unlikely that I shall reap any such harvest. But I thank you for the thought." He did not acknowledge the letter, but several months later alluded to it. "Good Lord!" he began, with his conventional tushery. "How did you get shanghaied into that election business? [I had declared my candidacy for mayor of New York.] Did you ever stop to think that through some strange twist of fate you might be unlucky enough to win? It isn't likely, but the possibility is frightening. At least you have the editors of the *Times* pulling for you to come out safely in the end. As for myself, I'm almost afraid to send you a contribution—it might help. Oh well, if nothing else, I can now agree with you when you say you have as many problems as I do."—June 25, 1965.

The final appeal of Edgar Smith will be based on several points. The first is that the proceedings by the police against him on March 5 and 6 were inquisitorial, rather than accusatory, that inordinate pressures were put on him, so much so as to cause him to say anything at all rather than endure the agony of further questioning, further harassment, further fatigue. The second is that Smith was denied counsel at a moment when the proceedings had clearly progressed beyond the investigative point on over to the accusatory point. The third is that incriminating information was got from him without regard to his rights under the Fifth Amendment. Still another, and perhaps

167

most crucial, has to do with the question of the volun-
tariness of the statement Smith was, in effect, tricked into
giving. And, finally, there remains to review the circumstances of the trial. The prejudgment of Smith by the
press was as final as almost any in the recent history of
criminal proceedings.

The legal fight, provided the money can be raised to pay
a lawyer's fee, will go, almost inevitably, to the Supreme
Court—for the final time. The District Court will predictably have turned down Smith's appeal by the time these
words appear in print. The Court of Appeals will hear
Smith's appeal and dispose of it probably unfavorably,
considering the flux caused by recent Supreme Court decisions and the conventional indisposition of a lower court to
apply Supreme Court rulings that are considered, if not
elusive, at any rate socially disruptive. If *Escobedo v. Illinois,* for instance, is to be applied retroactively, will our
jails suddenly empty? And will new trials, some of them
many years after the crime, need to be conducted? In the
spring of 1965 the Third Circuit Court of Appeals, ruling
on the prisoner Russo, who occupies the same death house
as Smith, took the bits and pieces of legal flotsam washing
about in the legal seas and attempted to lay down a firm
position. I asked Smith, at the time, to explain to me the
meaning of the Russo decision, and he wrote me as
follows:

"The Third Circuit decision at issue is a new and truly
far-reaching holding only insofar as it represents a sort of
amalgamation of all past State and Federal Court holdings.
In combination, these holdings add up to far more than
they do when considered separately. In all fairness to the
Third Circuit, one must note that each statement in this recent decision is supported by a previous decision of some
other court.

"The decision deals with two specific issues. The first is
the factual question of when the right to counsel obtains;
the second is the question of whether the right depends
upon a request.

"1) The prevailing standard for judging the point at
which a suspect becomes the accused, and the right to
counsel thereby attaches, is *Escobedo vs. Illinois.* In
simplest terms, Escobedo holds that the right obtains when
the crime is no longer 'unsolved,' when the suspect is in

custody, and when he has not waived his right to counsel. This is a difficult series of circumstances for an appellate court to determine in retrospect; it might have been better to say 'when probable [prima facie?—W.F.B.] cause to arrest is present.' The problem of determining when the suspect becomes the 'accused' is akin to determining when a book or movie is 'obscene.' In both cases, everything depends upon the particular circumstances of a given situation."

"Example: If the police have a confession from the suspect's partner, implicating the suspect, and there is independent evidence placing the suspect at the scene of the crime at the time of the crime; it may then be said that the crime has been solved, that the suspect has become the accused, and he is entitled to the assistance of counsel. This may not mean the police have sufficient evidence to convict, it simply means the police have probable cause to arrest; and that continued interrogation in the absence of counsel is impermissible, since the obvious purpose of that interrogation is to secure from the mouth of the accused the necessary evidence to convict. (Wretched phrasing!) Nothing prevents interrogation if the purpose is to solve a crime, and counsel at this stage is not a constitutionally secured right. However, when the interrogation is for the demonstrable purpose of eliciting a confession which will complement other evidence and assure a conviction, the constitutional right to counsel obtains. Finally, the police may interrogate any person at any time if that person has been advised by counsel, or has waived that right, and still wishes to 'bare his breast.'

"2) Having determined that the petitioner had become the accused, the Third Circuit turned to the question of whether their failure to request counsel militated against a finding that they had been deprived of counsel, and concluded that it did not. Citing the Supreme Court decision in *Carnley vs. Cochran* (1939), and a host of subsequent Federal and State decisions, the Court came to the obvious conclusion that the right to counsel is secured by the Constitution, not by any request. If the accused has that right, it is his whether or not he has asked for it; if he does not have the right, a request does not give it to him. This particular holding was taken from *People vs. Dorado,* California Supreme Court, Jan. 18, 1965. The State appealed and the Supreme Court refused to review June 2, 1965. The Ohio Supreme Court ruled to the contrary but the United States Supreme Court reversed that decision May 24, 1965.

"In all jurisdictions, the right to counsel may be waived. Many State Courts have considered silence to be a waiver, but this has never held up in the Federal Courts. The Federal Courts hold that the waiver must be knowing and intelligent, that to waive the right the suspect must know first that he has the right. Hence the recent holdings that police must advise suspects of their rights, and that any waiver must show that the suspect was fully aware of what a waiver would mean. For the Courts to hold otherwise would be to favor the habitual criminal over the first offender. The former 'knows the score' and is quick to request counsel; the latter is often confused, intimidated, or simply ignorant of his rights. Thus, in determining the intelligence of any alleged waiver, the suspect's prior record is a significant factor.

"Additionally, the Third Circuit Court reasoned that if a person has the constitutional right at trial, to counsel, notwithstanding his failure to request counsel, he should not be required to request counsel when the constitutional right obtains prior to trial. After all, why should a right depend upon a request at one time but not at another?

"I might add that many police officials argue that a 'warning' will prevent them from obtaining confessions from those suspects who desire to confess. This is ridiculous. If a suspect truly desires to confess, a warning will not stop him. On the other hand, if the confession is obtained solely because the suspect was ignorant of his rights and did not know he could remain silent, it should be thrown out. And this is what the Third Circuit has done.

"I could write a hell of a lot more, but it's getting late and I'm beat. Hope this rather sloppy and superficial rundown gives you some idea of what the decision was about. It's not Magna Carta, far from it, but it does help me."

It is only natural for laymen such as myself to wonder why a man who can write such expository paragraphs as these should need another man for a lawyer. One recalls, from time to time (without ever fully understanding it), the old saw about the man who serves as his own lawyer having a fool for a client. The key here is experience! How very necessary it is, and it's something Smith does not have. "Could you give me the benefit of your thinking, as to how I might best proceed," he asked me (March 28). "I hate like hell to put you to a lot of trouble on my account, but I have to plan ahead. . . . Quite frankly, Counsellor Smith is in somewhat of a quandary. Do I compromise my not too abundant principles and prepare the abject, bowing and fawning type of brief the State Courts have come to expect (prefer?) from indigent lay appellants? Or do I stand by what I know is right ('In your heart. . .'), and give the Court a lecture on the State's basic responsibility to uphold and protect the federally secured rights of its citizens? The first course is wiser, the latter is more honest. It's quite a problem in strategy. If I had been trained at 'Foggy Bottom,' I'd probably try to walk a thin line down the middle, and wind up losing on both sides. Oh, for a return to the simple days of my misspent youth!"

Smith never once asked me to help him raise the funds to retain a lawyer. Our single discussion of his needs centered on the purely mechanical problem of replacing an inadequate and slow prison typist with a professional legal stenographer accustomed to the proper typographical facade and to the irksome problem of supplying the dozens and dozens of copies that need to be furnished when complicated appeals are filed. I have never known a less importunate man, for whom the least favor is taken as a charitable act of great magnitude. "It is very kind of you people," he wrote a short time later, "to take such an interest in my situation." Much later, when I undertook to get his appeals typed and duplicated: "I know you are going to suggest that you will have the work done for me. Please, humor me; I am just conservative enough to insist on paying my own way for as long as I can." I replied that I would purchase the literary right to the letters he had sent me in return for the cost of duplicating his appeals. His next letter joked about the suggested deal. I persevered. He replied: "No, I didn't refuse you the 'litprop' in my letters. All I did was deny that any existed, and I still deny it. You'll never realize how happy I am knowing that you have to read my letters, not I. That isn't an opening into which you are expected to insert a compliment. I'm being perfectly candid when I say I haven't been able to figure

171

out what in hell there is about Smith that keeps you interested."

What indeed? It has not occurred to him that one can develop a friendship of a man in a death house or that a condemned man's friendship can be gratefully accepted. Probably it has not occurred to him because probably he suspects that any such friendships are emotionally condescending, that they are based on pity or morbidity. I suspect that that is the reason why his natural dignity has always prevented him from emotional self-revelation. Only twice has he exposed himself. I finished a letter about this and that (August 18, 1964) rather impulsively with the sentence: "My God, I wish I could be absolutely certain you didn't kill that girl!" "My God," he replied, "I wish you *could be* absolutely certain I didn't kill that girl"—but he recovered his composure before even finishing the sentence—"but you know what they say about death and taxes. I think, for now, that I am satisfied that you aren't certain that I did kill her. Besides, you really think it would do any good for me to tell you I didn't? Would that convince you? Disclaimers of guilt are a dime a dozen around this place." And then he was Lawyer Smith again: "From an idealistic [*sic*] point of view, if you are uncertain about my innocence, it follows that you must be uncertain about my guilt, as well, and I am entitled to the full benefit of your doubt. Where is your conservative belief in established judicial principles?"

The other time I riled him, he did not recover until the end of a long paragraph. I had written him that God was apparently "in" in the subways, to judge from graffiti I had come upon that morning. "God is Dead—Nietzsche," someone had written in chalk. Under which had been scrawled in block letters, "NIETZSCHE IS DEAD —GOD." I then made a second comment, coming apparently too close to the heels of the first, about his imperturbability. "I had not intended to write again so soon," he began glacially, "but I am, quite frankly, somewhat disturbed by your very apparent misapprehensions as to my state of mind. Your references to my serenity, imperturbability, etc., impute [*sic*] that I am some Buddha-like anachronism, fast approaching Nirvana. Tell me—does the fact that I am in the death house mean to you that I should be perpetually atop a soapbox, shouting my protestations to a cold, cruel, unhearing world? I assure you, my friend, if I thought soapbox oratory would serve me any good purpose, I would climb onto the closest box handy, and put George Wallace to shame. The fact is that what you mistake for serenity, or an air of detachment, is nothing more or less than the realization on my part of the fact that my situation is not going to be improved by breast-beating and lamentations, however loud or sustained—it can only be changed by and in a court of law. Perhaps my letters should be appropriately tear-stained when they arrive at your office, giving them a more pathetically desperate quality. Again, if it would do me any good, I would cry you a river—à la Julie London." Then, rapidly, the pulse slowed, and Queen Victoria remounted her throne. "I trust you will not misinterpret the tone of this letter. I was not especially unhappy that you failed to understand my feelings, but I did think it was worth clearing up.

"P.S. What ever were you doing in a New York subway? You're right, you do live more dangerously than I do—much more."

(AUTHOR'S NOTE: Edgar Smith has no funds to retain counsel, without which he cannot complete the final legal appeals that stand between him and the electric chair. A fund for this purpose has been started: donations should be earmarked "Edgar Smith Fund" and sent immediately to Mr. James Williams, Treasurer, New York Yearly Meeting of Friends, Oakwood School, Poughkeepsie, New York [a tax-deductible foundation]. Any surplus will be returned after the final disposition of the case.)

THE TROUBLE WITH POLICEMEN

May 28, 1967

THE BIG BLUE LINE. Police Power vs. Human Rights. By Ed Cray, New York: Coward McCann. $5.95.

Ed Cray's tractarian approach to the question of misbehavior by the nation's police is nonetheless useful, both to those who are convinced that there is a major problem—and to those who are not. The book appears

173

concurrently with the report by the President's Commission on Law Enforcement and the Administration of Justice, which like Mr. Cray, finds that the situation is deteriorating, though not, like Mr. Cray, because police brutality is mounting (it isn't, the commission says), but for other reasons. These include brusqueness by the police and little forms of corruption that Mr. Cray also condemns—and quite rightly. There are enough luridities in the book to satisfy anyone inclined to reason from the particular injustices committed by policemen to the general position that the police of America are a corrupt and unlawful breed about whom we must gravely worry and in order to restrain whom we must at the least set up everywhere, instantly, civilian review boards. Mr. Cray's exposition is, however, puzzling, because every now and again he gives us material that appears to belie his own generalities, as also, every now and then, he asks us to cry over an instance of police irregularity that simply will not bring tears.

He begins his book, for instance, by stating that "no accurate figures [have been] compiled which will demonstrate the prevalence or infrequency of police malpractice," and he assures us that although "the author is . . . a special pleader . . . it is to be hoped [that he is] one who has retained his objectivity." So much for objectivity—from that point on, the author catalogues instances of police brutality, discourtesy, and arbitrariness sufficient to rouse any man's indignation, without, however, answering persuasively the question, which he began by saying was moot and which this volume should ideally have removed from mootdom: Do the figures, or do they not, suggest that the incidence of police brutality is such as to warrant a wholesale review of existing procedures, or is police irregularity no more than that ration of ugliness the human race is cursed with in all its enterprises, to be likened to price fixing by businessmen, extortion by labor unions, corruption among bureaucrats?

Mr. Cray is greatly convinced that there is an urgent necessity for civilian review, but once again, he does not make it clear that the necessity for civilian review is any more urgent as regards policemen than, say, as regards bureaucrats or postmen—though it must be granted that the offenses of offensive policemen are more lurid than

174

those of offensive bureaucrats. It is more painful to be clubbed by the policeman on the beat than to be stolen from by Bobby Baker.

Mr. Cray's own figures are confusing. He dwells at considerable length in his final exhortatory chapter on the success of the Civilian Review Board in Philadelphia, and yet he does not appear to ponder his own figures. During the six years between 1958 and 1964, a total of 573 complaints were filed in Philadelphia against the police. The exemplary Civilian Review Board recommended action against the police in a total of 22 cases, or less than 5 percent. This suggests, if we are to generalize from the figure—and why not?—that less than 5 percent of the complaints against the police can survive the scrutiny of men whom Mr. Cray ratifies as qualified to pass judgment. Mr. Cray, perhaps inadvertently, goes further by saying that in Philadelphia "apparently most complainants have been satisfied." If one understands him, that means that 95 percent of those who complained against the police were apparently satisfied that they should not have done so! Not, in a word, the best argument for instituting a civilian review board, though one cannot doubt that the argument does exist.

And then Mr. Cray does his own case a disservice by citing here and there an episode which strains the reader's sympathy for his thesis. For instance, he recalls approvingly the extraordinary decision of Judge Leighton of Chicago upholding the right of two young men to resist arrest on the grounds that they knew they were not guilty of doing or intending anything wrong, and therefore, *ex-hypothesi,* their arrest could only be unwarranted—and shouldn't people have the right to resist unwarranted arrests?

The two police officers in question had accosted two young blades who were weaving down the street, one of them brandishing a broken beer bottle. The officers accosted them, and the judge's résumé was: "Officer De Sutter observed that the defendant Rodriguez had a broken beer bottle in his right hand. He was not doing anything unlawful with the broken beer bottle, and from the evidence in this record the conclusion that the defendant was seeking a place to dispose of it is as reasonable as any other. Nevertheless . . . one . . . of the officers shouted,

'Drop that bottle.' The defendant Rodriguez turned around, stepped back, and said to the two officers, 'Come and get it, you f—— cops.' At no time did either of the defendants attack or assault the two officers."

Quite true. The police officers moved first, and one of them wound up in the hospital, with permanent traces of broken beer bottle on his face. If I have not made it clear, let me say that this episode figures in Mr. Cray's book as another instance of police excessiveness.

It is too bad that Mr. Cray carries on so, because his onesidedness invites tedium, the same kind of distrust one feels after a few hundred pages of Mark Lane. Too bad, because the problem is real, and no doubt the community should be alerted to it. Mr. Cray's most convincing contributions are his recordings of the general condescension of many policemen toward minority groups, members of which they will address demeaningly.

This "verbal discourtesy," as Mr. Cray terms it, ought to be flatly and unsparingly extirpated (a) because it is wrong and wounding to the human pride and (b) because for the time being the highest per capita incidence of crime is among the minority groups Mr. Cray speaks of, and for that reason relations between those minorities and the police ought to be especially close. If civilian review boards are needed to bring about such reforms where needed, Mr. Cray has not made that case.

Still, where there is injustice, there is always the temptation to desire yet another agency to which to appeal. When one reads a sentence such as Mr. Cray's "Sauce for the black goose was apparently not to be sauce for the white ganders," one is tempted to ask for civilian review boards for book writers. Indeed, the generic case is appealing, and Mr. Cray's final pitch for an ombudsman, the citizen's defender against the abuse of authority, I find totally convincing.

THE CRIME COMMISSION REPORT

January 28, 1967

For some reason or other, it is being assumed that the conservative position on crime and crime prevention calls

for a thoughtless penology. President Johnson's Crime Commission has been delayed in issuing its report because of a last-minute flap over the question of eavesdropping (the commission wanted to authorize eavesdropping under strict control, but LBJ has come out flatly against it, except to track down plots to assassinate the President).

But enough people have seen the report so that we tend to know its gist, and the word is out that it will greatly offend conservatives, that it is, in the headline of the *Wall Street Journal*, a BOOST FOR THE GREAT SOCIETY.

The "boost" for the Great Society is meant to be twofold. The commission is going to come out four square in favor of the poverty program, and that certainly is a boost for Lyndon Johnson. But in fact, the commission is not likely to go further than to attack poverty, even as Lyndon Johnson repeatedly does.

"Poverty," he said recently, "there is the real enemy. Strike down poverty and much of crime will fall with it." Which is perfectly true. It is also true that if you were to strike down politics, the crime rate would greatly fall—all the graft, the bribery, the chiseling, the fixing. It is also true that affluence and crime have risen hand in hand in this country, though not true that the one causes the other, or, goodness knows, vice versa.

On the general question there is much explanation to be done. But on the concrete questions, also said to be distinctively liberal, the commission strikes me as having done excellent work by no means uncongenial to conservatives in pointing out that prisons make poor reformatories. Because Senator Goldwater called in 1964 for strengthening the police and prosecuting the criminals, he hardly committed himself or the conservative community to unintelligent and vindictive treatment for criminals once apprehended.

The Crime Commission's executive director, James Vorenberg of the Harvard Law School, points out quite correctly that "prison is a lousy place to prepare a guy to live outside a prison," though he adds, again quite correctly, "It's a good place to keep a guy who might kill somebody."

The Crime Commission will recommend that convicts be separated, on the basis of thorough research into their

177

background, their intelligence, the nature of their offense, into two categories, the one presumably reformable, the other less hopeful.

The suggested changes will concern primarily the former category. Many have been considered. They include great experiments with probationary arrangements. Why not permit certain kinds of offenders to work in the community during the day and return to jail at night (never mind the fun Hollywood will have with the concept)? There should be halfway houses that "seek to reintroduce prisoners to society gradually" by allowing them to live and work in a community before they are officially released from custody. Is there any purpose in requiring bail from people who are obviously in a position to furnish it, let alone requiring them to stay in the station house pending the materialization of bail?

The conservative is hardly opposed to the devising of means by which human beings can be rehabilitated. He has opposed, rather, the notion that society's debts to the criminal are requited by letting him alone to vent his resentments against innocent people. What has been wrong is that too many lawbreakers get away with breaking the law, and are neither detained in prison nor reformed in prison reformatories. There have been too many judges and witnesses and prosecutors who, worn down by the law's delays, have given up the hope of successful prosecution. There have been prison terms given, without effective probationary supervision, which have proved utterly inadequate and have resulted in fresh crimes. Whole areas of whole towns, such as Central Park in New York, for instance, are more or less formally ceded to criminals. The big crime syndicates are apparently untouched.

The commission's report should make for good reading, for criminals and noncriminals alike, for liberals and conservatives.

THE ASSAULT ON WHITTAKER CHAMBERS

December 15, 1964

I

The current assault on Whittaker Chambers has been in two parts, the first on his credibility, the second on his thought. Conor Cruise O'Brien has greeted the posthumous publication of Whittaker Chambers' essays, letters, and fragments as a singular opportunity to call to the attention of the literary world, or at least that part of it that reads the *New York Review of Books,* that Mr. Chambers was a "veteran liar" and to confess his own continuing surprise that, even so, Chambers "should have become a saint in the eyes of so many intelligent people who dislike lies, or say they do." Don't you see, says Mr. O'Brien, all of Whittaker Chambers was a living lie—lies, lies, lies, to which he was driven by all sorts of reasons, mostly squalid, not the least of which was the force of rhetorical pressure, which he never could resist, indeed, which was an aspect of that passion for melodrama that ruled his life?

For instance, Mr. O'Brien proceeds to give an example to which he devotes nearly one-third of his lengthy review. Consider, and dwell upon, a furtive little statement imbedded, almost invisibly, in Chambers' essay on the Third Rome, in which he speaks of Byzantium, known to the Russians as Tsargrad: ". . . the Imperial City, city of the Tsar (Tsar, the Russian form of Caesar). The depth of the special Russian feeling for Byzantium," Chambers went on, "is perhaps suggested by the fact that Tsargrad alone, among the names of foreign cities, is declined through all nine of the inflections of the Russian noun; is treated as a Russian word."

179

Now: "It [is] a fact, universally recognized by grammarians," Mr. O'Brien crows, "that the Russian noun has *six* . . . inflections: not *nine*. . . . The 'nine inflections of the Russian noun' are of course a mistake, not a lie, but the mistake is, I think, a revealing one because . . . there was a 'need,' a motive, for it. In this case—and I suspect, often though not always elsewhere in Chambers' writings and testimony—the pressure to distort is a rhetorical pressure. 'All nine of the inflections of the Russian noun' gives just the reverberation Chambers needed at this point in his boomy incantation."

What mattered to Chambers in this case, and indeed in his whole life, was the dramatic problem, Mr. O'Brien is saying. He invented the nine inflections because they give a special and mystical sonority to his sentence; "nine," with its tintinabulary sound, is such a number, by contrast with the pedestrian and unevocative "six." Just that is the key to Chambers' character. Whether he is talking about the inflections of a Russian noun, about which he is ignorant, or whether he is talking about Alger Hiss, of whose innocence he is not ignorant, Chambers is driven to untruth, unknowingly, and knowingly. The pressure of the age caused him to say things about Hiss that weren't true in order to make a grandiose historical point. A related pressure caused him, in order to perfect the rhetorical momentum of a paragraph, to say things about the Russian noun which are not so.

The charge that Chambers mishandled Russian grammar is, then, crucial to Mr. O'Brien's chimera. And so it becomes, by Mr. O'Brien's own terms, a matter of considerable interest to know whether Chambers knew something about Russian or whether he merely affected a familiarity with it, so exposing in himself that shallowness of nature which fortifies the assumption that he was a veteran liar, and a most mischievous one because he did not restrict himself to lying about Russian nouns, but lied also about American citizens. One of whom, on account of such lies, was sentenced to prison and discredited, along with a myth about the disinterested idealism of all of the votaries of the New Deal, which myth Chambers' witness mortally wounded.

I observed a Russian grammar at Chambers' bedside—he was recovering from a heart attack—when I first met him ten years ago. I have gone back over some letters I had from him. One of them remarked on an aspect of the Russian language one would ordinarily reflect upon, one supposes, only after mastering what is universally recognized by grammarians as basic about the Russian noun.

"I think," he added in a postscript to a letter in 1959, "I think I may have come on the key to the Russian mind, or at least a clue to the reason why the Russian mind will always remain elusive to the West. This requires a little background. In our Russian course [he was then studying the language formally] we have got to the aspect of verbs. There are two of these, the imperfective (which one learns first) and the perfective. The perfective deals exclusively with completed action, indicated by a structural change so special that there are, in effect, two of every verb in Russian. Sometimes the change is orthographic. More often, it includes (this is rather like German—with a difference) [undecipherable]. And here comes the clue to the thought process. One prefix is *za*. Our instructor counselled us to be careful to make a distinction between past time, and past time with the use of za, since the use of za indicates that an action, which has been completed, is beginning. *Le violà*. [Murray] Kempton should know that you can only read Dostoievski with the use of za."

On another occasion he wrote, "I have been expressly requested to convey to you the thanks of a delighted reader of *NR*. First, some rather elaborate background to make them intelligible. Recently, one of your writers exposed a plot somewhat like the one mentioned by Dostoievski—'a vast, unnatural conspiracy of two students and a poet which shook society to its foundations.' Your piece disclosed the cryptic corruption of the minds of language students by propaganda slipped into Russian text books. I own or have read all, or almost all, the books cited in the article, so that I can say that your writer's facts, so far as they went, were right. . . . Your writer went on specifically to exempt from his charges certain texts which he lists. Let me translate a short lesson from one of these honorable exceptions. [Chambers here translated a description of a day in the life of Comrade Volkhov.] That's it. First, grammatically, the passage is unexceptionable. It makes a number of important points. There is

181

the adjective 'hot' as applied to tea or to weather (two different adjectives in Russian). There are the distinctions among the prepositions: k, v, and na; and the preposition bez, 'without,' which (mischievously, as so often in Russian) governs the genitive, not the accusative. There is the indispensable idiom: 'There is not a cloud in the sky,' where the word, cloud, for reasons evident only to the Russian mind, is again in the genitive. Etc., etc. . . . Now I can get on with my mission of thanks. Among the exceptions cited by your writer was: *Essentials of Russian,* by A. von Gronicka and Helen Bates-Yakobson. Prof. v. Gronicka is credited to Columbia. I have never heard of him otherwise. . . . Prof. Helen Bates-Yakobson is the head of the Slavic Department at the George Washington University. Since she sometimes helps to supervise my exams, I have met and talked with her about the problems of teaching the linguistics of the [undecipherable]. . . . It is she who has asked me to thank you. And now I have done it. I hope you will not draw your writer's attention to this letter: there are trifles that wise men should keep among themselves for private smiling."

For private smiling, Chambers was not—shall we assume?—driven to untoward grammatical lies under the weight of rhetorical pressure.

It remains, finally, to ask and answer the gut question. An inflection, in American English, is a *change in form* to reflect differences in case, gender, number, etc. The pattern of inflections of a noun is known as the declension. The accusative case in the Russian declension is normally identical in form with the nominative. All other oblique cases—genitive, dative, instrumental, and prepositional—call for a change in form, *i.e.,* spelling. The word "Tsargrad," depending on the case, is variously written (1) Tsargrada, (2) Tsargradu, (3) Tsargradom, (4) Tsargradye, (5) Tsargradi, (6) Tsargradov, (7) Tsargradam, (8) Tsargradami, and, yes, (9) Tsargradach.

"So Whittaker Chambers," writes Mr. O'Brien, propelled by his own rhetorical necessity, "looked out and saw, flaring in imagination, a legendary vision: the Nine Inflections of the Russian Noun. On points of grammar it is always possible to get the facts; on historical episodes this is often less easy." Just so. On grammatical grounds it is very easy to shatter Mr. O'Brien's attempted tour de force; less so to hope to persuade him that just as he made his case by asking his readers to reason from Chambers' grammatical unreliability over to his historical unreliability as a witness against Hiss, it might be appropriate now to ask them to reason in reverse. It being unlikely that Mr. O'Brien will follow his own strictures, let us at least agree to deduce from the episode if nothing at all about Chambers the witness, at least something very considerable about Mr. O'Brien the prosecutor, as we observe him huffing and puffing to keep his soufflé from collapsing under the weight of those nine stolid Russian witnesses to his superficiality.

Nowhere else does Mr. O'Brien give any evidence of any disposition to learn from Chambers something about the nature of our time, as he might have learned from him something about Russian. Up against the weight of the evidence—the public trials, the appeals, the other witnesses—he is like Mark Lane and Thomas Buchanan confronted with the Warren Report, for it is true that Hiss is innocent as it is that Oswald was. Like Lane and Buchanan, O'Brien tries diligently to turn the most readily explainable anomalies into crushing evidence of his client's innocence, and he is as convincing as Mark Lane.

"Perhaps the most flagrant example [of Chambers' lying]," Mr. O'Brien goes on, tucking in his shirttail after the grammatical holocaust, "is that of his original charge against Hiss's brother, Donald Hiss, whom he said he knew as a Communist and from whom he said he collected Communist dues. Donald Hiss flatly denied that he had ever met Chambers, and no attempt at all was made to prove that he had; the thing was simply dropped."

Here and there Mr. O'Brien shows that he has mastered some of the minutiae of the Hiss case and so makes it difficult for the active-minded reader to conclude that this passage on Donald Hiss might have been simply ingenuous. It is quite true that Chambers originally named Donald Hiss, just as he named Alger. The ensuing difference is this: Alger sued Chambers for libel, and Donald did not. It was in order to defend himself from the charge of libel that Chambers produced the evidence that hung Alger. Donald never challenged Chambers in the libel courts, and the government chose not to prosecute him. If Donald had gone after Chambers as Alger did, why should

183

one suppose the result would have been different?

Again and again Mr. O'Brien insists on exposing his mindlessness. "Chambers made the charge—subsequently demonstrated to be altogether false—that Alger Hiss had swindled his stepson Timothy for the benefit of the Communist Party. . . . Chambers testified that Thayer Hobson (the boy's father) was paying for his education, but the Hisses had told him, Chambers, that 'they were diverting a large part of the money to the Communist Party . . . and they took him out of a more expensive school and put him in a less expensive school for that purpose.' This was actually the reverse of the truth. Thayer Hobson has recalled that 'When Timothy was transferred to a far more expensive school, he protested . . . and the Hisses paid the additional money out of their own pockets.' (Fred Cook, *The Unfinished Story of Alger Hiss*)."

"*This was actually the reverse of the truth.*" How easy it is for the chancellor of the University of Ghana to discover the truth! Let us assume that *both* Chambers and Hobson were telling the truth. Chambers would have got his story from Hiss, who told him version A, while Hobson got his story from Hiss, who told him version B. Unless Hobson and Chambers had exchanged notes, they could in clear conscience have repeated their stories, believing them to be true, even though they are mutually exclusive. It does not, in other words, follow that in order to believe Hobson, one need disbelieve Chambers. Or vice versa.

If, however, one were disposed to believe the testimony of only one of the two gentlemen, such points as the following would reasonably influence our choice: (1) Chambers' testimony, given in court, was checked out at every turn by the Federal Bureau of Investigation, which subsequently announced, giving the reasons why, its total confidence in his veracity; (2) Thayer Hobson was never able to contribute a scintilla of evidence to help his first wife, Priscilla Hiss, deny convincingly Chambers' version of the record of his association with the Hiss family; (3) the Hisses did not produce Timothy as a witness at the trial, electing, instead, to send him abroad; and (4) to the extent that we have only Fred Cook's word to go on, it is relevant to bear in mind that over the years Fred Cook has been for Alger Hiss as Mark Lane is for Lee Harvey

184

Oswald and that none of the "evidence" marshaled by Cook has satisfied a single judge, when submitted in an appeal for retrial, that the trial was unjust, or that Chambers had lied.

Thus, O'Brien's case disintegrates, and it is with the sense of relief a swimmer has on reaching the surface after a lung-breaking rise through the water that one arrives at the peroration, in which there is only rhetoric to get through, not facts or analysis. Alger Hiss is here compared to Dreyfus, Chambers to Titus Oates; Chambers' God to the Father of Lies; and Chambers, again, to Richard Piggott, the key and mendacious witness against Parnell. Mr. O'Brien has a wonderful time with all this and proves himself a fine rhetorical advocate—just the man, to judge by his endowments and availability to queasy causes, to come before the court of the world opinion and state the case for his boss, Kwame Nkrumah of Ghana. No doubt he could prove to the editors of the *New York Review of Books* that the Osagyefo is really divine. No doubt he could show quite plausibly how come it is that he, a man of such flagrant gentility, who is horrified by the lie Whittaker Chambers once admittedly told to shield Alger Hiss from prosecution, can work with such peace of soul for Nkrumah.

It is a commonplace of psychology that one tends to exaggerate an aversion to that vice which one most notoriously practices. Mr. O'Brien will be remembered as the field commander who launched the war against Katanga in 1961, Dag Hammarskjöld having brazenly lied—or so the world was subsequently informed by the same O'Brien—when he announced in the UN that the Katangese troops had launched an attack on the United Nations army. Eventually they got rid of O'Brien, after he had disported himself somewhat ineptly on the field of battle, sending bombers to obliterate Katangese civilians and hospitals. A raging discussion took place during those crucial weeks on the question of whether or not the UN troops had legally proceeded against Katanga. Mr. O'Brien, uniquely in a position to know, kept his normally irrepressible mouth snapped shut. Fifteen months after he was fired, he published his book *To Katanga and Back,* in which he insouciantly revealed that Hammerskjöld had lied, and that he, O'Brien, had done nothing about it, not until he wrote the book in question. Defenders of Dag Hammarskjöld may, after the present performance, conclude that the situation looks better than they feared, that, O'Brien having accused him, perhaps Hammarskjöld was innocent after all.

II

Irving Howe is a more serious critic of Whittaker Chambers than Conor Cruise O'Brien, and lets the Hiss case strictly alone, as cautious men should. He does not call Chambers a liar; he is satisfied to call him merely mad and stupid—an "intellectual manqué," says he, savoring the highbrow's dysphemism for the relatively inoffensive "stupid." Indeed, although he entitles his review in the *New Republic* "Madness, Vision and Stupidity," he quickly forgoes temperance to inform us that—and not simply because in his later years Whittaker Chambers "seems to have gone a little mad"—he greatly regrets that Whittaker Chambers should have undertaken to write anything at all. "He treasured a note André Malraux had sent him after the appearance of *Witness:* 'You are one of those who did not return from Hell with empty hands.' Whether Malraux remarked on the value of what Chambers brought back or the possibility that after a conspiratorial-ideological debauch it might be a nice touch of modesty to return with 'empty hands,' Chambers does not say." Chambers did not say; Mr. Howe seems to be trying to say what Malraux would have said to Chambers if Howe had been Malraux—which is most unlikely ever to happen—merely what Malraux *did* say to Chambers, which Chambers should not have repeated, because Malraux did not say to him what Howe would have said to him, which gives some insight to what Howe means by a "nice touch of modesty," if you see what we mean.

Understand, Mr. Howe would have us know that he, unlike certain others, is an open-minded critic of Chambers. He even finds, and wants us to understand his courage in saying so, a certain virtue in Chambers—namely, that Chambers *did* suffer a little bit. He wants us to know that this admission is dangerous, in the circles he moves in. "To grant Chambers any virtue, even a trace of humanity, is to risk"—and here Professor Howe enjoys a fine piece of brinkmanship—"a *hissing* of anger

186

from certain liberals who need to see him as the complete contemporary villain. But why?" he wonders. "If such people encountered Chambers in a novel, say in Trilling's *Middle of the Journey,* they would insist on granting him complexity of motive and shading of character." Chambers is, one concludes, somebody *others* should have written about (Krafft-Ebing? Max Lerner? Erich Fromm?), not somebody Chambers should have written about. For several reasons. In writing about himself, "most of the time, Chambers does his best to keep the reader from making the discovery . . . that there is a man [there]," a fact most difficult to discern from his "grandiose solemnity, his stunning pretentiousness, his oracular incompetence." Really, "appalling."

And because—and here is the principal trouble with Chambers—he simply *could not think.* Witness the conclusions he drew—which are not only wrong, but infuriatingly wrong, which are, well, unthinkable. These conclusions have to do with the world we live in and the universe of which we are a part.

There is, to begin with, Chambers' profound despair. That view, says Mr. Howe, "is not highly regarded in this country. Few of our intellectuals share [it.]" That is certainly true. Few of our nonintellectuals share it, for that matter.

Chambers *was* a pessimist. And his sense of drama and his style put him in the way of saying his darkest thoughts in ways so resonant that they rankle. There are many doomsayers in our age, as in other ages, whose expressions of gloom turn up as regularly as the stock market tables, and are about as eyecatching. But Chambers had the power to say things which stick in the unreceptive mind like foreign matter, which demand conscious, even violent, efforts to excrete them. No one will notice, or greatly object to, the man who says, with the usual humdrum variations, that the world is doomed, that our civilization is falling to pieces. Chambers' way of saying much the same thing was much different, because what he said was never ritualistic but wholly spontaneous, issuing out of the very genes of his thought and being. In a casual letter to a world-saving friend, he once remarked that "it is idle to talk about preventing the wreck of Western civilization. It is already a wreck from within.

187

That is why we can hope to do little more now than to snatch a fingernail of a saint from the rack or a handful of ashes from the faggots, and bury them secretly in a flower pot against the day, ages hence, when a few men begin again to dare to believe that there was once something else, that something else is thinkable, and need some evidence that what it was and the fortifying knowledge that there were those who, at the great nightfall, took loving thought to preserve the tokens of hope and truth."

Against such rhetorical power the *Zeitgeist* must defend itself and men turn ferocious. The passage in question, for instance, was several years ago quoted by the late Bishop G. Bromley Oxnam in a volume (*A Testament of Faith*) devoted to the bishop's love of everyone, and he fairly snarled after reproducing it. ("How dare such a voice speak of tokens of hope and truth!") One does not, after reading the reviews of Chambers' books, need to imagine what that kind of thing does to the little rationalists who measure progress by the spoonfuls that are added to the diet of Latin Americans by the Alliance for Progress and the purrs that emanate from the Kremlin between diatribe and pogrom. Such a man as Chambers cannot think, in our time, any more than Galileo could think in his, and Chambers knew it, never guessed otherwise. That is one of the reasons why he could never bring himself to finish the present volume, which was put together from fragments only after he died. There is no common vocabulary between the Howes and Chambers, and there is no doubting the age is the age of Howe, no surprise at all, therefore, that Howe cannot understand Chambers even though Chambers understood the Howes and their world all too well, which is why he retreated to his farm in Maryland and shielded himself, as best one can in our time, when the fallout of the age is everywhere.

"You cannot replace God with Point Four"—Howe singles out the passage as one of the examples of Chambers' appalling inability to think. "If you fed the starving millions four square meals a day and studded their primitive lands with automated factories, men would still die of despair." "No ordinary person," Howe fumes, "only a special kind of besotted ideologue, could say anything so stupid. Can one put under the same rubric the despair of a Brazilian peasant watching his children starve and the despair of a well-fed American who finds life aimless? Suppose the Brazilian peasant, suddenly lifted to plenty, were then to learn the malaise of a sophisticated New Yorker: he might indeed die of despair which, by the way, even in New York is not quite so easy."

Here are men passing each other on opposite sides of the street. God knows, no one who reads this passage will ever call Mr. Howe a Philistine *manqué*. For here he is, arisen in the twentieth century, who wonders at the stupid, mindless ideologue preaching, over in Judea, that men do not live by bread alone, who, because his philosophical amplitude is so greatly restricted by the materialist limits of his vision, sees in such a statement evidence that Chambers is indifferent to the pain of starvation. Merely because Chambers knew keenly that the well-fed also die, are dying by great numbers, and that their spiritual misery is in fact the cause of much of the physical misery—war, starvation, torture—that is the trademark of our well-fed age—where the principal agents of physical misery have for the most part been men who themselves were never hungry. "Would that we could live in the world of the fauves, where the planes are disjointed only on canvas, instead of a world where the wild beasts are real and the disjointures threaten to bury us," Chambers once wrote me. But the *fauves* run Grub Street and howl their orthodoxies in magazines with names like *Dissent*.

"If God exists, a man cannot be a Communist, which begins with the rejection of God. But if God does not exist, it follows that Communism or some suitable variant of it, is right." "This nonsense," says Mr. Howe, "Chambers first advanced in *Witness;* he was repeatedly challenged and answered. The statement is false in fact, inept in logic, impudent in morals, and un-Christian in spirit."

As much could be said of almost any one of the Beatitudes, as read by the vulgarian. "Blessed are the meek, for they shall inherit the earth." Suppose that were told today to the congregation of American Negroes and it were left to Mr. Howe to make comment. He would denounce the passage as false in fact (have the Negroes, meek for so long, inherited the earth?), inept in logic

189

(how does it follow that meekness conduces to ownership of the earth?), impudent in morals (it is wrong to urge on a people acquiescence in their servile condition), and un-Christian in spirit (should not a Christian hunger and thirst after righteousness?).

Passages which are allegorical, let alone paradoxical in structure, are not written for social anthropologists to stare at dumbly. The passage would presumably have got by Professor Howe only if it had been written: "If God exists, a given man cannot be a Communist for so long as (a) he recognizes that God exists and (b) he understands Communism to be founded on a negation of God. But if God does not exist, it follows that Communism or some suitable variant of it is right, if you understand that Communism or some suitable variant of it is the secularist derivation of a nonbelief in God, which, having the effect of denying the individual a divine spark, tends naturally to advance the claims of the collectivity over those of the individual, as the focal point of social effort." But no poet ever wrote that way.

And Chambers was above all a poet, with a poet's understanding of political affairs—which is both good and bad—good if you know and like and learn from the poet's vision, disastrous if you read a poet the way you would read the Kinsey Report, with a dramatist's understanding of political affairs—which is, again, both good and bad. No one could with any success extract a *Weltanschauung* from Chambers' writings, complete with neat and elegant trim. No more than from Bertolt Brecht or Alexander Pope, both politically minded men of letters.

It remains extraordinary that at a time when intellectuals can grasp the complexity of the statement that E equals mc squared, so many of them should have so much difficulty understanding what, for instance, Whittaker Chambers means by asking the question of "whether the West deserves to be saved." What, Professor Howe demands to know, immediately, *is* the West? "The Salk vaccine or Jim Crow? Anesthesia or torture? Shakespeare or Spillane? The seven-hour day or child labor?" Whittaker Chambers or Irving Howe?

Chambers is intelligible to the same people to whom "the West" is intelligible, and the latter are not, for the most part, running the affairs of the West, although, hap-

190

pily, they continue to influence the public policy of the West to a greater extent than they run the book review media of the West. A man who can catechize Whittaker Chambers while serving as chancellor of the University of Ghana, another who gives sincere evidence that he *literally* does not understand what Chambers can be talking about when he speaks of the West or when he makes disjunctions between God and Communism—they make the land stranger and stranger for any psalmist who wishes to sing the Lord's song.

"They will get what they want," Chambers wrote me, "and it may well kill them. If I did not believe that men make their own history, I could say loftily: a judgment. Since I do believe that men make their own history (though not, as we are reminded, just as they please), it is even worse. The result (judgment is an unnecessary concept) will simply parse the interactions of what really is, of reality. The consequence will be more terrible because quite merciless. What does energy know of mercy?"

But there are still those for whom Chambers' books, like his life, will be forever exalting, and on account of him, their numbers will grow. It is quite enough that there are some such left. The others are not yet writing all the books and do not yet make all history.

THINKING BACK ON ELEANOR ROOSEVELT

December 29, 1962

I have been sharply reminded that I have not written about Mrs. Roosevelt and that only a coward would use the excuse that when she died he was in Africa. There there are lions and tigers and *apartheid*. Here there was Mrs. Roosevelt to write about. Africa was the safer place.

People get very sore when you knock the old lady. And it isn't just the widow who thinks of Mrs. Roosevelt as the goddess who saved her children from getting rickets during the Depression. It is also the left intellectuals. "When are you going to stop picking on Mrs. Roosevelt?" a very learned writer asked me at a reception a few years ago after one of my books was published. (I had a sentence in it that annoyed him, something like: "Following Mrs. Roosevelt in search of irrationality is like following a

191

lighted fuse in search of an explosion: One never has to wait very long.") I answered: "When you *begin* picking on her." I meant by that that people are best reformed by those they will listen to. Westbrook Pegler could never reform Mrs. Roosevelt or her legend. But Adlai Stevenson or Max Lerner might have.

The obituary notices on Mrs. Roosevelt were as one in granting her desire to do good—she treated all the world as her own personal slum project, and all the papers, of course, remarked on that fabulous energy; surely she was the very first example of the peacetime use of atomic energy. But some publications, I think especially of *Time,* went so far as to say she had a great mind. Now is the time for all good men to come to the aid of Euclid.

Does it matter? Alas, it happens to matter very much. For Mrs. Roosevelt stamped on her age a mode. Or, it might be said by those who prefer to put it that way, in Mrs. Roosevelt the age developed its perfect symbol. Hers is the age of undifferentiated goodness, of permissive egalitarianism.

Mrs. Roosevelt's approach to human problems, so charming in its Franciscan naïveté, was simply: Do away with them—by the most obvious means. The way to cope with Russia is to negotiate. . . . The way for everyone to be free in the world is to tell the UN to free everyone. . . . The way to eliminate poverty in Latin America is to give them all money. . . . The way to solve the housing shortage is for the government to build more houses. . . .

All that is more than Mrs. Roosevelt writing a column. It is a way of life. Based, essentially, on unreason, on the leaving out of the concrete, complex factor, which is why they call it "undifferentiated" goodness. Negotiation with Russia, you see, implies there is something we are or should be prepared to yield. . . . And everyone in the world cannot be free so long as freedoms are used by whole nations to abuse the peoples of other nations or the freedoms of their own people. . . . Latin American poverty is something that grows out of the pores of Latin American institutions and appetites and cannot be seriously ameliorated by mere transfusions of American cash. . . . And the way to get houses built is to reduce their cost, so that poor people can buy them, without paying crippling wages to monopoly labor unions or crippling

192

prices to manufacturing concerns that have to pay the taxes of a government which, among other things, decides it needs to get into the housing business. . . .

Mrs. Roosevelt's principal bequest, her most enduring bequest, was the capacity to so oversimplify problems as to give encouragement to those who wish to pitch the nation and the world onto humanitarian crusades which, because they fail to take reality into account, end up plunging people into misery (as Wilson's idealistic imperialism plunged Europe into misery for years and spawned Hitler) and messing up the world in general (under whose statecraft did Stalin prosper?) Above all, it was Mrs. Roosevelt who, on account of her passion for the *non sequitur*, deeply wounded the processes of purposeful political thought. "Over whatever subject, plan, or issue Mrs. Roosevelt touches," Professor James Burnham once wrote, "she spreads a squidlike ink of directionless feeling. All distinctions are blurred, all analysis fouled, and in the murk clear thought is forever impossible."

Someday in the future a liberal scholar will write a definitive thesis exploring the cast of Mrs. Roosevelt's mind by a textual analysis of her thought, and then history will be able to distinguish between a great woman with a great heart and a woman of perilous intellectual habit. "With all my heart and soul," her epitaph should read, "I fought the syllogism." And with that energy and force, she wounded it, almost irretrievably—how often have you seen the syllogism checking in at the office for a full day's work lately?

A POLITICAL BIOGRAPHY
OF JOHN VLIET LINDSAY

November 12, 1967

THE ROAD TO CITY HALL: How John V. Lindsay Became Mayor. By Barbara Carter. Illustrated. Prentice-Hall. $4.95.

The editor's invitation to review this little book, so patently dedicated to the greater glory of John Vliet Lindsay, was clearly mischievous. He must have known that he was being naughty, but what the hell, we only live once.

193

He has, of course, put me on the spot. I remember resenting it when another editor—of the one remaining book section in Fun City—assigned a work of mine to Arthur Schlesinger, Jr., to review, a commission which I compared, in high dudgeon, to assigning to John Wilkes Booth the collected works of Abraham Lincoln.

I must guard carefully then against the manifestation of any bias and will attempt this entire review without once criticizing Mr. Lindsay, an exercise in self-control which will, one hopes, be duly recorded in the annals of endurance.

It would have been fine, having thus set the stage for a display of chivalry, if I could have gone on to say that Miss Carter's book is informative and readable. Alas, it is a most dreadful book. Poor Mr. Lindsay! How unfortunate he has been in his hagiographers. First Daniel E. Button (*Lindsay: A Man for Tomorrow*) and now Miss Carter.

Miss Carter does not add anything at all to such knowledge of the mayoral campaign as is had by anyone who is likely to read this book in order to learn something about the campaign. There is nothing here for the political analyst or the social anthropologist. But it soon becomes clear that it is not the purpose of the book to inform the professional community. That much is made plain by the inclusion of sixteen picture pages of Glorious John, which are posed rather like the saint pictures the children put in their first holy communion missals, and at that I think Miss Carter showed restraint. If I had been commissioned to write a favorable book on John Lindsay, it would consist exclusively of pictures.

How does one, in chivalry, cope with the matter of Miss Carter's prose style? If only she were a he, it would be so very much easier!

How many people who care about language will press on, beyond the sentence in Miss Carter's introduction which says, "This banquet of books [*i.e.*, the reference books she consulted while writing her own] will long remain at the table, their pages marred by arrows and asterisks, their corners thumbed-down and underlined everywhere. I wish only to acknowledge I enjoyed the feast: I don't mean to class myself as part of the company"? Had enough?

Don't go away. On page 25 we learn that when Hubert Humphrey went to New York to encourage Abraham Beame, with whom he rode ceremonially down the length of Manhattan, "If the Democrats looked good coming down Broadway, it was only the transient magic of Manhattan that made it so." The only thing we learn on page 40 is that Miss Carter hasn't the remotest idea what the word "alchemy" means. On page 46 we are told that Daniel P. Moynihan is the "possessor of an enviable sense of humor that permits him to walk lightly through [sic] subjects where [sic] angels fear to tread." (That's what *I* call alchemy.) "Are there many Irish politicians, for instance," Miss Carter, doubled up, asks, "who would suggest that 'the Irish did not know what to do with power once they got it'?" (Answer: yes). "Or many Catholic Democrats who would choose to believe that Al Smith really asked, 'Will someone tell me what the hell a papal encyclical is?' " One doesn't have the least idea how this crack relates to Mr. Moynihan, who has at the least a hell of an idea what a papal encyclical is. Miss Carter is obviously in search of levity. As obviously, she fails to find it in a study of how Mr. Lindsay became the mayor of New York.

It is not worth the trouble to recount Miss Carter's analysis of how come it was that Mr. Lindsay won the election. Among her difficulties is that she roundly contradicts herself.

On the one hand, Miss Carter patiently explains that Mr. Lindsay's victory was the result of his luminous qualities as a political candidate; on the other hand, she patiently explains that Mr. Lindsay would not have become mayor except for the (adventitious) arrival on the scene of the reviewer of this book ("If Buckley hadn't run, Beame would be living in Gracie Mansion today"). Both contentions are half-truths—Lindsay's performance, by contrast with that of a colorless Republican predecessor, was not impressive, although there is no doubting his superior appeal.

Although toward the end the Conservative candidate took more votes from Beame than from Lindsay, he (I) accumulated preponderantly Republican votes in the first couple of months of the campaign, so that it is safe to say that if the Conservative candidate had not entered the

195

race, Mr. Lindsay would have won not narrowly (he took only 44 percent of the votes), but overwhelmingly.

The best Miss Carter can manage by way of analogy not only is not good enough, but is a perfect syntactical reflection of her analytical powers: ". . . Lindsay had taken just enough cupfuls from each bucket the Democrats had to fill his own, and then Buckley, following after with a teaspoon, took just enough more to give Lindsay the edge."

All in all, for the kiddie library.

GORE VIDAL ON JFK

March 25, 1967

Gore Vidal has got around to saying (eloquently, in *Esquire* magazine) what a lot of us have been saying for years about the Kennedy political philosophy (it doesn't really exist) and about the Liberal Intellectual Establishment (it is vain, power-hungry, cynical). Mr. Vidal says so many things that are true, almost all of them in a contradiction to his own positions taken over the past, that it is a pity that his piece will be discounted so widely as the spiteful ejaculation of a discarded courtier.

For those who came in late, Gore Vidal was once an ardent champion of John F. Kennedy and, derivatively, of all lesser Kennedys. Vidal was, in fact, a member of the family in the extended sense of the word—Vidal's quondam stepfather is Jacqueline Kennedy's current. And when Vidal ran for Congress in 1960, he asked Bobby to campaign for him, which Bobby did, and everything was cozy as could be.

Then there was *the* episode. Never mind the details, but it ended in Vidal's being courteously but firmly escorted out of the White House, vowing internal vengeance on Bobby. And the current article in *Esquire* is an installment of that threat. But whatever the motive, here is some choice analysis, of major concern to those of us whom the Kennedys seek to govern, which is to say to every American, from sea to shining sea.

Mr. Vidal makes a number of observations, among them that the Kennedys' trinitarian (family, money, image) grasp on American life has proved enormously successful because it engages the gears of a middle-class society that has pretty well abandoned its ideals, theological and moral. The Kennedys accordingly tend to view everything personally. "In 1960," Vidal recalls, "after listening to [JFK] denounce Eleanor Roosevelt at some length, I asked him why he thought she was so much opposed to his candidacy. The answer was quick: 'She hated my father and she can't stand it that his children turned out so much better than hers.'

"It was significant," Vidal comments, "that he could not take seriously any of her political objections to him (*e.g.*, his attitude towards McCarthyism); he merely assumed that she, like himself, was essentially concerned with family and, envying the father, would want to thwart the son."

Vidal then examines JFK's credentials as an authentic hero of contemporary liberalism and discards them on the grounds that his liberalism was purely opportunistic, indeed that the highest testimony to the unity of the family is that it persisted notwithstanding the diametrically opposite course struck out by the son from that of the father.

"JFK was . . . very much his father's son even though, as all the witnesses are at pains to remind us, he did not share that magnate's political philosophy—which goes without saying since anyone who did could not be elected to anything except possibly the Chamber of Commerce." And the idealization of the Kennedys by the liberal intellectuals, Vidal concludes, is nothing more than one more tiresome reenactment of the traditional servitude of the intellectual class to anyone of rank who will permit them to participate in power. Thus, Schlesinger's threnody on JFK is dubbed by Vidal "the greatest piece of political fiction since *Coningsby.*"

The liberals are infinitely forgiving of the reactionary background of the Kennedys, Vidal reminds us. "That consistency which liberals so furiously demanded of the hapless Nixon need not apply to any Kennedy. . . . The McCarthy friend and fellow traveler of one year emerges as a New York liberal in another, and between these two happenings there is no thread at all to give a clue as to what the man actually thinks or who he really is." The emptiness of the Kennedy world view was best captured, Vidal reminisces, by the astonished look on the face of the

newly inaugurated President when James Reston "naively
. . . asked [him] what his philosophy was, what vision did
he have of the good life."

About the good life it is given to us to know only, in
this age of doubt, that a Kennedy must sit at the head of
the table. It is of course ironic that Mr. Vidal, the
superliberal superthinker who in pursuit of the good life
has tried everything, but everything in the world, including
icon smashing with a vengeance, now engages an icon he
had a hand in molding. He has a tough job ahead of him.
Who knows? It might even make a Christian out of him.

THE INEVITABILITY OF BOBBY

March 31, 1966

It should be noted that sometime between the fall of
1965 and the spring of 1966 Senator Teddy Kennedy
yielded to his older brother, who has successfully effected
what the political scientists call the problem of the succession. During 1964 and much of 1965 the operating
assumption was that it would fall to Teddy to inherit his
brother's mantle, that Bobby would never qualify because
of the brutalizations of his own political experience. It is, I
believe, at this point manifest that Robert has made it in
his own right and is no longer thought of purely as a
political technician, useful only for organizing the armies
or poisoning the rivals' soup.

During his lifetime it was of course never widely
speculated that any Kennedy other than John F. would sit
on the throne. The dynastic cracks were mostly to the effect that John-John would be the next threat. But on one
occasion Gore Vidal, the playwright, caused a considerable sensation. In the winter of 1962 he published a
piece of speculation in *Esquire* magazine projecting, most
gloomily, the utter inevitability of Bobby—*i.e.,* after John
had run his two Presidential terms. The article in question,
even though it was honed on personal spite, caused the
political world to contemplate for the first time that
awesome possibility. But mostly the professionals concluded that though Bobby was many things, he was not
Presidentabili, that he was a little short of the bigtime
dimension that people tend to require of their Presi-

dents—either that, or a perfect embodiment of the national mood, a Warren Harding. Bobby had neither the greatness nor the roots deep enough in his party or his nation's esteem to succeed to the Presidency in the mechanical sense that the sun succeeds the dawn. It was the cranky thesis of Mr. Vidal that the national addiction to Kennedys exceeded the national reserve concerning Bobby and that, therefore, in 1968, when John stepped down, Robert would step up. The article provoked considerable alarm both because it heightened the general suspicion of Bobby and because it warned that Bobby would indeed get us if we didn't watch out. A lot of good Americans took the pledge on that occasion never to serve as instruments by which to advance that awful prospect. Many of those same Americans have by now renounced that pledge. What did it?

Unquestionably the tragic death of the President was primarily responsible. It left a nation which, somehow in expiation, felt it couldn't do enough for the Kennedys. One result was Bobby's great ovation, given at Atlantic City, as if to say to Lyndon Johnson "You are the boss, and we concede that; but never suppose that you can occupy the place your predecessor did." And his election over the popular Senator Keating a few months later.

But Bobby himself must take a great deal of the credit himself. It was not alone the hagiolatry that surrounded his brother that worked for him. Through his own efforts, he succeeded in acquiring important and discriminating allies, most of them among the liberal intelligentsia. Arthur Schlesinger, Jr., can be a powerful friend, and he has unmistakably cast his lot with Bobby.

Bobby's organizing skill permitted him a tight hold on a half dozen Senators, whom he deployed with deftness, constant testimony to his raw power in the legislature. He is strong with the party, not only for the obvious reason that he is a Kennedy, but because he does his duty, as when he campaigned industriously in the lost cause of Abraham Beame.

He is developing a personal flair, demonstrated by his visit a fortnight ago to the University of Mississippi, which greeted him with tears of joy, even as Berlin, looking up from the rubble, greeted General Eisenhower.

So history worked for Bobby, and Bobby worked well

for Bobby. There has been a third factor. He is indestructible. He can say silly things, as he did all over Latin America, and somehow not be taken as silly. He can say outrageous things, as, for instance, that he would not object to American blood flowing into Vietcong veins, and when the public winces, he will issue a torrent of explanations and modifications (I didn't mean that I said it; I mean that I said I didn't say it; is that perfectly clear?— that kind of thing) which are gratefully and instantly accepted. He can back the machine, as he did in New York, and somehow escape the normal consequences of the association. He can propose excruciatingly inapposite solutions for Vietnam and emerge as the forward-looking thinker.

It is, so far, a winning combination. Teddy is out. And Hubert Humphrey is on the defensive. It might even be safe to say that the country is on the defensive.

BOBBY FOR KING

June 2, 1966

Bobby, Bobby, everywhere. It drives a man to drink. Open the paper, and there he is. A marvel of industry, a brooding omnipresence, the determining factor (it is said) in the nomination of Mayor High in Florida for the governorship, deeply involved in Oregon, and in Kentucky, and in a dozen other states, stitching together a heliocentric alliance of disciples. No one, so far, dares say him nay, not even the government of South Africa, which is, if not exactly about to welcome him there, at least about to tolerate him to propose a civil rights bill, or whatever it is he plans to do, to the cheers, predictably, of the whole world.

In New York State, Senator Kennedy recently served notice on great big grown men who aspire for the Democratic nomination for governor that unless they would accompany him in a sort of political fashion show about the state, he would decline to endorse the winner. Faced with this insurmountable threat, they dutifully appeared for classes at the appointed hour and time, and the seminar began at Cornell University. Franklin Delano Roosevelt, Jr., was among them, and the redoubtable Frank O'Connor, president of the City Council of New York City, who rode into office with several hundred thousand votes more than John Lindsay himself last fall, but whose prowess isn't such as to embolden him to advise Bobby that he will seek the Democratic nomination in his own way and that he is much too busy to do bumps and grinds around the state under the choreographical direction of Senator B.

Most recently Senator Kennedy resolved to challenge the nomination of a judge designated by the regular Democrats for the important office of surrogate. The Republicans, rather surprisingly, decided to endorse the same man. But Senator Kennedy, no doubt influenced by howls from local editorial writers deploring the alleged incapacity of the Democratic-Republican designee, announced his backing of another judge, who will run on a Reform Democratic ticket. (Bobby doesn't go for hack judges, unless nominated by Teddy for the District Court.) Meanwhile, the Liberals in New York are committed to a third candidate, and the Conservatives to a fourth. So that not inconceivably, it will be Bobby against the field. If he wins this one, he will emerge as invincible as Caesar returning victorious from Gaul.

Herewith a constructive suggestion. Why not a constitutional amendment or, just as good, an edict from Earl Warren, instituting a monarchy and designating Bobby as the first incumbent?

The rules should declare that all successors must be lineal descendants of Joseph P. Kennedy. But—mark this—the rules should not stipulate that the successor should be the firstborn son of the king. Anyone directly descended from the founding father would qualify. The advantages are that this would give scope to the competitive political instincts of the Kennedys.

Upon the death or retirement of the incumbent, all qualified Kennedys, male and female, would put forward their claims; perhaps they all could appear at seminars around the country, at which they would stress their qualifications for the throne. A great national election could be held to decide when Kennedy would succeed. The new king or queen would then take office for his or her lifetime and preside over the country as chief of state, while the practical affairs of the government could be administered by an elected President or Prime Minister.

201

John Adams remarked that the Constitution was badly mistaken in forbidding American citizens to receive titles of nobility, since such titles are a relatively innocent way of sating human ambitions, the dread substitute for nobility being power over other men. Think of the trouble we would be saved! It would be beneath the royal dignity to specify what should be the procedures by which mere governors of New York should advertise their qualifications, let alone who should be the next surrogate of Manhattan. And the adulation all good subjects owe to their sovereign would come more easily than that which goes to a mere politician whose earthly concerns tend to stain the purity of his radiant presence.

IS LYNDON JOHNSON CUCKOO?

July 17, 1965

President Johnson is getting it in the neck. Every President of course does; but there are criticisms and criticisms, and what is going the rounds these days about LBJ is all the way. I have in mind, for instance, a confidential report, internationally distributed, by an immensely influential English publication which all but reports that the President of the United States is loco. He is described, for instance, as having approached the point where he simply doesn't know what is and what isn't true, which, if it were so, would make him certifiably insane. He is described as having grown so irritable as to lose sight of the irreducible dimensions of social intercourse. And he is said to have become incontinently emotional, so much so as to embarrass and deeply worry his closest associates.

Believable?

Of course not. There is no doubt that the President has weaknesses of which the charges in the English publication are a hideous exaggeration. He *is* vain; he *is* sensitive to criticism; and he does, occasionally, let fly at his detractors. But these attributes, which after all are hardly unusual in political eminences, are being abnormalized by two groups of people. The Communist press seizes on them for the obvious reasons. *U.S. News & World Report* reports that the new Communist line on Johnson is that he is "ill, both physically and mentally." Any weakness in any public figure who inconveniences the Communist movement is instantly exaggerated, and if, *per impossible,* no weakness exists, the Communists will, of course, invent one, no matter how wildly implausible. The non-Communist left, although it has a weak ear for Communist propaganda and not infrequently finds itself acting as an echo chamber for it, ventilates its own vilifications of men in public office who take drastic steps in contradiction of their view of sanity in foreign affairs. And sanity in foreign affairs consists (can you name an exception in the postwar decades?) in yielding wherever the Communists set up pressure points. Whether in Greece, or China, or Hungary, or Spain, or Katanga, or Lebanon, or Quemoy, or Cuba, or—Vietnam.

When in 1964 the machinery of the left was in high gear to elect Mr. Johnson as President of the United States in order to dispose of the singular threat posed by the candidacy of Senator Goldwater, it was more or less agreed that the foibles of Senator Johnson—his ambition, his intensity, his megalomania—were, when all is said and done, no more than the incandescence of man afire with concern for righteousness. His criticisms of other people and other ideas, it was said, were motivated by his intense attachment to social truths. His impatience with his staff and associates was passed off as altogether understandable in a man on the march to a great society. His arm twisting of Congress, when the arm twisting was done in behalf of, say, a civil rights bill, was an inspiriting example of the Executive Seizing the Initiative and Exercising His Powers of Leadership. His arm twisting of Congress, of the Secretary of State, and of the Pentagon for support for his opposition to a Communist take-over in South Vietnam or in the Dominican Republic is, of course, something altogether different. It is a sign of a psychic derangement.

Malice is not necessarily the motive of Mr. Johnson's detractors. Some people consider it a charitable explanation for another man's dissent from their own point of view to say of him that he is not, poor thing, actually quite all there. The editors of the English journal and those others who are whispering the same things about Lyndon Johnson are so utterly convinced that it is nothing short of madness to resist the Vietcong in Southeast Asia or to land the Marines in the Dominican Republic that they look rather wistfully to extra-rational motivations for such conduct. No man in his right mind, they are saying in effect, could risk a great war with the Red Chinese or resort to dollar imperialism in Latin America; therefore, does it not follow, as neatly as *B* follows *A*, that anyone who so reasons, has lost his faculty for reasoning?

I do not deny that Lyndon Johnson's ego corresponds to his fearful appetite to run our lives for us, to arrange for our education, for our old age, for our poor, for our rich, for our culture, for our labor union policy, for our droughts, for our floods, for our bridges, and for our subways, and conservatives in this country have every reason in the world to project from that vanity a true threat to the survival of our local institutions. But all conservatives must, I think, join in resenting the insinuations that Mr. Johnson is just plain off his rocker. We can do this safely without being drawn into the orbit of Jack Valenti's recent paean on Mr. Johnson, which he should indeed have saved for such a moment as it becomes relevant to nominate Mr. Johnson for sainthood. But I for one, and you, I hope, for another, will denounce those of Mr. Johnson's critics who, by concluding that he is overgone in megalomania because he disagrees with them, prove nothing less than that this is their particular difficulty.

SENATOR FULBRIGHT GOES ON

July 2, 1966

What happens in the current issue of the *Reporter* magazine is an event of considerable psychological significance. It was greatly overdue, but one cannot help hoping that the process, finally launched, is well and finally under way. A tough-minded British journalist, Henry Fairlie, has written an article ("Old Realities and New Myths") analyzing the intellectual, historical, and emotional content of Senator William Fulbright's two most famous utterances of the past years: his speech in 1964 ("Old Myths and New Realities"), and his lectures in the spring of 1966 at Johns Hopkins University. The Senator does not survive the examination.

Consider, for instance, the most blatant, though not necessarily the most striking, of the Senator's inconsistencies. In 1964 he said: "To the best of our knowledge there is no evidence that wars are necessary and inevitable consequences of human nature." But in 1966, not much having happened to human nature in the interval, the Senator intoned at Johns Hopkins: "We must recognize, first of all, that the ultimate source of war and peace lies in human nature."

Mr. Fairlie goes on to analyze a number of historical analogies offered by Senator Fulbright in warning the United States against the "arrogance of power." Fulbright reported that "an exaggerated sense of power and an imaginary sense of mission" caused the Athenians to attack Syracuse, and Napoleon and then Hitler to invade Russia. The journalist Fairlie patiently explains to the former university president and Rhodes scholar Fulbright that the Athenians were dominated by a centrifugal ethos utterly alien to the America's current and thoroughly anti-Wilsonian distaste for ideological imperialism, and that Napoleon and Hitler were moved by a fanatical desire to pursue power for the sake of it, again utterly unlike the United States' tortured role in Vietnam, a theater we entered as ambivalently and indecisively as Hamlet undertaking to reorder the affairs of Elsinore Castle.

Not only the inapposite historical analogies but the insecure and contradictory grasp of revolutionary history and metaphysics. Fulbright in 1964 seemed to be saying that our interference in foreign revolutionary situations, though often justified by the vital interests of the country, should be measured against our capacity to wield power—which is certainly correct. But then in 1966 the Senator takes the position that revolutions are inevitable and follow predictable patterns, eventually reaching *Thermidor* (the stage at which the moderates, having executed their Robespierre, domesticate their revolution), that Russia has reached *Thermidor,* and so probably has Cuba. That Red China hasn't, but that there isn't much to be done about that, except wait.

Henry Fairlie shows that the dialectic of the Senator's two general positions reduces to this lesson: "Thus, America must not undertake the full responsibilities of its power, otherwise it will court ruin as surely as Athens and

Napoleon and Hitler; and America must not search for ways of encouraging peaceful and democratic changes of government, because resolution, and especially contemporary revolution, will probably be violent and undemocratic." And Fairlie concludes: "Between 1964 and 1966, [Fulbright] seems to have moved to a position from which he regards it as all but inevitable that the consequences of exercising world power must be ruinous; all but inevitable that revolutions must be violent and undemocratic; and all but inevitable that war follows from human nature. Such a formidable construction of inevitability," sighs Mr. Fairlie, "is, of course, a traditional argument for withdrawal from action."

Such detached analysis of Senator Fulbright is long overdue. That it should be published in a magazine whose featured speaker on the occasion of its tenth anniversary was Senator William Fulbright is not merely piquant, but greatly reassuring to the cause of intellectual courage. A syndicated liberal journalist, Pete Hamill, writes that the article's publication "will not change Washington's ideas about Fulbright, because [Washington] is inhabited by people who prefer to believe in the idea they have constructed of a man, rather than face uncomfortable truth." But then there are those who do not find it all that uncomfortable a truth that such an apodictic scholar-moralist as William Fulbright is, much of the time, talking through his *chapeau*.

THE HARDENING OF FIDEL CASTRO

January 12, 1967

The January issue of *Playboy* magazine carries a remarkable interview with Fidel Castro which is at once reassuring (Castro's rhetoric is more weathered, and he clearly isn't bent on seizing the Panama Canal next week), saddening (he is absolutely convinced that the Cuban people are better off than they once were), and revealing (the older he gets, he says, the more radical he becomes).

The interview took place over a period of days, and before he was through, Castro had spoken twenty-five hours' full of tape. He has a great deal to say, and he says it all, and although there are clear traces of guile, we walk

206

away with a better knowledge of the dictator of Cuba than we had before. And on the way, we learn things about our own country we didn't learn before.

On the eternally interesting question—was Castro or was he not always a Communist?—here is the way Castro now puts it: "If you ask me whether I considered myself a revolutionary at the time I was in the mountains, I would answer yes. . . . If you ask me, did I consider myself a Marxist-Leninist, I would say no. . . . If you ask me whether I considered myself a Communist, a classic Communist, I would say no, I did not yet consider myself a classic Communist. But today, yes, I believe I have that right. Today I see clearly that in the modern world, nobody can call himself a true revolutionary who is not a Marxist-Leninist. . . . With the passing of time, my thought has become more and more radical."

This is not, of course, the final word on the subject, and indeed it contradicts an earlier autobiographical pronouncement by Castro. But it is not inconceivable that Castro is telling the truth, and on this point there is a convergence of opinion from two bitterly divided quarters: Herbert Matthews of the New York *Times,* who when last heard from was still taking the line that we drove Castro to Communism by being somehow unpleasant to him when he took to shooting people and confiscating American property, and those soldiers in arms of Castro who fought with him in the Sierra Maestra under the illusion that they were fighting for a free Cuba. They too refuse, or most of them in any case, to believe that the Castro they fought with was all along secretly committed to the abolition of freedom in pursuit of his bloody Communism.

Castro informs us that President Kennedy did indeed promise not to invade Cuba if the Russians would remove their missiles and adds: "The United States has since alleged that because we haven't permitted inspection, there is no such agreement; but *de facto,* they accept it. . . . And I can say to you that even more agreements exist besides, about which not a word has ever been said. However, I don't think this is the occasion to speak about them. . . . I am a prime minister in active service. One day, perhaps, it will be known that the United States made some other concessions in relation to the October crisis besides those that were made public."

Playboy: "In a written, signed agreement?"

Castro: "It was not an agreement in accordance with protocol. It was an agreement that took place by letter and through diplomatic contacts." An interesting area of inquiry for the Senate Foreign Relations Committee next time Secretary Rusk heaves in.

Perhaps the most interesting passages concern Castro's recognition that Cuba is an agricultural paradise. He appears to have fought his way free of the common ambitions of little agricultural countries for prestigious industries and services (Ghana Air Lines). He will in due course find out what other socialist countries have found out, that somehow the agriculture doesn't come up out of the ground in socialist countries, even if well irrigated by Marxist-Leninist rhetoric. And then what? Will Castro become less and less radical? Unlikely, since it is clear that he is in love with his noxious little dogmas. Marxism-Leninism is still clearly his God, and he will no more abandon his faith, because of repeated crop failures, than a Christian will his because the world continues to be a vale of tears.

Castro is not in love with himself, he stresses—only with his faith. He has convinced himself that there is more "real" freedom in Cuba than in the United States, and he has ways of squaring all the little circles you have to square in order to defend that proposition. He is, like his own subjects, a slave to his own unreason.

HAROLD WILSON AND GEORGIE BROWN

London, October 10, 1967

The political news here is of the triumphant performance by Prime Minister Harold Wilson (who in the view of some observers intimately acquainted with British history is the worst Prime Minister who ever presided over the Mother of Parliaments) at Scarborough, which is where the trade unionists meet every year to pass judgment on the performance of the Socialist Party.

Mr. Wilson is up against it because his prestige is very low, very, very low, for several reasons, many of them of his own doing. He has been in power for three years now, and confronting national bankruptcy, he has been forced to institute a program of economic austerity, among whose effects has been considerable unemployment.

Full employment is, of course, the cornerstone of socialist economic policy, but the trouble is that in order to have full employment, one needs employers, and in order to have employers, one needs customers, and in order to have customers, one must produce salable goods at salable prices, and this means you need to cut down on your overhead, and how do you do that if you are committed to effusive welfarism?

The trade unionists were gunning for their Prime Minister, but he had them, in a matter of minutes, jumping through his hoop, cheering delightedly. He spoke about the great accomplishments of the Labour government, which he described statistically, using the base of 100 pounds. "For every 100 pounds that they [the Conservatives] spent, we are spending 144 pounds." Cheers. "For every 100 pounds they spent on education, we are providing 142 pounds." Double cheers. "For every 100 pounds they provided for housing and slum clearance, we are providing 155 pounds." Standing ovation.

Although the conference voted by a narrow majority to censure the government for supporting the U.S. effort in Vietnam, it all was thought to be a considerable personal achievement for Harold Wilson, particularly inasmuch as the figures he gave, which so solaced the audience, move in exactly the opposite direction from what is needed in order to reduce the economic austerity of which they all are complaining.

Mr. Wilson's principal assistant, George Brown, is not doing quite so well. He pleaded for a vote of confidence in foreign policy, *e.g.*, to permit him to deal with the Vietnam war other than as an enemy of the United States position and to permit him freedom of action vis-à-vis Greece. Nothing doing.

Concerning Greece, the unions demanded no less than the instant withdrawal of relations and the ousting of Greece from NATO. One has the feeling that if the conference had gone on another hour or two, the socialists might have voted in favor of sending U.S. Marines to Greece.

And then, too, George Brown has been having some rather personal troubles. The gentleman likes his occasional whiskey, as most gentlemen do. But it has become part of the game over here to try to get pictures of the Foreign Secretary in particularly uninhibited postures —e.g., doing the frug with that special abandon which fine spirits uniquely induce. This, said George Brown over television, is unfair. Did the press do it to Churchill? Everybody knew that Churchill drank, didn't they? He works jolly hard, he reminded his countrymen, and if they want a Foreign Secretary who doesn't drink, they can jolly well look elsewhere.

Booze is much on the mind of every British toper because the government has decided to crack down on drunken driving, and beginning yesterday (October 9) a law went into effect which permits policemen to examine suspect drivers, who, if they believe that the breathometers with which the police will be equipped unfairly register, and to their disadvantage, the amount of alcohol in their system, can be required by the magistrate to submit to more clinically revealing tests. That violates the sense of privacy of many Englishmen, not to say the tradition against giving evidence against oneself. One columnist obviously prepared to take arms against the government sums it up this way: "It is a fine comment on modern Britain: you can now be sent to jail for refusing to pass water when a policemen tells you."

People are beginning to wish that the voters had been given breathometer tests when they voted in the present government.

DOINGS AT DR. HUTCHINS' ZOO

September 2, 1967

Remember I told you about the Episcopal Bishop of Washington who a month ago turned over a church for H. Rap Brown to teach hate in? Here is a parallel. Doc Hutchins, head of the Center for the Study of Democratic Institutions and Keeper of the Dialogue, hosted a three-day meeting of students at which among other things it was proposed (a) that "the institutions of this country must be destroyed" and (b) that "the dialogue wastes a lot of time. . . . [D]isruption [is] more advantageous."

The latest visitors to Mr. Hutchins' tax-exempt zoo

210

were nineteen charmers from the academy who met to discuss ways in which students might successfully assert themselves. Devereaux Kennedy, the student body president of Washington University in St. Louis, called, in the words of an observer, "for outright revolution and the overthrow of the United States government. He advocated terrorism on such a scale that it would 'demoralize and castrate America.' "

Stan Wise, who is secretary of SNCC and a recent graduate of Howard University, boasted that his organization was "absolutely without doubt responsible for the race riots throughout the country." (This, repeat, was a boast, not a confession.) "The only way to stop the war in Vietnam," Mr. Wise explained to Mr. Hutchins' attentive staff, "is to kill those institutions behind it."

Jeff Alexander, from Harvard College, was introduced as a moderate, and he merely proposed "the boycott of classes [as] the students No. 1 weapon and a boycott . . . on a nationwide scale to bring the university to a halt."

David Seeley, of the University of California at Santa Barbara, promised that "the revolution is coming. We're bound to destroy the university," he said gleefully. "Not pull it apart, brick by brick, but bring it to a complete stall." Young Mr. Seeley wore sandals and his hair "just short of the shoulder." His old man was a professor of sociology at Brandeis but is now a staff member of the Center for the Study of Democratic Institutions and must have burst with paternal pride.

I almost forgot Mr. Saltonstall. Yes, one of *the* Saltonstalls. He is twenty-three. And very optimistic. "We have," he said speaking for his fellow students, "the power to bring the American juggernaut to a halt. Let us paralyze the university; let us ball up the economy. One day soon, Congressmen and Presidents may petition us, not us them." He had a lot of specific proposals, such as immobilizing ROTC by breaking up drills and harassing instructors, stopping defense research by blocking government advisers from their offices and harassing them at home.

But surely, Mr. Saltonstall's most interesting suggestion was "the introduction of a small quantity of LSD in only five or six government department coffee urns"—it "might be a highly effective tactic." Indeed. On the other hand, how do we know it hasn't been done already? How could you tell? Mr. Saltonstall is going on to graduate work at Yale, no doubt to replace the terrible void felt by the leave of absence granted to Staughton Lynd.

Some members of Mr. Hutchins' staff expressed themselves mildly in opposition to this or that position of this or that student, but they did not apparently make much of an impact and were dismissed by one student as "quaint," which is not exactly how others would dismiss Mr. Huchins and his staff.

Bruce Levine, from a New York high school, found Dr. Hutchins "naïve," which is one way of putting it. One center consultant, Scott Buchanan, expressed "anger." He thought the students were "playing house with the idea of power." "You act," he said, "like children. I get a little frightened."

Ah, yes. But what is frightening is that a center staffed by apparently civilized people should sponsor three days of such types. As for the children, I think of Russell Kirk's suggestion that increasingly he is tempted to found a Birch John Society.

JEAN-PAUL SARTRE WINS THE NOBEL PRIZE

October 29, 1964

There is something about Jean-Paul Sartre's rejection of the Nobel Prize that is wonderfully pure. Because there is something about accepting a prize offered by anyone at all that suggests an acquiescence—unwise, in some cases—in the prizegiver's standards. If you are offered an award by a committee that previously had given the award to Tom, Dick, and Harry, there is a sense in which you become a part of the community of Tom, Dick, and Harry. Sartre recognized this—and said no. I honor his stand as a refreshing act of individuality and wish that others who have been tendered the prize had refused it along with Mr. Nobel's 53-gees as grandly. It is, of course, a pity that M. Sartre advanced the wrongest reasons for gainsaying the honor.

The Nobel Committee is, to begin with, a semi-mysterious group of intellectuals and bureaucrats who appear to be influenced alternately by sentimentalism (the award to Cordell Hull), pseudocosmopolitanism (Halldór Laxness of Iceland), literary proletarianism (Italy's Quasimodo), and out-and-out left pacifism (Linus Pauling). Any red-blooded Westerner should think twice before accepting a Nobel award, precisely because to do so is to lend the recipient's prestige not merely to the idiosyncratic criteria the committee uses, but to its political relativism. The committee's choices are increasingly greeted as signs of divine approval. Yet the committee has shown neither artistic prescience (T. S. Eliot got the award twenty-five years after he had earned it), nor courage (Ezra Pound is yet to get it), nor a high regard for justice (Adenauer never got it). The committee has come to expect an ayesaying heavenly chorus every time it releases its thunderbolts of approval. It has hardly earned any such thing.

It was a public scandal that it did not award a prize to Robert Frost, even while handing them out to such mediocrities as Quasimodo. John Dos Passos would certainly have got one if only he had been careful not to follow his conscience into the American conservative movement. No one, but no one in our time, has contributed to literary craftsmanship more than Evelyn Waugh—but he is a traditionalist, and so unqualified. You do come across Yeats and Eliot and Faulkner, but one has the feeling that their overpowering performances required as a matter of self-preservation that the committee recognize them. Shakespeare would have got a prize from the Swedes. But they would probably have found an excuse for not giving one to Milton.

And now the remarkable M. Sartre advances as his reason for not accepting the award not merely that the Nobel Committee is ideologically tendentious, but that it is tendentious in the wrong direction, no less. " 'In the present East-West confrontation,' " he said (I quote from the New York Times), " 'my sympathies go undeniably to Socialism and to what is called the Eastern bloc.' " And the Nobel Committee, Sartre claims, has not sufficiently honored the Communists. For instance, he complains, the Nobel Committee has not given prizes to Pablo Neruda, the Chilean poet, or Louis Aragon, the French poet, or Mikhail Sholokhov, the Soviet novelist. All three of them, observes the Times, "are Communists." Indeed, Sartre

213

says, the only Russian the Nobel Committee has honored is Boris Pasternak—"a rebel of the East," who was forbidden to accept the prize by Nikita Khrushchev.

"My sympathies go to what is called the Eastern bloc." M. Sartre has been loyal to his friends. He has joined in common causes with sympathizers of the Soviet Union and of Soviet Cuba on any number of occasions. Recently he traveled to Cuba to celebrate his enthusiasm for that country's new regime. Sartre calls himself an existentialist. He is primarily a superverbalist, who spins his teeming thoughts into plays, novels, autobiography, creative philosophy, biography, essays, criticism. He is one of the foremost creative literary men of our time, and although at the center of his philosophy is the importance of the individual, he is stubbornly atheist—and so denudes the individual of the divine spark that is his surest claim to individuality—and he is stubbornly socialist—and so denudes the individual of the privacy which best reflects the dignity of the human condition. It is these philosophical and social confusions which render Sartre ultimately a dull man, a man truly disoriented, whose concern for individualism tends to reduce to a kind of ascetic hedonism: It is not so strange that his lifelong mistress should have written the definitive defense of the Marquis de Sade or that he should have undertaken the definitive defense of the pervert Genet. Recently, Evelyn Waugh sardonically defended the Catholic Index as "a convenient excuse for not reading Sartre." It is a convenient time for those who cherish the notion of the superidealism of the Nobel Committee to meditate on the character and work of Jean-Paul Sartre, the committee's hero of the year.

KENNETH TYNAN SAYS A NAUGHTY WORD

January 13, 1966

A few weeks ago on the BBC, no less, an unmentionable word was mentioned by, no less, the literary manager of England's National Theatre, and, once again, Kenneth Tynan was in the news. He has been newsworthy for a good many years in dramatic circles because he is, if not a first-rate critic (he is impeded from being that by his world view, which is materialist and egoistic), at least a very, very good one, in that he is a shrewd observer and expert verbalizer who disposes of a pyrotechnical vocabulary and abundant wit and is, therefore, fun to read, whatever one thinks of him, of drama, or, indeed, of the universe itself.

He is extremely interesting to theater folk because of his exemplary technical skills as a critic; but it is, alas, not these but other exhibitions which have caused him to become an international figure, recognized as such by the New York *Times Sunday Magazine* which has devoted an admiring spread to him, triggered—O sweetest of ironies!—precisely by the commotion that resulted from his violation of a taboo, for the maintenance of which the New York *Times* would go to the electric chair.

Mr. Tynan is interesting to us ordinary folks, we learn, because of his freewheeling iconoclasm and because he is, thereby, a part of that wave of the future which good gray editors dutifully cover on the grounds that in due course it must inundate us all, and we may as well be good sports about it when the time comes.

The philosophy of Kenneth Tynan is not by any means original, although he depicts it refreshingly in his quite ungovernable effluvia, most of them published in this country in the cleavages of *Playboy* magazine. It is the usual kind of business. Man is born to enjoy himself. The acutest pleasures in life are cultural and sexual, or maybe sexual and cultural. From the time he was a schoolboy, Tynan was on to the instant scandal value of manifestos in favor of sexual permissiveness, and it is recorded that he resigned as an independent candidate for a school election when the headmaster denied him permission to make his stand in favor of free homosexuality. Unlike some of his friends and admirers, he himself is not a practitioner of the freedom he advocates, but he finds it a constant source of amusement to toy with the subject.

A few years ago he wrote a piece for the highbrow English periodical *Encounter,* in which he took great delight, a delight he apparently believed was communicable to his readers, in recounting an episode with a tailor whom he visited to hire a costume for the annual affair given by the Lord Mayor of London and before whom he declined to undress on the ground that he (Tynan) was a homosexual. That, believe it or not, was the punch line of his long essay, which suggests that as a critic, he has his own second act problems.

In the United States he made great publicity for himself a few years ago by signing the Fair Play for Cuba Committee's manifesto to the effect that we were being beastly toward Fidel Castro and then writing a whimpering piece of self-pity when Senator Dodd of the Internal Security Subcommittee had the nerve to question him about his knowledge of where the funds were collected to pay for the publication of the manifesto. For a man who was so unbrave with Senator Dodd, whom he esteems less than his tailor and over whose impending questions he worried greatly, wondering even whether the result of Senator Dodd's interrogation might be that he would never, ever be able to earn a living again ("economic fears welled up," he wrote, ". . . would my American earnings be jeopardized?"). It didn't hurt him, of course, and he has been too busy ever since to apologize to Senator Dodd, whose pertinacity absolutely established that the money for that particular Communist front had indeed been provided by a Communist—no less a man than Fidel Castro's own ambassador to the United Nations.

But Tynan went back to England and continued his chatter about sex and revolution, calling, among other things, for capitulating to the Soviet Union at the time of the Berlin crisis, lest he should die in the holocaust that would result if we stood firm. ("I would rather live on my knees than die on my knees.")

In England he lives contentedly among the literati, available to all interesting people, save only for his reservation that he "couldn't be friendly with a convinced Tory . . . all the people I know and like are Liberal or Socialist."

The syndrome is complete when we learn that he can't be friendly with God either, which is, one hopes, an unrequited attitude and, in any case, an especially sad one, considering that Mr. Tynan was exposed to the most persuasive Christian scholar of his generation, C. S. Lewis, at Oxford. "I hope," says Mr. Tynan, "I never need to believe in God. It would be an awful confession of failure." Rather like a show that closes after the first week, which is the dramatist's idea of hell.

ROBERT LOWELL'S SIT-OUT

June 9, 1965

Certain people—very few of them, but some—ought to be immune from criticism. As far as I am concerned, Robert Lowell, the poet, should be treated like the bird of paradise he is, and no matter if he advocates returning Arizona to the Indians, emptying the Atlantic into the Pacific, or pulling out of South Vietnam and the Dominican Republic. The trouble is, as so often happens when birds of paradise start opinionating about the doings of us chickens, the polemical opportunists seize on their statements and blow them up with synthetic authority. As, for instance, neutralists-fellow travelers were always doing to the empty political vaporizings of Albert Einstein, which they asked us to accept as solemnly as the proposition that E equals *mc* squared.

Mr. Lowell is a superb poet, translator, critic, and I cherish the hope, human being. But along comes an invitation from LBJ to Mr. Lowell, as to other literary men (most of them his artistic inferiors) to come read his works on the White House lawn in celebration of Art in the Age of Lyndon or something.

At first Mr. Lowell said yes. Then he reconsidered and wrote a letter which made many of the front pages, informing the President that he wouldn't come after all. Why? Because, he said, he views our present foreign policy "with the greatest dismay and distrust" and fears that his appearance at the White House ceremony might have the effect of piping the Marine Corps into some new foreign country. He feels that, by accepting the invitation, he would in some "subtle way" appear to be implicated in programs in fact he disapproves of.

Most extraordinarily, it was *not* widely reported that Mr. Lowell is a conscientious objector who spent time in prison as the result of his refusal to participate in the Second World War. One honors him for his fidelity to his convictions. But surely it is not surprising if a conscientious objector declines to endorse the Vietnam war? If you decline to sanction the use of force anywhere, it must follow that you decline to sanction the use of force against

217

the Communist guerrillas in South Vietnam—so what else is new?

What isn't new, unfortunately, is the ravenous desire to publicize every cuckoo of dissent against the foreign policy of LBJ without recording such qualifications—such as that Mr. Lowell is a conscientious objector—as help put them in focus.

A few weeks ago, Lewis Mumford, the prominent ecologist and author, while presiding over a meeting of the American Academy of Arts and Letters, took the occasion to blast off against Johnson's policy in Vietnam. Headlines. Thomas Hart Benton, the artist, not only took exception there and then to Mumford's usurping his prerogatives as chairman of a gathering convened to discuss belletristic goings-on, he subsequently resigned from the august organization in a huff. Minimum notices.

There are several points to meditate. Principal among them is the perennial question of the artists and intellectuals and their depressing political unintelligence. That is a theme for the ages. At least we should comfort ourselves, if comfort is indeed to be derived from the fact, that it is a continuing problem. The intellectuals in Hitler Germany curled up and died in acquiescence when Hitler moved in. The refugee intellectuals did a very good job in arousing the consciences of our own intellectuals. And one would hope these same intellectuals might be aroused if they permitted themselves to consult and talk with some of the many intellectuals who are refugees from Communism. One hopes that would happen—though there are grounds for pessimism.

STEVE ALLEN REPLIES

January 23, 1965

It develops that I was premature in imputing a creeping sanity to Mr. Steve Allen, who now writes plaintively in the *Progressive* magazine that not nearly as many people will see there his clarification as saw my original column on the subject. The column in question contained my proposal that the Strategic Air Command obliterate Communist China's nuclear installations and that Steve Allen, who is famous for his almost superstitious fear of any

218

direct military action, was so dazzled by the cogency of my proposal when put to him that he nodded his acquiescence in it and, moreover, authorized me to quote him.

Poor Mr. Allen. How the boys went to work on him! He has now done his best, which is very good, to extricate himself from the commitment he made—by the use of two methods. First, he hammed the thing up, suggesting that the conversation was one of those abstract after-dinner things like "How many angels can fit on the head of a pin?" No one present, he said, took the subject seriously, so that his formal acquiescence (he does not deny having acquiesced) was really nothing more than a sort of acknowledgment of the abstract neatness of a discrete proposition wrenched out of time and space. And second, if Mr. Allen had known that I would construe his giving me permission to quote him as his giving me permission to quote him, he'd have said the thing differently, or better, or more completely, or something.

Having done with that, Mr. Allen takes the offensive. He wonders out loud: (1) Since I and my friends are known to be close to Senator Goldwater, could it be that the Senator had it in mind, in the event he had been elected President, to advance this "dramatic proposal"? (Answer: I haven't the slightest idea.) (2) Was the bomb-China plan actually conceived *before* the election? (Answer: As a matter of fact, yes, if we are to stretch a point and believe Drew Pearson. The plan was conceived—as distinguished from executed—two years ago by President John F. Kennedy, and was exhumed after the detonation of the Chinese bomb by President Lyndon Johnson.) (3) Is it possible that the plan originated with Chiang Kai-Shek, who "commissioned [remember that word, friends] his China Lobby friend, Mr. Buckley, to initiate a public debate" on the subject—and to embarrass Mr. Allen? (Answer: I don't accept commissions from foreign governments, to advance any point of view, and as for the demonstration of my friend Mr. Allen's fuzzy-mindedness, I fear that the job was commissioned not by Chiang Kai-Shek, but by an elfin nature.)

But within the cracks of all this lapidary nonsense, Mr. Allen attempts to forward the reasons why, on reflection, he opposes the program which first he was willing to endorse. And it is, as one feared, a list of those arguments which have the effect of absolutely guaranteeing that the United States will remain paralyzed in her foreign policy. Not quite—he is all in favor of talking to the Red Chinese about the necessity of improving. But to bomb Red China's bomb? No. Why? "We have . . . no way of knowing—really predicting—what the response would be. It would seem reasonable to assume that such an attack would render it impossible, in our lifetime, to ever develop a rapprochement with the Chinese."

This sentence contains a greater density of fatuities on foreign policy than I have ever seen since President Johnson last addressed the United Nations. (1) The response of the leaders of Red China would be a spasm of rhetorical outrage. The kind of thing they have done every week or so against the Soviet Union for about two years. Only this outrage would drop all references to the West's being a "paper tiger." (2) The Red Chinese leaders would instantly find that all their current military and guerrilla aggressions—against South Vietnam, against Laos, against Thailand, against Malaysia, against the Philippines—had become much harder, as the result of the remoralization of the anti-Communist peoples, who also would have learned that the United States is not a paper tiger. (3) Since when have we taken to referring to Mao Tse-tung and his fellow slavemasters as "the Chinese"? "The Chinese" are a captive people whose workaday misery is the direct consequence of the ideological mania of their leaders. To suppose that "the Chinese" would hate us for depriving their leaders of the ultimate weapon by which that misery can be perpetuated and spread to other outlying areas is to fall prey to the most exaggerated presumptions of Communist propaganda. Steve Allen should precisely aspire to be a noncommissioned advocate for the China lobby—*i.e.,* for that movement which seeks by bold and courageous means to do something *for* the Chinese people, which is to say, to do something *against* their leaders.

ROBERT VAUGHN FROM K.O.O.K.

Los Angeles, July 13, 1967

The story on the front page is that undisclosed Washington observers are gloomier than ever about the Vietnam war, that General Westmoreland's greeting to Secretary McNamara in Saigon—"We are winning, slowly but steadily"—was considered by them almost perversely inaccurate ("We are steadily making no progress, at great cost" is their position).

In California anti-Vietnam passions—like all others —are especially volatile, and would you believe it, an emerging spokesman for the doveish left is Robert Vaughn, the same gentleman who fights with T.H.R.U.S.H. in behalf of U.N.C.L.E. every Friday evening, on coast-to-coast TV. Mr. Vaughn, although he opposed the candidacy of George Murphy for Senator, was grateful when Murphey won, and perhaps also grateful and for the same reasons when Ronald Reagan went on to win the governorship. It meant that gentlemen from the theater would be taken more seriously in the world of politics, and it is the world of politics that most greatly fascinates the man from U.N.C.L.E.

"Both Aristotle and Plato," he has said, "believed that the good politician is also the good philosopher. I agree with them."

I asked Mr. Vaughn if there were matters on which Plato and Aristotle agreed, with which Mr. Vaughn disagreed, and he replied: Oh, yes, he had written papers for the University of Southern California—which he is attending in pursuit of a Ph.D., which will be his as soon as he completes his doctoral dissertation on McCarthyism and the theater—outlining the errors Plato and Aristotle fell into.

In his most celebrated speech, delivered before the California Democratic Council, Mr. Vaughn explained that he took off a great deal of time to study the Vietnamese situation. "When this academic research was completed, it was my unfortunate lot to adjudge the facts and find the Establishment in error. Hence"—and these words, believe it or not came from the same mouth that spoke the words of Hamlet in the Pasadena Playhouse last summer—"a moral judgment was now incumbent on my responsibility as a citizen to voice my conclusions publicly."

Alas, Mr. Vaughn's analyses of the Vietnam situation are in perfect harmony with his prose. Among his most remarkable conclusions are:

(A) That John F. Kennedy totally misread what was going on in Vietnam when Mr. Kennedy in 1956 warned against "an election obviously stacked and subverted in advance, urged upon us by those who have already broken their pledges under the agreement that they now seek to enforce."

(B) That if there had been an election in 1956, it would have been a genuinely free election, and Ho Chi Minh would have won it.

(C) That the million refugees who poured into the south during 1954-1956 did so less because they sought sanctuary from the persecutions of Ho Chi Minh than because they desired to be governed by Ngo Diem, a fellow Catholic.

(D) That if the Communists in Southeast Asia launch an assault on Thailand, the United States should not go to Thailand's aid—unless the United Nations sanctions our doing so.

And (E) That the crucial decision to continue the war in Vietnam was reached not by the President of the United States and his advisers in the Cabinet and the leaders of the Senate and House of Representatives—but by Cardinal Spellman at a secret meeting (presumably with the Holy Ghost and Lyndon Johnson, or vice versa) at Ossining, New York, several summers ago.

On and on it goes. "On August 6, 1945," Mr. Vaughn said in his speech, "a new world was born. It was named the Atomic Age. And with that first fleeting heartbeat in the new babe, all the ages that came before were rendered unmeaningful." Certainly all the rules of English that came before were rendered unmeaningful to Mr. Vaughn, and all the ages except those relics from them, here and there an insight of Plato and Aristotle which happily coincide with the conclusions of Mr. Vaughn which are now incumbent on his responsibility as a citizen to voice publicly.

Mr. Vaughn has been named head of the Speakers

222

Bureau of the Democratic Party of California. It is as though an illiterate Robert Welch had been named head of the Speakers Bureau of the Massachusetts Republican Party. Truly the Democratic Party is coming apart, which may prove to be the most urgent reason for ending the Vietnam war.

SPELUNKING WITH NORMAN MAILER

September 25, 1965

The life and art of Norman Mailer are discussed all over the pages of Life magazine this week by an intelligent and gifted writer, Brock Brewer, who had the sense to acknowledge even before setting out on his twelve-page journey that he doesn't know (and neither does Mr. Mailer) what in fact is the goal of Mr. Mailer's "reckless quest." The heavy recognition of Mr. Mailer by the editors of *Life* is final confirmation that he is big on the literary scene—and more: that he is big on the American scene, for reasons that most critics do not know how to explain but, by their friendly activity in trying, go so far as to acknowledge that the Quest to Explain Norman Mailer is itself worthwhile.

And indeed it is. He is probably the single best-known living American writer, second only to John Dos Passos. It doesn't mean his books have sold as well as Erskine Caldwell's or John Steinbeck's, merely that far more of the people who read Mailer's books wonder about who he is and what he is trying to get at than ever have on reading Caldwell or Steinbeck.

Mailer is interesting in two respects. The first—and here is why I love him as an artist—is that he makes the most beautiful metaphors in the business, as many as a dozen of them on a single page worth anthologizing. The second reason why he is interesting is that so many who read him hungrily (and perhaps too seriously) he represents present-day America. He expresses their feelings that America today is shivering in desolation and hopelessness, is looking for her identity after a period of self-alienation marked by a couple of world wars, a depression, and a cyclonic advance through technology and automation.

223

It was Mailer who developed the cult of the hipster—the truly modern American who lets the bleary world go by doing whatever it bloody well likes, because nothing it does can upset the hipsters' inexhaustible cool. It isn't that Mr. Mailer's characters are without passion; on the contrary, they tend to be so highly strung that no matter how gently you stroke them, they emit twangy, sharp tones. It is that the workaday pressures of civilization don't affect them. They aren't influenced very much by tradition, or by the venerable arguments for continuence and moderation, or by the recognition that other people's existences and hopes abut against our own ambitions and self-concern.

In every categorical sense, Norman Mailer is an utter and hopeless mess. If there is an intellectual in the United States who talks more predictable nonsense on the subject of foreign policy, I will pay a week's wages not to have to hear him. On the domestic scene, he is a so-so socialist. So-so because even though he finds he can float only in the cool waters of the left, he is transparently unhappy, really, as a socialist, although he is more docile toward that barren religion than toward any other. As a citizen, he is wild, defying not only those starched conventions that are there primarily to stick out your tongue at, but at the other conventions, the real McCoys—those that are there to increase the small chance we have, whether as children or as adults, for a little domestic tranquility.

As a philosopher, however, Mailer is—dare I say it?—in his own fashion, a conservative. Wrestling in the twentieth century with the hegemonies of government and ideology, the conservative tends to side with the individualist. In his savage novels, Mailer's titanic struggles are sustained by the resources of his own spirit (plus booze). In his novel *An American Dream,* a hero as screwy as Mr. Mailer lurches from Gomorrah to hell and back, but always depends upon himself to get out of the jam.

Mr. Mailer is properly denounced by philosophical taxonomists as a solipsist—a man for whom reality is confined to himself and his own experience. Still, it is a relief—sort of a halfway house to the proper blend of the individual and tradition—to read a novel in which the protagonist doesn't depend for his salvation on life rafts cast out into the sea of hope by Marx, Freud, or U Thant.

I confess that Mr. Mailer's tours through the night spots of hell are not my idea of recreation, even with pad and pencil in hand to jot down what one has Learned About Things. I do not enjoy spelunking in human depravity, nor do I wish my machine to tape-record the emunctory noises of psychic or physical human excesses. Even so, there is hope in Norman Mailer's turbulent motions.

THE VIOLATION OF ARTHUR SCHLESINGER

March 30, 1963

Just after Mr. Kennedy's inauguration, I met with Professor Arthur Schlesinger, Jr., historian and dogmatic theologian for the Americans for Democratic Action, in public debate in Boston on the subject of the welfare state. It was on that occasion that Mr. Schlesinger, countering some point or other I had made, announced that the "best defense against Communism is the welfare state." Now everybody expects that professors will say foolish things from time to time, but Professor Schlesinger had just then taken leave of Harvard to accept a position as special assistant to the fledgling President of the United States, so that a great deal of publicity was given to that remarkable statement. And those who felt a decent interval would surely be allowed to elapse before an egghead academician would presume to press such homeopathic nonsense about how to deal with Communism on practical men of exalted station must have sobered on witnessing the professor's grand entry into the lecture hall, twenty minutes late, escorted by screeching police cars; it obviously hadn't taken long for Mr. Schlesinger to acquire princely habits.

And along with them, it is my sad duty here to report, he seems to have lost—an occupational risk for humble folk who suddenly find themselves supping with the great—whatever sense of humor he once possessed.

Mr. Schlesinger had been accustomed to such fawning audiences as he regularly came upon at Harvard and elsewhere in the academic world, where they preach academic freedom and practice liberal indoctrination, and was visibly disconcerted on discovering from the audience's reaction that one-half of those present were adamantly opposed to his views and those of the New

Frontiersmen. Under the circumstances, he thought to curry the opposition's favor by handing me, as their spokesman of the evening, a most redolent bouquet. Quoth Arthur: "Mr. Buckley has a facility for rhetoric which I envy, as well as a wit which I seek clumsily and vainly to emulate." The crowd (or my half of it) purred with pleasure. As an old debater, I knew exactly what he was up to, and determined, when my turn came to rebut, to say something equally oleaginous about Arthur. But I had only fifteen minutes, before getting up to speak, during which to compose a compliment, and I guess my imagination failed me—I forget.

And indeed I forgot about the whole incident until a couple of months ago when I received a letter from a lady in Boston who had been there that night. She cited Mr. Schlesinger's cream puff to illustrate his exemplary "fairness to the opposite political camp." It happened that at just that moment I was supposed to furnish my publishers with some quotations for the jacket of my new book, *Rumbles Left and Right*. I thought it would be mad fun to include the words of Arthur Schlesinger—you know, sort of the literary oxymoron of the year.

Well, sir, you'd have thought this was the biggest swindle since the Donation of Constantine. A few weeks ago, while minding my own business, I received a frantic telegram from my publisher announcing that Arthur Schlesinger, having seen the blurb in an advertisement for my book in *National Review*, demanded to know where and when he had said any such thing about me. I wired back: "MY OFFICE HAS COPY OF ORIGINAL TAPE. TELL ARTHUR THAT'LL TEACH HIM TO USE UNCTION IN POLITICAL DEBATE BUT NOT TO TAKE IT SO HARD: NO ONE BELIEVES ANYTHING HE SAYS ANYWAY." Needless to say, I sent a copy of the telegram to Mr. Schlesinger, with the postscript: "Dear Arthur: I am at work on a new book which, however, will not be completed until the spring of 1964, giving you plenty of time to compose a new puff for it. Regards." And then, on the upper left-hand corner of the letter, properly addressed to Mr. Schlesinger at his august quarters (The White House, Washington, D.C.) I wrote, "Wm. 'Envy His Rhetoric!' Buckley," with my return address.

That, apparently, did it. Before even Arthur could say "I-believe-in-free-speech," the firm of Messrs. Greenbaum, Wolff and Ernst let it be known to my publisher and to *National Review* that they would demand an apology—or Schlesinger would sue. Now there is a very good case to be made for everyone's apologizing who has ever quoted Arthur Schlesinger; but isn't it droll to be asked to apologize *to* Schlesinger for quoting *from* Schlesinger? Messrs. G. W. & E. have solemnly announced that I have "invaded Mr. Schlesinger's privacy." A most interesting complaint, considering that Mr. Schlesinger's words had been uttered before an audience of 1,500 or so, before television and radio, and before members of the press and the wire services. For someone who wants what he says to be kept private, and as I say, all the world should cooperate in securing Mr. Schlesinger's privacy, that's a strange way to go about it, wouldn't you say?

Though, I dunno, lots of things about Schlesinger seem strange, and I intend to have a very interesting time with Messrs. Greenbaum, Wolff and Ernst going into some of them. Ernst, by the way, is the great Morris Ernst, the free-speech specialist who so strongly believes in free speech that now his firm threatens an injunction to keep my *Rumbles* from being published and *National Review* from being distributed, unless I apologize to Schlesinger for exercising my right of free speech by quoting Schlesinger.

Ah, well, it is a mad world. But I shall certainly put in for next year's Freedom Award. On the ground that the more time Schlesinger devotes to me, the less time he has left over to devote to public affairs.

SCHLESINGER PROTESTS USE OF QUOTE
IN PROMOTION OF BUCKLEY TITLE

EDITORS, THE PUBLISHERS' WEEKLY:

The publishing house of G. P. Putnam's Sons placed an advertisement in the February 12 issue of the *National Review* which read, with appropriate typographical flourishes, as follows: "Watch for a new book by W. F. Buckley, Jr. . . . Here's what the critics say." There followed quotations from a number of critics, including a

227

quotation ascribed to me expressing uncontrollable admiration for Mr. Buckley's rhetoric and wit.

Having never seen—or indeed heard of—Mr. Buckley's book, I was naturally startled to find myself listed among its critics. And, having no great admiration for either Mr. Buckley's rhetoric or his wit, I was equally startled to find myself listed among his fans. On application to Putnam's, I learned that the quotation ascribed to me came from the transcript of a debate between Mr. Buckley and myself—a debate which took place in January 1961, some two years before the new book was announced. It is further evident from an examination of the transcript that the remark was entirely ironic in nature—that, in fact, it reeked with sarcasm—and therefore that Putnam's use of it in promoting Mr. Buckley's book was invalid not only because it had no application to the book but also because its meaning was opposite to that implied in the advertisement.

When I pointed these things out to Putnam's early in February, Mr. Peter Israel, the editor-in-chief, finally wrote me (on February 26), "I am going to see to it personally that no further use of the quotation is made in our publicity or advertising for Mr. Buckley's book." He declined, however, to do anything about the use of the quotation on the jacket on the ground that "since the jacket has already been printed there is literally nothing I can do about its use at this point." He did not explain how Putnam's happened to put the quotation on the jacket without authorization in the first place or why, after I communicated with Putnam's on February 8, nothing was done to stop the use of the jacket. I thereupon directed my lawyers to take up with Putnam's the question of the jacket or, alternatively, the possibility of working out with Putnam's a statement which would make clear that the quotation attributed to me was used without authentication or authorization and did not express my view of Mr. Buckley or his book.

The discussion with Putnam's was recently interrupted by Mr. Buckley, who seized the occasion to put out a release stating (a) that I had announced my intention of suing him and (b) that I was trying to keep not only his book but his magazine from being published. Both claims were false.

My desire remains a simple one—that is, not to be cited

as among the enthusiastic "critics" of a book which, to this day, I have never seen, nor to have my sardonic statements in a debate presented to the book-buyer as solemn and rhapsodic praise. I might add that, speaking as an author, I would even think there might be a matter of publisher's ethics involved here—though it must be stated that Putnam's while it has agreed under pressure to stop the use of the quotation, has continued to act as if the unauthorized application of a questionable and ambiguous quotation to a book unread by the supposed critic is in accordance with the highest traditions of the publishing profession.

ARTHUR SCHLESINGER, JR.
3123 O Street, N.W.
Washington 7, D.C.
April 13, 1963

April 19, 1963

The Editor
Publishers' Weekly
62 West 45th Street
New York 36, N.Y.

Dear Sir:
  Mr. Arthur Schlesinger, Jr., wrote you in the last issue to register a series of complaints centering upon the appearance on the dust jacket of my new book, *Rumbles Left and Right,* of a quotation from Mr. Schlesinger, to wit, "He has a facility for rhetoric which I envy, as well as a wit which I seek clumsily and vainly to emulate."
  (1) Says Mr. Schlesinger: The statement was made "some two years before the new book was announced" about a book "which to this day I have never seen." Say I: Estimates of an author's generic skills are not self-lapsing, like soufflés. The author must do something concrete to change the critic's mind about him. If I have done any such thing, Mr. Schlesinger has yet to remark it, and if I have done such a thing in my new book, Mr. Schlesinger is unaware of it, having said repeatedly that he has yet to read it.
  (2) Says Mr. Schlesinger: When I made the state-

ment about Mr. Buckley in the first instance, it "reeked with sarcasm." Say I: As a matter of fact, it did not—and the vast audience who heard it clearly interpreted it as sincerely intended, perhaps because it took for granted Mr. Schlesinger's general sincerity. If he intended it sarcastically, then it must be said that his powers of sarcasm are becoming as dull as his wit, which by now everyone surveying his recent behavior knows is approaching the dimensions of a depressed area, worthy of federal intervention. But I should not want my word for it to be automatically accepted and would risk a thousand copies of *Rumbles* against a thousand copies of *The Politics of Hope,* to be sent to college libraries, that an impartial jury reading the transcript and listening to the tape recording, would rule that Mr. Schlesinger's sentence was *not* rendered with obvious sarcasm.

And a couple of supplementary observations of my own:

(3) Mr. Schlesinger is perfectly free to change his mind. Indeed, I wish he would change his mind about things much much more often than he does. But he is not free, having changed it or having been caught up in an act of hypocrisy, to go rampaging about making a nuisance of himself, getting lawyers to harass us, and planting the suggestion that either I or Putnam's behaved unconventionally or unethically. Under the circumstances,

(4) Putnam's has decided to bring out the next printing of *Rumbles,* which has already gone to press, without replacing the original jacket copy, and I shall continue to circulate Mr. Schlesinger's quotation until I have from him a letter (a) admitting he said it without sarcasm, (b) admitting I had every right to use it, and (c) requesting me to do him the personal favor of removing it. So long as he tries to get me to drop it under the pressures of Messrs. Greenbaum, Wolff and Ernst, I'll go to the electric chair first and instruct my heirs to put on my tombstone,

Wm. F. "Envy His Rhetoric" Buckley, Jr.

IX. *Manners (Mostly Bad) and Morals*

THE POLITICS OF BEAUTY*

July, 1966

It is a thesis of the literature of protest against the way
physical America is shaping up that external harmony is
necessary for the repose of the soul. I suppose I am not
absolutely certain that this is so, but I do know that it is so
for some people (for instance myself), though not
necessarily for those people who, according to fashion's
book, are the most to be admired in the human race.
These last include the inner-directed types, of whom the
absentminded professor is the most widely caricatured example, who are generally oblivious to external surroundings. And there are the hard intellectuals, whose physical
life is mostly spent inside the cavernous libraries and
whose intellectual life is in the mind, who could not care
less whether one, two, or a dozen trees grow in Brooklyn.
   One's own experience counts greatly. Mine, during my
childhood, was a continuing confrontation with beauty. I
do not know whether I'd have recognized it as such or
even whether I'd have thought back about it as such, except that my father was constantly calling attention to it,
wherever we were—and that was, on account of the
travels to which his work took him, all over the place. He
had lived, after college, in Mexico and intended to settle
there and would have, except that he backed the wrong
revolution, which was easy enough for a political activist
to do since during that period there was almost always an
incumbent revolution. So he left, escorted to the border by

* Reprinted by permission of *Esquire* magazine.

armed guard, in 1921, and took with him the plans for a beautiful house and garden he had just begun to build and on which he had lavished infinite attention. He bought a large house in Sharon, drawn to the little town in northwestern Connecticut for the simple reason of its extraordinary beauty. We went to Paris and Switzerland and London for protracted stays when I was a boy but kept popping back to Sharon, where we settled more or less permanently during the thirties, spending winters in Camden, South Carolina, where my father undertook the rehabilitation of a derelict antebellum house which is surrounded now, the fruit of his diligent supervision, with whole terraces of flowers, red and white and lavender. I remember as a boy my older brothers and sisters giving vent to the underworld amusement because, notwithstanding my father's vigilance, a red azalea had had the nerve to raise its head smack in the middle of a bed of white azaleas, quite against my father's orders, which no vertebrate had ever been known to defy.

But such acts of insubordination were rare even among the flowers, and shrubs, and the trees, which performed prodigies under his direction. In Sharon we lived among many acres of green, on a property called Great Elm, after a tree of noble girth and stature which was reputed to be the largest elm in Connecticut, under whose irenic shade a treaty with the Indians was said to have been concluded shortly before the Revolutionary War. The town itself was—is—an elongated rectangle, with rows of majestic elms going the length of it and extending a mile or more to the south. The Garden Club of Connecticut once classified it, after Litchfield, as the most beautiful town in Connecticut, and it was a source of constant pleasure to my father, who loved it even as he loved the trees on his own property, which he looked after with pride and loving care. The Dutch elm disease struck Sharon before he died, and one of the first casualties was the great elm, and we all knew the pain he experienced on account of its loss because, when the time for fortitude came, as when there was a death or illness in the family, he fell into a preternatural silence, and the decision was made to cut the tree down. But he saved the trunk, which stands even now about twenty feet high, to remind someone, by its enormous waistline, of the splendor of its maturity. All those elms, the whiteness of the town, the coordinated vision, did, I think, communicate something to our lawless brood, indeed so much so that most of my ten brothers and sisters, though it is infinitely inconvenienient for them to do so, continue to live there, and I do not think this is merely a matter of desiring to live in the place where one grew up. For one thing, their background was cosmopolitan; for another, they have, most of them, continued to care very deeply about the elms and the shrubs and the flowers, and the stillness, and the town, which continues to look as though it was hewn out of a single, pleasant dream. They did, I think, come by that repose of the soul, about which we hear more and more, as related to one's surroundings.

During the thirties my mother was active in the Dutchess County Garden Study Club, whose principal effort was to guard the Hudson River against the irruptions of billboarders who had designs on its banks for large and garish announcements of their magical contributions to modern commerce. After an extensive war the Garden Club won, and I remember cheering the victory against Coca-Cola even when I was too young to be permitted to drink it, though I may merely have been acting as echo chamber for my father's enthusiasm. At about the same time, without any notice whatever, all of a sudden a large billboard sprang to life about a mile and a half north of Sharon, interrupting the theretofore uninterrupted stretch of New England landscape that coaxed the tourist up toward the Berkshires. On seeing it, my father was seized with indignation, which he communicated to us at dinner. Activists that my older brothers and sisters were, they promptly volunteered to go out and burn the sign down. My father's allegiances were in conflict. On the one hand, he himself had once been a revolutionary, or rather counter-revolutionary, who, as a young man, undertook nothing less than the replacement of the order of things in all Mexico. On the other hand, he was the conservative who believed in law and order. The dialectic did not yield altogether convincing results: We were to do no such thing. However, he said, if the town of Sharon itself rose in popular uprising against the billboard and marched against it, our sympathies would clearly be on the side of

Sharon, rather than on the side of BBD&O or whoever the villain was.

So, in loose application of the Machiavellian law that insurrections, in order to be justified, must be successful, we were to wait on the day when insurrection galvanized the whole of the population. We sulked at the enforced inactivity, in part because we had an anarchic streak within us, in part because we felt it would be a fine way to demonstrate our admiration for our father to proceed on our own initiative, at our own risk, to do his implicit bidding. As often happens in such situations, we ended up doing the thing halfway and ignobly. Caught up in the post-Depression exuberance of 1939, the owner of the local soda fountain and cigar store abutting the local post office hoisted a spectacular Coca-Cola sign above his building, an unnecessary piece of exhibitionism, considering that there was only one other place in all Sharon to go if you wanted to buy Coca-Cola at the fountain, and we stole there late one night, with mops and a bucket of white paint and streaked the sign into unrecognition, a venture in beautification which we found especially easy to perform, inasmuch as the gentleman in question was the town's premier grouch and, quite coincidentally we supposed, republican lord of all he surveyed. The next day a horrible communal silence fell on the town, as the question was moot whether the omnipotent republican would call in the National Guard to detect the malefactors or whether he would submit to the implicit censure of the community, always assuming the expression had indeed been the community's. He did neither. He merely, within a matter of days, hoisted a fresh sign, whereupon, after a council of war, we reasoned that, unlike Hercules, we were not equipped to cut off Hydra's head. So he won; but a demonstration of sorts had been made, and now I no longer feel I can theoretically defend what I had a hand in doing at age thirteen; but, come to think of it, the sign is no longer there. Neither, on the other hand, is the old republican, though I cannot quite remember whether he went off to his reward having first renounced Coca-Cola.

I am, then, myself committed to the notion that attractive external surroundings can mean a great deal, and to the corollary that something ought to be done about it, just how and just what being, of course, the question. Next in order of consideration is the question: Who knows what is beautiful? Perhaps it boils down to the easier question: Who will decide what is beautiful? That, after all, is merely a matter of political arrangement. The Congress of the United States, for instance, is absolutely in charge of deciding what is beautiful and what isn't in respect to its own quarters. Sam Rayburn was in charge of the Congress of the United States at the time the plans were drawn for a new House Office Building, and so it came about that the sovereign legislature of the United States, representing all the people, devised and constructed a building not merely lacking in beauty, but positively drunk in its featurelessness, $86,000,000 worth of white neoclassical blah. The thing was, presumably, designed by an architect, which therefore raises another question: Is there an expertise in beauty? To which the answer, of course is, yes and no, yes in that some people's eyes are better than other people's; no in the sense that there is continuing disagreement on just whose eyes are operatively better. And this, in turn, makes insufficient the recommendation of Daniel Patrick Moynihan, a very fashionable intellectual who also happens to be very bright, that the architectural "profession" form a lobby. "There wasn't a special interest in America that didn't have a hunk of [the highway] bill except the architects," he observed at one of our regular conferences of disgust over the deteriorating face of America, enjoining the architects to become "a lobby." Why not? The most beautiful buildings in the world are designed by architects. But so are the ugliest buildings in the world, and it isn't that the beautiful buildings are beautiful because they are free of the pressures of the marketplace, though those pressures do figure, often for the worse, in certain types of buildings. Disagreements about architecture—and indeed about all art—are often written about as though they were being fought between the beautiful spirits and the Philistines, which is all very well until the moment comes when with absolute confidence we are asked to distinguish between the two in such a way as is esthetically or politically acceptable. The monster that rises over the Grand Central Building in New York is despised by Norman Mailer and adored by August Heckscher. Heckscher is "in," culturewise; indeed he was

JFK's number one on-duty esthete, and Mailer is concededly erratic; but he is in very steady company in his dislike of the Pan Am Building and, quite apart from that, greatly respected for the occasional jewel that washes in with the flotsam and jetsam that inundates us from his ongoing collision with the world he lives in. The most galvanizing words recently uttered on the matter of saving America the Beautiful came from the President of the United States, whose superb French cook, inherited from JFK, recently resigned in despair after the superordination of a dietitian from Austin, Texas, who ordered him to serve beets with cream on them at affairs of state. Can a man who thus misorders his own kitchen be trusted to design the Acropolis?

It is not safe, in a word, to assume that great and beautiful buildings are automatically what happens when you allocate more money to be spent on great and beautiful buildings—even when you give the money to those among our highest political authorities who bloviate most regularly on the subject of the beautiful life. To say that taste differs is not to concede, to be sure, that all tastes are equally defensible. It is merely to say that the demonstration of the poorer and the better taste is not easy to make, that it often depends not merely on a blackboard demonstration whose at-onceness overwhelms the Philistine, but on a lengthening perspective—the kind of thing which over a period of several hundred years came absolutely to establish that Westminister Abbey and Chartres, both built about the same time, were respectively a catastrophe and a thing so sublime as might have been designed by God Himself. There weren't any art critics in the thirteenth century who attended cathedral openings, but it isn't necessary, in order to make the point, that there should have been. The "finest" available designers and craftsmen were called together at about the same time to construct the two Elysian Cathedrals. They did their best, and there is no reason to believe that a talented designer doing his best doesn't, during the period of his absorption with his fancy, proceed with as much conviction—and as much of a right to his conviction—as the critic. If a well-trained architect can act on a defective impulse, so can a well-trained critic. It is time that gradually erodes the dross, settling the impression and making possible the universal judgment. When Johann Sebastian Bach died, the obituarists acclaimed him as a choir-master and organist and his son Carl Philipp Emanuel as the composer. Obviously this is not an argument against all public buildings. Familiarity breeds contempt, a Cambridge debater argued before the First World War, opposing the maximization of contact between His Majesty's and the Kaiser's subjects. "True," his opponent observed, "but a lack of familiarity breeds nothing at all."

Well, then, if we cannot necessarily expect beautiful buildings to arise from an act of political will, can we hope for better luck from Authority in City Planning? Edward Durell Stone remarks that most of the cities of the world intended to be spectacularly beautiful—Leningrad, Paris, Washington—were designed by the assertion of central authority. Louis Napoleon hired Haussmann to redesign Paris in 1853, and the result was certainly smashing. The czars recognized that the Russian talent was not for visual beauty, so that when St. Petersburg was made, Peter the Great called in a Frenchman, and behold the result. Washington, says Stone, was conceived as a "white city," and even that elementary conceptual commitment gave it what character, what beauty it has. It is a pity that more cities aren't thus conceived—*i.e.*, that there isn't a master planner around, with a first-rate sensitivity for the natural character of the place and the people, to require a kind of loose-footed uniformity, which is nothing more than a respect for harmony. A spontaneous cultural homogeneity is an adequate substitute. It isn't always a master planner who is responsible for beautiful cities. Charleston, South Carolina, has that harmony, and it is a joy forever. On one of its main streets there sits, interrupting the tall white-wood pleasure, a squalid concrete two-story office building in Modern-Austere that looks like a raised cement fill and could only have been built by (a) someone who hated Charleston or (b) by an institute for the blind, intending to interrupt the prevailing reverie so as to compel attention to the plight of the less fortunate. Salamanca, of course, has it to perfection—the special yellow, everywhere, that turns to gold when the sun is on the horizon—and only the anarchist will resent the municipal coordination that made it so.

It is, of course, a tricky business to regulate, in behalf

237

of an overarching esthetic idea, what a man may build on his own plot of land; but even so, I'd be for taking that risk, and, I shall argue, libertarian theory would, I think, accommodate the requirement, provided that titles were devised and exchanged with the impediments clearly prescribed. Thus, the idea is widely accepted that if you buy a lot which is not business-zoned, you may not transact business on that lot, and there are no persuasive squawks, addressed either to the civil liberties unions or to the natural law, to deny the municipality the right to zone. What about the extension of the zoning right to regulate a building's façade? It is a dangerous business, because the doctrine of congruity, fanatically extended, very well might have the effect of discouraging those elegant variations which, expressing a disciplined individuality, sometimes give birth to the flowering of an idea and even to breathtaking mutations. But the rewards of running the danger can be very great, whether in a small town like Litchfield, Connecticut, a medium town like Charleston, or a very large town like Paris. In such towns as these one can walk about and know what it is that Ian Nairn, recoiling from the typical American city, means when he says that although "chaos occasionally is good fun and essential, chaos all the time is just chaos" and, pleading for relief from the "chaos of nonrelation, probably worse in America than anywhere else," reminds us as so many others have done that "townscape depends on two things, relationship and identity"—and promises skeptics that a walk in a properly expressive town "can be as refreshing and exhilarating as Scotch-on-the-rocks after a hot, tiring day."

Having acknowledged that something should be done about the problem, we need to ask what, concretely. What are the theoretical problems, and what are the practical problems? The first have to do with the role of the government; the second, with the capacity of the community to rise to the challenge.

As regards the first, I fear greatly that it is only a matter of time before some President will think to declare war against ugliness. He may very well be a President who couldn't care less about ugliness, but who is desperate for programs by which to confer democratic benefits on his people. When that happens, theoretical arguments will rage, even as, less conspicuously, they rage at this moment—for instance, on the question of what are the rights of the collectivity over the individual. Some hard thought should be given to that problem, and the sooner the better, and herewith a modest and, I hope, heuristic contribution.

The role of our various governments, local, state and federal, ought to remain primarily negative. Governments are as a rule better at reeling off prohibitions than fancying themselves as creative artists. I have mentioned the overarching problem: How is the government going to decide what is beautiful; will the Library of Congress send down a memo on the matter? And second, don't we need to understand that the kind of organic beauty we most greatly need to encourage in our towns and cities can issue only from the genes of the community? Infusions of federal money and federal bureaucrats tend, as Jane Jacobs has amply demonstrated in her book on the life and death of the great American cities, to upset the glandular balances of individual neighborhoods, and the baby is deformed.

In some areas, the federal government has intruded probably forever. One never quite realizes, in retrospect, why the federal government had to get into some of the acts, but so it happened. As regards highway building, for instance, the program arose like Venus from the Cyprian seas, ordaining that henceforth the government would pay 90 percent of the cost of building interstate highways. That, of course, gave the federal government a little leverage, which it sought to exercise, by happy accident, for the common good—by offering a bribe (an extra one-half of 1 percent) to those states which would agree to ban billboards along the banks of the highways. Only seven states have qualified for that subsidy.

The pressure from the billboarders in the other states was overwhelming. They used every weapon, including theory. Now here is something that needs to be done—some first-class theorizing in behalf of the esthetic order. The cynic will doubt that this is of any material importance, and the cynic will be wrong because ours isn't an altogether pragmatical community (if it were, the Commies, for instance, would long since have been exiled, or jailed, or something); it is very much theory-oriented. We brood, and I think it is good that we should do so, over the niceties of such questions as whether the individual has the quote right unquote to post billboards on quote his unquote land. Granted that human beings will produce fancy theoretical justifications at the clink of a nickel. But grant, also, that those justifications are effective weapons and that we have been delinquent in failing to shoot down presumptuous theory with better theory.

It is true that the billboarders survive primarily through political pressures and manipulations. But, draped in theoretical mantle, they seduce a not inconsiderable number of people who are convinced by the private property argument. Robert Moses, who has been fighting the billboards for almost thirty years, tells us it is "dirty fighting, with eye-gouging, rabbit-punching, bone-breaking, mayhem, and no holds barred." At the level to which he refers, nothing will do but the mobilization of the esthetic conscience followed by irresistible political counter-pressure. But meanwhile, the billboarders must be stripped of their theoretical armor. This one oughtn't to be difficult. Other problems are much more difficult, such as those that need to be attacked before we can pave the way for a harmonious architecture. Here the individual can say, with some plausibility, that his is an undisputed right to build a house exactly along the lines of his own potty choosing—on the ground, *tout court,* that he has the sovereign right to define the specifications of his own enjoyment. A very intricate case needs to be developed, wooing public acceptance, to knock down that argument, and I myself believe it can be done. "The quarrel between the individual's right to design his own home and the neighborhood's right to architectural unity can only be solved," a philosophic friend of mine has argued, "by an existential dialectic. If the community desires architectural harmony, it must win the argument by the exercise of power."

But the billboarders, I should think, are more readily disrobed. The display of hortatory commercial slogans is not covered by the same set of arguments used by the anarchical housebuilder—because the billboards are manifestly not directed at himself, but rather at others who pass by. As such the billboards are acts of aggres-

240

sion—like skywriting—against which the public is entitled, as a matter of privacy, to be protected. If a homeowner desires to construct a huge Coca-Cola sign facing his own homestead rather than the public highway, in order to remind him, every time he looks out his window, that the time has come to pause and be refreshed, he certainly should be left free to do so. But if he wants to face the sign towards us, that is something else, and the big name libertarian theorists should go to work demolishing the billboarders' abuse of the argument of private property.

As regards the maintenance of the natural beauty of great parts of the nation, the weight of the argument is, once again, on the side of the public. The present Secretary of the Interior Department, Stewart Udall, is, I think it is fair to say, as aggressive a champion of the necessity to maintain oases of natural beauty as anyone who ever held high federal office. Sometimes, to be sure, he does leave the impression that he resents any private dwelling at all, on the ground that it is liable to get in the way of a meandering buffalo. But his occasional excesses, unlike those of some of his own coadjutors, are tolerable in an age that very much needs to be reminded of the factor of beauty, natural and man-made. Mr. Udall has launched a great land-acquisition program, attempting to husband the natural parks to the use of the public. I must depart from the company of those conservatives who are always resenting the acreage owned by the government, always provided said government does not go hog-wild, and that the great reservations continue—as some of the city parks for instance do not—to be dedicated to the enjoyment of the public (42,500,000 people visited one or another of our natural parks during the last year, which suggests Udall must be doing something right). The withholding of land, to be retained in its supernal beauty, is a legitimate function of government, as Adam Smith was among the first to observe.

I would greatly welcome an exhaustive theoretical justification of an extension of the present zoning ideas. As they stand, they are, after all, widely accepted. Most towns and cities, as I have noted, have zoning laws, and some—for instance, New York City—use the power to discourage, for instance, the obnoxious ziggurat, which with its mechanical terraces has defaced so many buildings. But Mrs. Jane Jacobs has pointed out that the mere acquisition of power is not by any means a solution to the problem. New York City conferred powers on itself beginning in 1916 and subsequently did much, by the use of those powers, to damage the potential of New York for beauty. Circumspect use of power is supremely important, with a heavy respect for those domiciliary prejudices which are indispensable to beauty, preserving their individuation without which relationships are utterly lifeless. The practical problem with cities is infinitely complex, in large part because of the transient population—it takes awhile before an individual is incorporated into a city. Urbanization has greatly increased the difficulties. Since 1945 our cities have grown hardly at all—but the suburban communities have increased in size by almost 70 percent. The result has been to leave the cities at the mercy of the awful urban renewal programs.

Still, progress can be made, block by block, area by area, and the theoretical problems having been chased at least to the point where a respectful and considerate attention for theoretical differences is exhausted, the question will finally arise—my friend's existential dialectic: Will we, or won't we, do somethng about it? And at this point one needs, in a democratic society, to depend on the community.

The community. It is cursed by indifference. That indifference is perhaps exaggerated, but it is most certainly there. "Indifference," sighs Herbert Read, "is endemic . . . a disease which has spread through our whole civilization, and which is a symptom of a lowered vitality. The sensibilities are dulled and the average human being no longer cares to feel the keen edge of life, to have freshness in vision or zest and savor in the senses." Mr. Read is very largely correct, but it is demoralizing to take his conclusions as an absolute judgment on the current state of mind, because if one does, one faces a dilemma. It is, very simply, that the only way to do anything about the problem of natural beauty and architectural harmony is to do so athwart the people's indifference—indeed, by extension, athwart their will.

At this point a word should be said about the Very

Gloomy. The point can be made, as with Mr. Udall, that their exaggerations are galvanizing. But the opposite point can also be made, that their gloom is so total as to invoke not the impulse to reform, but the impulse to despair.

Herewith Miss Marya Mannes on her especial irk:

"Cans. Beer cans. Glinting on the verges of a million miles of roadways, lying in scrub, grass, dirt, leaves, sand, mud, but never hidden. Piels, Rheingold, Ballantine, Schaefer, Schlitz, shining in the sun or picked by the moon or the beams of headlights at night; washed by rain or flattened by wheels, but never dulled, never buried, never destroyed. Here is the mark of the savages, the testament of wasters, the stain of prosperity." And her climax: "Slowly the wasters and despoilers are impoverishing our land, our nature, and our beauty, so that there will not be one beach, one hill, one lane, one meadow, one forest free from the debris of man and the stigma of his improvidence."

Now: does that kind of thing make you want to give up beer cans, or does it make you wonder whether Miss Mannes has, as regards beer cans, the same kind of problem that the fellow had who went to the psychiatrist and kept brushing the mosquitoes off his arms and legs?

Or there is the crushèd poet, an anonymous employee of the Department of the Interior, who comes up with the grisliest metaphor of the season in, no less, an official publication of DepInt:

"The shift of our Nation from a predominantly rural to an urban population has made a sinister sandwich of much of our land, buttering our soil with concrete and asphalt, piling people on people, and then hanging a pall of polluted air over all."

And, not to be outdone by Miss Mannes, he reaches his own immolation: "If current trends continue unchecked, in another generation a trash pile or piece of junk will be within a stone's throw of any person standing anywhere on the American continent." Surely before that happens, the hungry cosmos will have gulped down the sinister sandwich and eliminated all our worries?

Another kind of criticism, more subtle but equally enervating, is *el fastidioso*'s, the kind of man who, because Shakespeare ever wrote, can't bring himself to see anything good in John Cheever; can't listen to an Appalachian folk song because the organ tones of Johann Sebastian Bach crowd his ear. Listen to Edward Durell Stone:

"Compared with us, the Italians are impoverished. They hold body and soul together with a few strands of spaghetti and are not pampered by creature comforts. But you hear opera on every street corner and people walk among fabulous things of beauty. Verdi, Titian, Michelangelo are spoken of with reverence by the taxi drivers and the waiters. They are more concerned with the well-being of the spirit than with material well-being. I once flew from Venice to Akron, Ohio, and when I landed and looked about me, I decided that the so-called poor people of Italy were a lot better off." Ho-hum. The so-called poor people of Italy happen to be very poor indeed, and a lot of them express their reverence for life by voting the Communist ticket at election time and prefer the Beatles to Verdi. And anyway, genius is genius precisely because it is not normative, but unique. To compare Venice to Akron is not only stupid, but outrageously irrelevant, the cant millenniarism which makes so many of our cultural critics, like so many of our politics critics, so very profoundly boring.*

In fact, things can be done; in fact, things are being done. Not nearly enough, but enough to permit, to admit, hope.

In Southern California a group of merchants and housewives, unsubsidized by the federal government and, I daresay, unread in Miss Mannes or in the literature of the Department of the Interior, have undertaken a program—they call it Los Angeles Beautiful, and let us not raise our noses; what would *you* call it?—which is doing what it can, where it can. "When we started out," the ex-

* Another doomsayer, with however restraint in his voice: "For some of our mountains at present will only support trees, but not so very long ago trees fit for the roofs of vast buildings were felled there and the rafters are still in existence. There were also many other lofty cultivated trees which provided unlimited fodder for beasts. Besides, the soil got the benefit of the yearly 'water from Zeus,' which was not lost, as it is today, by running off a barren ground to the sea." (Plato, on the despoliation of Attica.)

244

ecutive director, Fred Chase, commented to a *Newsweek* reporter, "my old friends thought I'd changed my sex or something. But we've shown everybody." The program is being emulated in more than two hundred Southern Californian communities.

" 'Plant-a-tree,' " *Newsweek* reports, is amont LAB's projects. "Converting abandoned trolley-car strips into landscaped traffic islands, sponsoring horticultural experiments to determine which plants have the highest resistance to auto-exhaust fumes; and promoting a 'plant-a-tree' campaign in the downtown area. A neighboring group, the Pasadena Beautiful Foundation, recently helped remove all but a few billboards from the main thoroughfares and persuaded the city to adopt 'sight-nuisance' and sign-control ordinances." Individuals and private associations can begin the work, and then enthusiasm can catch on.

At a formal level, it is not easy to devise the means by which to inculcate the appreciation of beauty. To some it comes naturally; to others it is intellectually received. I remember with great affection a chauffeur-companion of my childhood, a gentleman refugee from Russia—he was, of course, a nobleman, full of flossy ancestry, and married to Tolstoi's niece—who, finding himself impoverished in Paris between the wars, took a job as a bus driver on the condition that he be assigned the route to Chartres, so that he might adore it every day. How do you create such men as a class? As a nation? Nobody knows. I do believe that it is correct to make the effort—*i.e.,* not to leave such matters to fate. If I were a teacher I do not know what techniques I would use, beyond attempting to stimulate a mere interest in the question. Perhaps I would try showing the children slides of various buildings, and asking, "is this ugly? Is this beautiful?" and bringing down a cane on the knuckles of the blockhead who grunted the wrong answer. I would do so with due recognition of the hazard of my undertaking, because my own knuckles are constantly rapped, as, for instance, when I go see some of the work of our most prestigious artists and architects. . . . Still, I would take the risk, in behalf of the idea that a regard for beauty, an inquisitiveness about it, can be communicated, even as I learned about it merely by sensing

245

the pleasure in my father's soul as he walked among his azaleas or about the streets of the beautiful villages and cities of the world.

DECISION MAKING FOR CHRIST

February 7, 1967

Sociologists have a way of laboriously discovering a truism and then, having done so, going on to encourage, oh, so soft-spokenly, mischievous conclusions of a moral nature. A dozen years ago a humorless sexologist discovered at age sixty something less than Fanny Hill knew at eighteen, but that discovery he more or less parlayed, or at least allowed to be parlayed, into a sort of philosophy not merely of sex, but of life—Everybody Does It; therefore, it's okay.

Comes another sociologist who surfaced a few days ago at Arizona State University with the discovery that it is the unusual student who is religiously inclined in our secular culture. So what else is new? But Dr. Frederick L. Whitam uses certain key words of derogatory flavor from which we are subtly invited to conclude that those who are religiously minded are not so much unusual in the admirable sense as in the sort of queer sense. Dr. Whitam sent questionnaires to 1,600 young people who, as teenagers six years ago, made "decisions for Christ" at Billy Graham's Crusade in New York City. Analyzing the 290 returns, Dr. Whitam concludes that "the youths, particularly the boys, tended to be somewhat indifferent to social life and athletics."

Well, is there anything wrong with being indifferent to social life? Einstein was, and so was William Faulkner, and we're not against Einstein or Faulkner, are we? And surely those who are indifferent to athletics are okay, are they not? Wasn't that what Holden Caulfield proved to an entire generation of intellectuals?

But comes now the jargon. Says Dr. Whitam: Such students had "status problems"—and that, of course, in the public psychology clinches it. Anyone who has status problems probably has Oedipus complexes or life adjustment problems, and certainly isn't 4-H. "In making decisions for Christ at crusades, teenagers are setting themselves up in direct opposition to the peer group of which they are a part. A group emphasizing good times, cars, and liberal views on sex. . . . The grand crusades [note once again the loaded rhetoric. Crusades are out of style, and the adjective "grand" makes them especially so] . . . seem to attract kids on the fringe ["fringe" as in "lunatic fringe"—you know] of things—kids who aren't really 'in' with the crowd. In making decisions, they accept a set of values quite contradictory to that shared by their peer groups."

God, who is not in the peer group either, is a sort of negative symbol anyway. Thus, the decision makers are advocates of "adherence to don'ts—don't drink, don't smoke, don't engage in pre-marital intercourse. By subscribing to this list of don'ts they run counterclockwise to the hedonistic philosophy of their friends." Here is a minor rhetorical slip, since "hedonistic" sounds sort of like Nero and maybe even Caligula, though who knows, if Nero were around these days, say as Emperor of Hanoi, there'd be a lot of people saying, "Who are we to criticize Nero?" And, indeed, maybe Nero is the wave of the future. The likelihood of that is greater in proportion as there are fewer decisions taken for Christ.

It is an interesting aspect of the whole thing that if the identical poll had been taken of young people who enter the Peace Corps, it is probable that the results would have been much the same; the poll would have shown that those who enter the Peace Corps are not totally well adjusted to the hedonistic imperatives of the day, that they too care less for social life and athletics than for other things. But the trouble with loosing a psychological critique of the Peace Corps of the type that would tend to point invidiously at its members is that to do so would be to cast aspersions upon the founder of that order, John F. Kennedy, and that is to commit a sacrilege. If only Mr. Kennedy had founded Christianity, one could safely make decisions at Mr. Graham's rallies, without fear of aspersion by the social scientists.

JOHN LENNON'S *GAFFE*

August 18, 1966

John Lennon, O.B.E., the concert master of the Beatles, has got himself and his cartel into very serious difficulty which, in economic terms, can only reaffirm the international pessimism about the fate of the British pound. Scores upon scores of radio stations and dozens upon dozens of disc jockeys have declared at least a temporary embargo on the Beatles. Mr. Lennon's offense was to say that "the Beatles are more popular than Jesus." The reaction appears to be based on the assumption that Mr. Lennon was comparing not the relative popularity of himself and Jesus, but their related virtues. And this is, of course, to miscomprehend what Mr. Lennon said, which was certainly untactful and indubitably accurate.

There are, one supposes, a few—Christians?—who clamor for the crucifixion, *mutatis mutandis,* of the Beatles; but they are a minority. I myself ventured two years ago in this space to write critically of, not the Beatles, but the Beatles' "music," and received 100 times as many letters in protest as I have ever received before or since. More numerous, by far, one infers from Holy Writ, than the protests addressed 2,000 years ago to the executioners of Our Blessed Lord.

Mr. Lennon's rather coarse ejaculation was, to be sure, the plain truth, hardly shocking to students of the Bible, who know the relative attractions of Mammon over God. Secular deities always have it over just plain Deity, and one would think that inasmuch as the Bible confronts this commonplace with some fortitude, so might the disc jockeys even in the Bible Belt. Surely if someone were to observe that John F. Kennedy is more "popular" than St. Paul, an embargo would not be imposed on the literature of Kennedy hagiolatry? It is hardly anyone's fault, save possibly God's own, that we are so constructed as to worship more willingly at the altar of the secular divinity than at that of the Real Article.

The question of taste, of course, arises. Mr. Lennon's comparison of the divine and the profane suggested a certain self-elevation. It was this public shock that unques-

248

tionably drove the Beatles into a prolonged conference with their public relations experts, from whose deliberations emerged Mr. Lennon's dumbfounding exegesis of what-it-was-he-actually-meant.

At a press conference in Chicago he explained to the press, of course, he had not, of course, intended, of course, to compare himself with Christ. He had merely ventured a historical truism. And then he added: "Of course it is true that Christianity is on the wane." Now this, it appears to me, was even more gratuitous than the original observation. It is true that Christianity is on the wane. It is also true that the world is on the wane. And if Mr. Lennon ventures to project an observation in which both he and Christ are involved to another observation in which they are both still involved, to the damage of the latter rather than the former, it is only fair game to speculate on whether the decline of the one might not somehow or other be related to the advancement of the other. That is to say, the Beatles, who have more lavishly nourished their flock than ever the profiteers of Lourdes nourished the pilgrims to that sacred shrine, are, however inadvertently, self-anointed substitutes for rather more meaningful objects of adulation.

The Beatles do not, let us recall, peddle merely their records. They sit still for columns, articles, magazines, books, encyclopedias, which prey on the reserves of veneration in young people, which in healthier ages would be directed at objects more venerable than the Beatles. After my last foray in sacrilege, I engaged in a correspondence with a young lady who finally sent me, after a half dozen letters and an amorous epistolary reconciliation, a registered letter at Christmas. It contained a square inch, her affectionate note breathlessly advised me, of a bed sheet on which one of the Beatles had slept in San Francisco while there to commit nonmusic, and it was exactly one-half of her most treasured possession, which she had secured at a semipublic auction conducted no doubt by an enterprising publican at a local hotel. Of course, I acknowledged the gift with profuse exclamations of gratitude and indeed bartered it to seduce the eternal servility of a beloved ten-year-old niece. But it is, I judge, not altogether stuffy to observe that someone who remarks on the diminution of Christianity ought probably to go on to evaluate the suitability of some of Christianity's successors to fill the void. No doubt poor Mr. Lennon wishes at this point that he had never opened his mouth except to emit music, or rather nonmusic, but now that he has done so, one can only ask for more, more, more.

THE REPEAL OF THE HOMOSEXUAL LAWS

March 3, 1966

The House of Commons is about to repeal the old "Oscar Wilde" law, and there is all kind of hypocritical talk about the triumph of truly Christian attitudes concerning the question of homosexuality. Truly Christian in the sense that Christian lawmakers, by consenting to repeal the old antihomosexuality act, are acknowledging the division of responsibility between church and state. The argument is that it is the church's unique responsibility to govern the moral order, the state's to concern itself with the civil order, and that the relationship between the two is, of course, not identical, though the lines do cross. Murder is both a moral and a civil affront. Homosexuality between consenting adults, it is argued, is not: It is merely a moral affront.

It is that hypocrisy which has annoyed the prestigious English editor with my favorite name this side of the *Pickwick Papers,* Peregrine Worsthorne. He believes that the old law should be repealed, because it is ineffective, because it encourages licentious methods of detection by police (peepholing, etc.), and because the opportunities for blackmail are so great.

But, Mr. Worsthorne observes, the real reason why the House of Commons is finally repealing the law is not that it confidently hopes "that the Almighty will do a better job than the Director of Public Prosecutions" in punishing malefactors. The reason why the law is being changed is that homosexuality has ceased to shock. Mr. Worsthorne gave as an example a reference in the course of the debates in Commons to homosexuality as an "unnatural vice." "The House quite noticeably stiffened with embarrassment, rather as if some old-fashioned member had referred to Great Britian's 'imperial mission.' Plain homosexuality is no longer thought of as 'unnatural vice.'

The whole idea of sex having anything to do with sin is alien and slightly comical."

In New York the legislature is, depending on how you look at it, either ahead or behind the Mother of Parliaments, in that it recently refused to repeal either the antihomosexuality law or the antiadultery law, but certainly ahead on the question of frankness. One legislator, during the heated debate in Albany last year, when asked why he favored repealing the adultery laws but not the homosexuality laws replied: "After all, there are more of us than there are of them."

So far. According to any number of reports, the rise in the homosexual population is enormous. And, inevitably, there is a new morality that comes in to justify and even to honor this abnormality. Theologians who talk about "unselfish love" as the sole criterion have got on the bandwagon. "Homosexuality permits a rise to a higher level of conscience for one who cannot experience sexual love with one of the opposite sex," one minister writes. And from a philosopher: "The merits and demerits of sexual union rest properly upon personal rights and values, not only natural processes. We human beings are psychosexual creatures. Our spiritual and moral relationships, our responses to others, are most complete and genuine when they are voluntary surrenders and mutual commitments, including physical as well as spiritual comradeship. It is for this reason that we regard sexual love as good, not for any reason of naturalistic utility or physiological mysticism. Therefore, when there is good and sufficient cause to eliminate the possibility of reproduction against our rational will, in order responsibly to fulfill the obligations of love, we are more than justified morally in doing so."

The appeal of such arguments explains why the honorable gentlemen in the House of Commons are acting as they do—not because the arguments against the homosexuality law are actually persuasive, which they are. It is another historical example of the capacity of the species to generate a morality to keep the conscience easy. It is, however, in an ironic way, a tribute to the endurability of the conscience, that it should always insist on a means of justifying itself and that it should continue to have the power to compel hypocrisy.

251

A PLAYBOY'S PHILOSOPHY

October 1, 1966

I bring the news, which I had from Hugh Hefner's own lips, that the last issue of *Playboy* magazine sold 4,000,000 copies and ran $2,000,000 worth of advertisements, a phenomenal achievement; indeed, it is just possible that Mr. Hefner is making more money from *Playboy* and related enterprises than any other publisher in the country, at least from a single magazine.

Mr. Hefner's *Playboy* is most widely known for the raciness of its prose and the total exposure of the female form. It is more than that, Mr. Hefner insists—and many agree, including professors and ministers and sociologists. It is a movement of sorts, and its bible is an apparently endless series, published monthly by Mr. Hefner, entitled "The *Playboy* Philosophy," the key insight of which is that "a man's morality, like his religion, is a personal affair best left to his own conscience." The phrase sounds harmless enough, and the tendency is to cluck-cluck one's agreement to it.

The trouble with Hefner's law is that society is composed of nothing more than a great number of individuals, and if each man's morality is defined merely to suit himself, then everyone will endure the consequences of the individual's autonomously defined ethics. Mr. Hefner's philosophy notwithstanding, there *is* such a thing as the public morality, and that morality has throughout civilized history been primarily sustained by religion.

The so-called sexual revolution, of which *Playboy* is the slickest harbinger, asks in effect that sanctions be removed against what used to be known as "illicit sexual behavior." The *Playboy* group correctly skewers the conflicting and vague laws that lie in the dusty statute books of the individual states, and a case could be made, let us say for removing criminal sanctions against homosexuality between consenting adults. But the modernists want to go further and, in effect, remove the moral sanctions against such behavior—and that is something else again.

All that is good is not embodied in the law, and all that is evil is not proscribed by the law. A well-disciplined society needs few laws, but it needs strong mores. And the kind of solipsism that is encouraged by the sexual revolution goes further by far than to encourage a loosening of the laws. It encourages the loosening of public attitudes.

How Mr. Hefner shrinks from the consequences of his own position, though he is quick to insist that he does not, that a general moral breakdown would not necessarily follow upon the acceptance of the *Playboy* philosophy.

I am struck by a recent book, advertised in the *New York Review of Books,* called *The Erotic Minorities.* It is a plea, written by a Swedish doctor and introduced by the same kind of argumentation used by Mr. Hefner, for total sexual permissiveness. It is, in the publisher's words, "A Bill of Rights for erotic liberation of the 'sexually different.' " Note the stolen base—"sexually different" is put in quotation marks to suggest that what we now think of as "sexually different" is really rather arbitrary, a hangover from old and useless Puritanical codes that presume to suggest there are right and wrong ways of making sex. The book lists some of the sexually different categories and suggests that provisions be made, if necessary at government expense, to provide them the means for their gratification. My favorite category is ". . . the necrophiles, who require a corpse as the object of their passion."

If my eyes do not deceive me, and alas they do not seem to, it is the insight of Dr. Ullerstam that laws against necrophilia should be repealed and that necrophiles should be permitted, indeed encouraged, to sate their appetites as best they can. Indeed, says the doctor, we need "mobile brothels" to provide for the sexually different.

Professor Benjamin DeMott of Amherst has said that the *Playboy* philosophy is "the whole man reduced to his private parts." I do believe that he misses the larger point of the philosophy, which is not so much a call to total lubricity as it is a renewal of the old personal Utilitarianism of John Stuart Mill and his apostles, carried to anarchical lengths. It is a theory of ethics, by the way, to which such modern "conservatives" as Ayn Rand seem fully to subscribe. Its principal deficiency, I mean other than in the eyes of the God to whom increasingly infrequent references are made, is its neglect of the social reality.

253

John cannot behave exactly as he desires, because he will inevitably affect James, not to say Jane, if those desires are not contained by reference to the great prescriptions of human conduct which are the most valuable part of the national patrimony.

THE CASE OF THE UNFETTERED PORNOGRAPHER

October 17, 1967

I recently met Mayor Samuel Yorty of Los Angeles, and having found him attractive and decent, I thought a few weeks later to take a problem to him directly, and so I wrote:

"Dear Mayor Yorty:

" . . . I enclose an envelope from a bunch of pornographers who hide out in your fair city. Some while ago they got the name of my fourteen-year-old son to whom they now send, on an average of once a week, an invitation to share in their perversions. From time to time they piously announce that anyone who wants his name removed from their lists may effect this by simply writing to them enclosing the addressographed dick strip. I have done this several times, but, of course, they continue to send their literature.

"Would you do me the favor of putting the gentleman in jail? Or, failing that, giving him a poke in the nose? Or, failing that, advising me when and where I might administer that poke without being declared unconstitutional? Yours cordially . . ."

The mayor referred the matter to his incisive and able assistant, Captain H. A. Nelson, of the Administrative Vice Division of the City of Los Angeles, from whom I have received a most revealing communication, to wit:

" . . . The pornography unit of this Division is fully aware of the company and its owner Dale Packer Ewing.

"Ewing was arrested on September 21, 1966, and charged with 311.2 of the California Penal Code (Distributing Obscene Matter), to wit, bondage books. He was again arrested on April 20, 1967, and charged with 311.2 P.C. (Sale of Obscene Matter), to wit, a bondage-

254

flagellation movie involving five nude females, titled 'Five Red Butts.' Neither of these two pending cases have come to trial due to legal delays as a result of the defense attorney motions.

"Ewing's criminal record also includes statutory rape, grand theft (2), traffic violation warrants (4), narcotics (2), and possession of counterfeit and fraudulent documents. He is thirty years of age and is compiling quite a background for himself, as well as a small fortune in his mail order business.

"We regret that your son is being exposed to this type of unsolicited matter through the mail. We coordinate our investigations with the Postal Inspectors who are also aware of Ewing's activities. Unfortunately, under existing laws within which we must work, we are unable to curtail Ewing's mailings. You may be assured that we will continue our efforts in prosecution whenever we can prove a violation of the law.

"We cannot administer the poke in the nose for you, but Ewing's whereabouts are known to us, if you wish them the next time you are in the Los Angeles area."

It is obvious that Los Angeles needs one additional red butt; however, it is dismaying that the Supreme Court appears to have left the disciplining of Mr. Ewing to the free enterprise system. The state courts are listless against the likes of Mr. Ewing. True, last May the Court overturned three state pornography convictions. But the same majority authorized convictions by the state if either of the following three circumstances applied:

(1) If the state statute showed "a specific and limited concern for juveniles" (that would apply in the case of a fourteen-year-old boy).

(2) If it involved an assault on individual privacy "in a manner so obtrusive as to make it impossible for an unwilling individual to avoid exposure to it" (that would apply in the case of a mailed communication, the opening of which is impossible to avoid).

Or (3) If there is evidence of "pandering" in the "context of prurience not science" (the mailed literature is conclusive here. Science not being a dirty work, Mr. Ewing has probably never heard of it).

Only one count is necessary, but all three counts would

appear to apply, which point I respectfully commend to the attention of the prosecutors of Los Angeles, if only to spare them a rise in cases of assault and battery.

THE WEED

January 21, 1964

Smoking. What do we want the government to do about it?

Suppose we argue by analogy and ask: What ought the government to do about alcohol? I can, without even trying, whip up a sentence or two about alcohol that would earn me honorary membership in the Anti-Saloon League. Watch: There are (the figures are improvised, because I do not have the stomach to ring up Alcoholics Anonymous to have them cross my statistical *t*'s or dot the *i*'s) 5,000,000 American alcoholics; several thousand deaths per year from biological failures whose proximate cause is alcoholism; 100,000 divorces and 200,000 broken homes per year that result from alcoholic excess; several hundred thousand children traumatized by a childhood spent with alcoholic parents; $50 billion per year lost to the economy as the result of the diminished productivity of men and women who drink too much; 75,000 serious crimes per year committed under the licentious influence of alcohol . . . enough? But it all is true, and the government does practically nothing about the sale or distribution of liquor.

Once upon a time it tried to do something, and we know all about the miserable failure of the experiment and the damage it did to the prestige of the law. Granted there is a minority opinion that continues to believe the contrary—and not all who hold it are teetotalers by any means. Henry Mencken used to say that a sizable number of Kansans would continue to vote dry every election day so long as they could stagger to the polls and locate the right lever.

While we are at it, we know as an established fact that obesity is a great killer. The doctor who cured Dwight Eisenhower after his awesome heart attack and whose word on the subject has, I am told, influenced Lyndon Johnson—who also came to the brink because of an un-

256

steady heart—he said flatly that there are three basic rules for longevity. One must not smoke cigarettes, one must exercise one's body, and one must not gain weight after the age of twenty-five. The latter is the most important of the three, according to settled medical testimony.

What then should the government do? Have the census takers weigh us in, like prizefighters, and commit offenders to Main Chance, until the avoirdupois melts away? Along, of course, with extra subsidies for farmers, to compensate them for those of their products that go unconsumed as the result of the program?

We speak nonsense, of course. Yes, Of course. Yes. . . . But we are left feeling a great void, because we are nowadays trained to believe that the government is charged with all matters that deal with the common health. With the common everything, let us face it, and I for one do not doubt that except for the fact that the majority of us are sinners, as regards smoking, as regards alcohol, as regards cholesterol, as regards layer cakes, and apostles of central authority would be calling on the government to do just that—tell us how much, or whether, we can smoke, drink, eat. But let's face it, a political party that takes on all the smokers in this country or all the drinkers will die, if not a more hideous death than those of us who will succumb to lung cancer or cirrhosis of the liver, a much speedier one. We would be entitled to look such a political party in the eye and say to it what one of Rabelais' besotted characters said to his censorious physician: "Forsooth, sir, I do believe I know more old drunkards than I do old doctors."

I do not mean to make light of the subject. My wife is an inveterate cigarette smoker. Need I say more? I suggest only that the government cannot, for reasons that go to the womb of freedom, do anything, anything at all, about smoking. I would not endorse a law requiring the cigarette companies to advertise the dangers of smoking. But I would consider it consistent with the laws of a free society to hold that any company that declined to specify the known dangers of the use of its product become liable to damage actions by victims. But the courts should then hold immune from prosecution those tobacco companies that emblazon, on every pack of cigarettes, the warning:

SMOKING CAN CAUSE LUNG CANCER. SMOKE AT YOUR OWN RISK. From there on, it's up to the individual. It pays to remind ourselves that the most important things of all are up to the individual, who can opt, after all, for heaven or hell. That is the way the rules were written well before the Surgeon General's report.

RESPECTING PRIVACY

April 29, 1965

The current issue of a mass magazine offers, for a mere $18, to send you a little ("Weighs only 4 lbs.!") device that looks like a miniature radar antenna and guarantees to bring to your ear private conversations being held a full 500 yards ("Five times the length of a football field!") away. And wait a minute, lest you spend the full measure of your delight at the mere prospect of being able to eavesdrop: There is a jack behind the instrument into which you can plug your tape machine so as to be able to record said conversations and play them back ("Be the life of the party!") to your friends! Not bad, is it? For a mere $18 you can violate the privacy of anybody within five football fields' distance of you and arrange to preserve that violation forever on magnetic tape.

And this, of course, is only one of a number of gadgets being assembled for the wars against privacy. The little microphone I have in mind is not yet being offered for sale to anyone, over twenty-one or under, but it does, we know from testimony before a Congressional committee, exist and no doubt will be on the market soon: a mike so small that it will fit inside the olive you plunk into the mark's martini. It was not made clear what happens in the event the mark decides to swallow the olive. Presumably you would then be able to record all the emunctory noises of the body processes. That contingency is not spoken of. Presumably you will not want to spy on anyone so uncouth as to swallow the olives that go into martinis.

And, of course, we have known for years about telephone bugging devices. Slightly technical, these: It takes at least a half hour's instruction to learn to install then, an intellectual labor most snoopers would not desire to subject themselves to. But there are those who do know how

258

to handle them, and we are told it is as easy as can be to rig the little bugs up and stow them away someplace where they can sit day after day and record everything you have to say, to your wife, to your neighbor, to your partner, to your doctor, to your priest. What fun!!!

Conservatives are presumptively opposed to the passage of new laws telling people they can't do things. But here is a classic situation where the affirmation of an individual's right overpowers the presumption against the passage of new laws and, indeed, dictates their passage. More and more it becomes plain that privacy is the key to liberty. Privacy considered in the larger sense, as the right, not only to insulate yourself against the importunities of a bustling, hustling order, but to preserve to yourself the ground within which to maneuver.

How shrewd the man who observed that Sigmund Freud did more to deprive people of their privacy than any man who ever lived! How? By popularizing a set of categories of disturbed behavior into which we tend to slot people whose syndromes we vaguely recognize, inviting ourselves to ignore the infinitely various characters of individual human beings. Our psychologized, anthropologized concern for other people tends to be skin-deep, to be a manifestation of our concern for ourselves. We give ourselves the illusion of understanding other people's illusions, projections of our own self-pity and self-absorption. "Tiresias," Professor Hugh Kenner has written, referring to the man who, for seeing things he shouldn't have seen, was changed into a woman for one year by an angry god and thereafter has served as the symbol of the insider's knowledge of the other sex, of other people, is "he who has lost the sense of other people as inviolably other." The fact that we cannot ever really know other people is merely one of several ways by which we reason to the necessity of their privacy: their right to inviolability against any effort by others to intrude, uninvited, into their private world. So far have we come from privacy that we consider as perfectly routine instruments of amusement the paraphernalia for assaulting the innermost thoughts of *other* people.

Let us, then, have yet another law. Rather, fifty state laws (why a federal law?), forbidding the sale or purchase or ownership of antiprivacy devices, with a penalty attached that will guarantee to any miscreant user thereof the privacy of a jail cell for a couple of months. Meanwhile, if you desire private conversations, you will apparently have to walk out into the woods six football fields away from any house with $18 to spare and a young Tiresian in residence.

THE POLITICS OF TRUMAN CAPOTE'S BALL *

December, 1967

The vote on the affair was pretty much unanimous. There was one guest, a banker—according to the commentator—who left early. He muttered that he had never before attended a party at which there were so many intellectuals and, one gathers, would not, eyes open, do so again. Of course, there are lots of possibilities to explain the fermentation of that sour grape. One of them is that it was all in the imagining of a writer who reached out for a little cream of tartar to stir into her story: Anonymous people are so very, very useful: ("One observer, a close friend of Mr. Capote, noted that . . ."). Another possibility is that the banker had ridden up in the elevator with John Kenneth Galbraith and that Mr. Galbraith asked him why in the hell interest rates were so high. But, that, too, is inherently implausible: The Galbraiths, and indeed most intellectuals, or at least most of the intellectuals who would have been invited to *that* party, would consider such a question vulgar. In the new industrial state interest rates sort of set themselves, everybody in the business community is everybody else's prisoner, and it is hardly the doing of individual bankers that the interest rates are high. On the other hand, Galbraith *is* a tease, and some bankers *don't* tease lightly; so maybe this one was there, *did* go up in the elevator, *was* offended, and *did* go home muttering about the overpopulation of intellectuals at Truman Capote's party.

And then, of course, a third possibility (actually, the possibilities are endless). Maybe the banker found himself seated next to a dumb blonde and figured she must have

---

* Reprinted by permission of *Esquire* magazine.

been an intellectual, else why was she there, inasmuch as everyone there was said to have been a personal friend of the intellectual and artistic Truman Capote? But in order to play with that explanation, it becomes necessary to ask how come the banker (that square) got into the Plaza Hotel in the first place? Surely no friend of Truman Capote would (a) object to intellectuals or (b) expect that out of the mouths of statuesque blondes stock market tips cascade.

And on and on, and the likelihood is ever likelier that the banker didn't pull out cantankerously or that, if he did, he had an ulcer or something. Because by everyone else's reckoning, private and public, the party was a smashing affair, so much so that here we are a year after the 500 met at the Plaza as guests of Truman Capote, and very bright editors of very bright national magazines are wanting more copy about a subject—yesterday's party—which doesn't generally sustain the curiosity for more than a day or two. What happened on November 28, 1966, at the Plaza Hotel?

The reviews—setting aside the anonymous banker —were raves, sure enough. CAPOTE'S BLACK AND WHITE BALL: "THE MOST EXQUISITE OF SPEC-TATOR SPORTS." That was the *Times'* headline, and the quotation was from Mrs. Alice Roosevelt Long-worth, a surviving daughter of President Theodore Roosevelt; indeed, she was married at the White House and, at the age eighty-three, is thought to be qualified to judge, from a long perspective for that sort of thing, which social affairs are truly classy, and her enthusiasm about Capote's was, as we have seen, unconfined. And then a few days later the New York *Times,* apparently judging that the affair was of more than ephemeral interest, did yet another story, this one quoting the producer David Merrick, who tends to reserve his raves for his own productions, to the effect that Capote's ball was such a stand-out affair that he, Merrick, was decided to give another such a thing himself in the near future, presumably at Radio City Music Hall, before a packed audience. "What a wonderful thing," said Mr. Merrick, "to have a party not for any reason. It was always shimmering. It was never still, nor was there a static moment. I guess you'd call this a rave review." I guess we would, and moreover, this time, for once, David Merrick was on the side of practically all the critics.

Practically all the critics—let's dispose of that problem once and for all. Unlike the anonymous banker, there was an identified, if not readily identifiable, columnist, Pete Hamill, who reviewed the affair most awfully sociologically, from his desk at the New York *Post* (from where else?). The device was to contrive wisps of frivolous conversation, à la *The Women,* and juxtapose them with horror stories from the Vietnamese battlefront (get it?), so as to effect a Stendhalian contrast that would Arouse the Conscience of Versailles. Sample: "And Truman was just marvelous! He was the first to arrive, along with Mrs. Kay Graham, who was the guest of honor. You see, *she* threw *him* a party in Washington and he did get on the cover of *Newsweek,* and she *does* own *Newsweek,* and. . . . Well, anyway, she looked just gorgeous in a white Balmain gown. . . . Truman is a little fat fellow, you know, and he was so nice and round and sweet and polite that, God, you just wanted to *hug* him. . . ." ("The helicopter landed in a scrubby open field six miles north of Bong Son. It was very quiet. The young men began moving silently across the field, when the machine gun started hammering from the tree line. You could hear the phwup-phwup of a mortar and the snapping of small arms fire and then when it was quiet again, you realized that the young man next to you was dead. His right eye was torn from his skull.") In other contrapuntal passages from Vietnam Mr. Hamill contributed a girl whose "face, arms, chest and back were burnt away by napalm. There was pus forming where her eyes had been. . . ." The demonstration was on the order of subtlety of Carl Foreman's film *The Victors,* in which, just in case you are under the impression that war is a game of soccer at Eton, he sets up an execution of an American deserter (must have been Private Slovik, since he was the only one) during the Second World War, with music blaring out of an adjacent PX, "Have yourself a merry little Christmas/Through the years we all will be together. . . ." The implicit point, in case the banker happens to be reading this, is that one shouldn't enjoy oneself publicly while there is a war on, and of course, such advice would be easier to accept from an evangelist of continence who less visibly than Mr. Hamill enjoys weaving the luridities of Vietnam through his editorial loom. But it is true that certain functionaries intimately involved in the Vietnam war deemed it inappropriate to frug-with-Kay at Truman's blast; indeed, that was just the reason why Secretary McNamara did not come; at least, that is the reason he gave to Truman Capote for, regretfully, declining his kind invitation.

But he was one of few who did decline and the only one on record to have given that reason for declining, and he did not, Mr. Capote informs us, make that point censoriously. After all, one of the reasons why there is fighting in Vietnam is that people can have fun together back home. And besides, if society accepted the dictum that so long as some people are suffering, others may not party together, there would never be any partying at all, especially not on the evening of Mr. Capote's ball, when the agony experienced by some of the uninvited almost certainly exceeded that of the calm and resolute young men in Vietnam, who, if polled, would, almost surely, produce much more contempt for Pete Hamill than for Truman Capote.

And anyway the guests at the party, if called upon, could have conducted a very long spontaneous teach-in against Vietnam, so there was no presumption that only the insouciant were there. To be sure, Dwight Macdonald wasn't there and didn't, therefore, have a chance to demand that everyone leave when Lynda Bird Johnson came into the room—all the protesting he could do on the occasion was presumably at his own exclusion. But there were scads of others there who could, at a rap of Peter Duchin's baton, have gone effortlessly from a fox-trot into a fully orchestrated Teach-in Against Vietnam. My God, Norman Mailer alone would have been good until 5 A.M. the day after the day after. And to back him up there was Arthur Schlesinger, the redoubtable Galbraith, Walter Lippmann, Drew Pearson, Norman Podhoretz—only Susan Sontag was missing, but No Man is Indispensable.

Beyond that, there seems to have been no general sociological criticism, though no doubt if the society editors had thought to telephone the Reverend William Sloane Coffin of Yale collect, he'd have given them a very good argument for the abolition of Truman Capote, which one supposes he has programmed after he gets around to abolishing Skull and Bones, which he is now working on, so as to Prevent Watts. The rest thought it a great deal of fun. Suzy, who never ever has been caught short of cool, was at one point positively schoolgirlish. "Truman Capote," she wrote, "was the host of the year, the decade, the era . . . and all his friends like and love him—not because he's a big literary lion, not because it's the thing to do, but because Truman is Truman. . . ." To be sure, the inimitable Suzy recovered her equilibrium even before the paragraph was out. The party, she went on, was for Kay Graham. "She's Kay Graham, who owns the Washington *Post, Newsweek,* and part of the Paris *Herald Tribune.* She tries." And the impressiveness of the impregnable receiving line didn't dampen *everyone's* spontaneity. "Rose's little girl, Mrs. Sargent Shriver, really fooled our Truman. She told the announcer in a throaty French accent that she was Madame de Quelquechose. The announcer repeated her name to Truman, and Mrs. Shriver from behind her mask trilled a few more French pleasantries. Truman hadn't a clue to who she was (he wasn't wearing his glasses) and Mrs. Sargent Shriver got a very fast shuffle." But then back with the diapason. "It will be a long time before anyone gets around to a private ball like this again. Bravo, Truman, bravo."

That was the word. *Life* magazine said it, quote unquote: "Depending on which masked and bejeweled guest was talking, it was the party of the decade, it was the party of the century, or plainly it was the biggest and most glorious bash ever."

Why? Everyone asked Capote that question, and he came forward modestly with the conventional punctilio. The orchestra had been *wonderful.* The people who gave the dinner parties before the ball had been *so very* obliging. The decorations by Mrs. Backer were *so* appropriate. The service at the Plaza was so *very* good. The ballroom was *beautiful,* perhaps the only beautiful ballroom left in the *whole* country.

And, of course, all that was true, and all of it so irrelevant. It was the people who went. To which Capote demurely acknowledges that he *does* have nice friends. Is it as simple then, in order to have a successful party,

264

merely to invite people from the long register of Truman Capote's personal friends? Or if that is reasoning backward, how does one go about *becoming* a friend of Capote? Does one begin by heeling the *Yale Daily News* and making it into Deke? And then just staying in your room that spring evening of your junior year, confident that Capote will tap you? Are there things that meanwhile you must not do, must not say? Ways in which you may and may not say that which you may say? Was Proust correct in suggesting that society is the most sensitive indicator of fluctuating power values within society, so that, for instance, a sociological examination of the invitation list broadly limns the regnant hierarchies in American life?

Such questions are not answered by Mr. Capote, who likes to talk about his party but adamantly refuses without ever using so drastic a word to theorize about it: except to make one point, pointedly and, one suspects, teasingly banal. "I have always observed," he says, "in almost every situation, and I have been in almost every situation, that people tend to cling to their own types. The very rich people, for instance, tend to like the company of the very rich people. The international set like international socialites. Writers writers, artists artists. I have thought for years that it would be interesting to bring these disparate people together and see what happens. What happened is that Henry Ford sat down at my party with Walter Lippmann and had a hell of a good time." Is that right? the visitor asked. But isn't Mr. Lippmann a, uh, monologist? "Well, in combination with Mrs. Lippmann, yes." Laugh. "She is a very active conversationalist, and is usually telling Walter what he *really* means. . . ." Giggle. DANGER. (We're getting away from the pursuit of theory.) The visitor asks grimly whether any transcendent relationships were established. Yes, indeed—he heard only the other day of a wedding between a young lady and a young gentleman who had met at his party. . . . NO FAIR, the visitor objects; that isn't what he meant by *transcendent;* what he meant was: Did any *Henry Ford* become a buddy of any *Walter Lippmann?* Had businessmen discovered artists, or artists politicians, or politicians philosophers, beyond the stroke of midnight when everyone scurried back to the comfort of his *status quo ante* (plus Capote's ball)? A totally irrelevant reply. (An amusing anecdote about an amusing person, amusingly told.) One more game try: Somebody pointed out that there were members there of every Presidential family of modern times: Margaret Truman Daniel; three Kennedys (mother and two sisters); Lynda Bird Johnson. What about the Eisenhower family? "I don't happen to know any Eisenhower"—touch of ice, and the emjambment all but articulated: "Do *you*?"—as if to say: "If you do, really, I wonder that *you* were invited. . . ." The visitor made his final attempt: If you don't know any Eisenhower, that can hardly be put down to chance. Surely if you ever had wanted to meet an Eisenhower, that could have been arranged? Is there anybody anywhere you'd like to meet, but haven't? "Oh, lots of people," and he dove into the swimming pool and came up laughing about the difficulties of composing a suitable stag line.

"I decided that everyone invited to come stag had to be either very rich, very talented, or very beautiful and, of course, preferably all three. So I worked for weeks—I decided in June to give the party. I was with Kay, and she was feeling low, and I said to her, 'I'm going to give you the nicest party, darling, you ever went to.' *Blood* had really washed me out at about that time, and I found I just couldn't write. On the other hand I couldn't do *nothing,* so I worked literally for months on the party, getting the people lined up to give the dinner parties, telling them who to invite, and, oh, how many hours on the list. But on the stag business, there were three categories of replies. The first was 'Mr. Joseph McGoo accepts with pleasure the kind invitation etc., etc.' The second was 'Mr. Joseph McGoo accepts with pleasure the kind invitation etc., etc. and will be bringing Miss Josephine Flip.' The third category would say: 'Dear Truman: Great. Look forward to it. But I'll have to bring Josey, you know. Been banging her for eighteen months. You understand of course. See you there.' " Laugh.

"So, to the second category I promptly sent out a note: 'Mr. Capote is delighted Mr. McGoo has accepted his invitation but deeply regrets that he cannot on this occasion receive Miss Flip since he does not know Miss Flip.' Right mixture there of firmness and courtesy, don't you think? And anyway"—he was indignant—"what is the *point* of a stag line? The point is to have *unaccompanied* men. So I held out in every case. Category Two, which was tough. But also Category Three, which was *really* tough. Most of them capitulated. But some didn't. Some got so angry at me they *still* aren't speaking to me!" Laugh. "One person—you can tell this, if you don't use his name"—he began to break up when he thought about it—"announced to his staff—he has a large staff—that there would be a meeting at his office at 5 P.M. on the twenty-eighth, and there were rumors *all* week long. Was the company going to dissolve? The boss retire? Well, at 5 o'clock everyone was tense tense tense, and"—the words were barely discernible through the merriment—"he announced that he wanted everyone to know that he *had* been invited to the party that night but had refused!" Gales.

The visitor pointed out that the New York *Times* the following day confirmed that Mr. X had indeed been invited—by publishing the list of all the invitees. SERIOUS POINT. *Time* magazine had written: ". . . in a moment of almost understandable weakness [Capote] gave The New York *Times* his guest list, not bothering to cross out those who had regretted or had not come. The published list changed the private ball to a public event, and gave the social columnists and sociologists a chance to move in." "That," says Capote, "is pure hogwash. I didn't give a copy of the list to *anyone*. There were two copies of the complete invitation list on the table at the entrance to the corridor, where guests' names were ticked off. It was way after midnight, and my secretaries left the table because everybody who had accepted had checked in. Then Charlotte Curtis of the New York *Times* went by the table, saw the lists, calmly took one, and, oh la, la, put it into her purse and walked off to the city room.

"It was awful, really awful. Who I felt most sorry for," he continued delightedly, "was the people who had left town. 'I *do* wish I could stay and go to Truman's party, but it's the only time Richard can get away for that little holiday we've been planning in Nassau.'" Laugh. "Or, 'I promised Johnny that if he did well at Groton in his midterms, I'd take him to Mexico for the soccer championships—even though I'll miss Truman's party. He wrote me *such* an understanding note. . . .' Then there was another category of people I'm sorriest for of all. They were invited, but for some reason I'll never know, their names *weren't* on the list that Charlotte picked up! You can imagine how *they* felt!"

Wasn't it the politics of Truman Capote's ball that there were no politics to Truman Capote's ball? But that, of course, would not answer the generic question: What are the politics of Truman Capote? In the liberal-conservative sense, there were no discernible politics, except insofar as the social *Zeitgeist* says that liberals are more beautiful than conservatives. See, for instance, the dictum of Dean Acheson that the Democratic Party is "the party of brains" ("Brains Acheson," Senator McCarthy [the bad Senator McCarthy] retorted, never made it altogether clear to the mainland Chinese what Brains would do for them!)—and hence more plentiful at Capote's party. But politics in the wider sense there was presumably a fair amount of that night at the Plaza. Politics isn't only who gets nominated or who gets the postmastership of Chicago, but also, check Webster (subpoint: efficacious politics could have got that changed to: check Random House), "a science dealing with the regulation and control of men living in society." Look up "science," and it means at least as many things as politics means, so that it is at least possible to contend that the giving of a highly successful ball is a "science" and that the "regulation," if not the "control" of society, is the business of that science. The regulation being that of ordering the attitudes, value judgments, and reflexes of society. In such a way, obviously, as is congenial to the gentleman practicing the science in question, the gentleman who is, in this instance, giving the ball.

Politics is also (Webster 4a[3]) "activities concerned with achieving control, advancement, or some other goal in a non-governmental group." Well, then, there were presumably politics in Truman Capote's ball, if you want to go all the way down to 4a[3] to find them. There is no doubting that Truman Capote advanced himself as a social arbiter and, derivatively, in every other way. Even Ethel Merman, or whoever her name was who played Ethel Merman in Washington, exercised, through her social power to invite or not to invite, a certain political (1a[1]) influence. So in this sense it could be said that

268

the politics of Truman Capote's ball were self-serving. But the trouble with such an observation is that it is ineffably vulgar. Rather like saying to Beethoven that unless he diminished the beauty of his final quartets, he might be accused of playing politics.

Well, then, was Capote playing politics in the negative sense—*i.e.*, was he gratifying political appetites? No doubt about it. Politics, viewed as the arrangement of hierarchies, is the process of superordination and subordination, and the former is primarily the act of exclusion, and the latter primarily . . . the identical thing. The thrill of becoming bishop has very much to do, alas, with the knowledge of the many who are called by contrast with the few who are chosen. And the consignment to mere priesthood is galling, when galling, only because there are those who are elevated from that station. The politics of Truman Capote's ball was largely that and only that —namely, that some were tapped, requiring, by definition, that some not be tapped. Like Yale: the politics of Tap Day was and is that—some make it; some do not. Nobody has succeeded, and Tap Day at Yale with all the sociologists peeping through the machicolations of Branford Courtyard is rather like Sally Rand working as a waitress at the Kinsey Institute—yet nobody has succeeded in giving the reasons why, and why not, the marginal candidate is included or excluded. What matters is merely that the *power* is retained to include or exclude. And the mere assertion of that power—whether by the college fraternity or by Truman Capote—is an enhancement of that power. By such standards, it could be said that the politics of Truman Capote's ball was the exercise of what was, to judge from the objective situation, nothing more than the subjective power to decide who was to be tapped on that particular occasion. And, of course, the importance of his decisions necessarily rested on the sense of deprivation in those who were not tapped. Otherwise, Capote's list would not have been noticeable. Not even to *Women's Wear Daily*.

What are the techniques by which he made that list noticeable and therefore—most important—noticeable to those who were excluded from it? A vulgar question. Or, rather, a question of interest only to the mechanics of public relations, a science whose formal mastery would almost surely exclude one from qualification for any future party by Truman Capote (can you imagine the damage that would have been done to Capote if he had invited Edward Bernays?).

And so one is left with the conclusion that, in the strictest sense, the politics of Capote's ball was that there was no politics.

Proust is undoubtedly correct, and the obvious can be said—applying Proust to our own time—namely, that in the Kennedy era verbalists, rather than doers, stepped into the limelight and, therefore, advanced in the pecking order. But even before Kennedy, it was generally true that verbalists are *better* at parties than, say, tycoons. Bolkonsky vs. Bezuhov. Henry Ford I was a genius, and Arthur Schlesinger, thank God, probably isn't; but there isn't any question which of the two would fare better at a ball. There wasn't anything Dwight Eisenhower could do to making interesting the presidents of all those Coca-Cola companies and not an awful lot he could do to get their names into the papers: He couldn't play bridge *all* day long. So what political overlay fits Capote's party? Not even a negative one. The regrets were as eclectic as the acceptances. *Life* had its list of "jarring juxtapositions"—"Marianne Moore and Henry Geldzahler; Frank Sinatra and Alice Roosevelt Longworth; Janet Flanner and Andy Warhol; Henry Ford and Norman Mailer; McGeorge Bundy and Douglas Fairbanks; Walter Lippmann and Roddy McDowall; William Buckley and Lynda Bird Johnson; Princess Luciana Pignatelli and the gentry of Garden City, Kansas. . . ." But as much could be done with those who regretted: Ralph Bunche and Marlene Dietrich; Arthur Goldberg and Samuel Barber; Harry Belafonte and Mrs. Murray Vanderbilt; Thornton Wilder and Jack Lemmon; Mary Martin and Paul Mellon. It *was* a party, for the most part, of Truman Capote's friends. And he does have friends in, as the saying goes, every walk of life, mostly in the garlanded walks of life, to be sure; but who doesn't like the shade? "As the day approached," said *Vogue,* "there was a growing conviction"—at least among the more imaginative editors of *Vogue*—"that the invitation list was not just friends but a new Four Hundred of the World. . . . A whimsical rumor that we were all being called together for some purpose—probably the announcement of the End of the World—spread by magic or telephone. Jerry Robbins wondered if we weren't the list of those to be shot first by the Red Guard: Kenneth Galbraith said no, not as long as *he* was on it." It was all, after all, very reassuring. "Clifton Daniel, for instance, jitterbugged with an expertise that increased one's respect for The New York *Times*. Arthur Schlesinger Jr. smiled beatifically as he performed a spirited fox-trot." And George Plimpton used a candelabrum to instruct his guest (not Miss Flip) in the mechanics of the Statue of Liberty play. It was all very loose-jointed, psychedelic, very apolitical, very anti-*arbiter elegantiarum;* all the guests sensed, sort of, that they were *hoffähig;* but it didn't matter much, and if there was politics in the situation, it was not explicit, or even implicit, or contrivable even by the most schematic imaginations. The PhD's will undoubtedly, in the future, discover a Pattern of Exclusion. War-wounded Negro nuns! Huh! Call the Equal Opportunity Commission! Call the Anti-Defamation League! Call Max Lerner! But don't—please—call me. Lynda Bird and I are transcending together and do not wish to be disturbed.

LET THE RICH ALONE

December 30, 1967

It was said in the *Saturday Evening Post* once upon a time about Nelson Rockefeller that although it isn't known how rich he is, it is known that he is "stupendously, redundantly rich." All this was said rather amiably, indeed by an admirer of the governor, but, of course, the knife was there, and blood was drawn: Why should we countenance redundancies in wealth any more than in poetry? Henry Ford awhile ago gave a party for one of his young daughters, and the estimate was that it cost Mr. Ford $500,000, which is concededly a lot of scratch to spend in order formally to announce the already obvious nubility of a dear young thing, but the oohs and the ahs were not all limited to the question of whether Henry Ford hadn't rather overdone the display of his affluence. No, the discussions, some of them public—those, for instance, in the journals explicitly favoring the redistribution of incomes—expressed shock at Mr. Ford's spending so much money at a time when people are in want. Others, members indeed of Mr. Ford's own social and economic class, whispered together about his extravagances and wondered whether the rich did not nowadays endanger their own future by such profligate consumption. A dozen years ago it was the ball in Venice of Carlos de Bestegui, at which the guests were instructed to appear in costumes appropriate to the time of Mozart, which the guests proceeded to do, some of them with facsimiles so exquisitely authentic as to cause one commentator to reflect that if the price of just one of those dresses had been available to mitigate the material misery of Mozart's life, he might have lived on another decade and left us another dozen symphonies. And again at Venice, a generation earlier, Cole Porter was the host, and the lights were out all over a world that wrestled with an international Depression. But not the lights at Cole Porter's *palazzo*. On that one evening he consumed 25,000 candles—just enough, he reckoned, to provide just the illumination he sought, and never mind the blackness of his conscience—he earned the money, didn't he? Tremors went out through the capitalist community, whose sense of history may be blurred, but whose knowledge of what happened to Marie Antoinette very soon after she suggested that the hungry eat cake is a vivid part of their personal psychological equipment.

And then there is H. L. Hunt. Winston Churchill is reported to have said about a tedious socialist of unconventional sexual disposition that he had managed to "give sodomy a bad name." Mr. Hunt has done his share, among capitalists he has known, to give capitalism a bad name, not, goodness knows, by frenzies of extravagance but by his eccentric understanding of public affairs, his yahoo bigotry, and his appallingly bad manners. It is especially ironic that Mr. Hunt, who may be the richest man in the world, has in the course of time employed any number of people professionally devoted to the capitalist ideal, almost all of whom found that their exposure to Mr. Hunt turned out to be the greatest test of their ideological devotion. But it isn't Mr. Hunt's behavior so much that rankles the socialist or the dogmatic redistributionist, it is the fact that he is so very rich, so stupendously, redundantly rich.

Norman Thomas, for instance, gets utterly carried away by the subject. One time, when I was exchanging views with him at the Bronx High School of Science, he almost lost his voice in indignation at the recently announced calculation that Mr. Hunt was worth $2 billion (give or take $100,000,000 as they say in Texas). Mr. Thomas roared, and fumed, and pawed the ground, and tore at the lapels of his jacket, and belched forth such indignation as the fires of Vesuvius showered upon the people of Pompeii.

It is the fashion, after asserting that H. L. Hunt is the richest man in the world, to say that, on the other hand, there is Paul Getty, and maybe he is the richer of the two—we'll never know for sure until probate time. Mr. Getty has distinguished *himself* by reporting that he personally examines every single request for funds addressed to him by every single applicant, that he has been doing this, week in and week out, ever since the word got round in the late thirties that he was stupendously, redundantly rich, and that only twice has he yielded to a written entreaty. Mr. Getty does not give us any indication of the especially efficacious flavor of these two appeals, even though it is probably the single most interesting piece of information he is in a position to communicate to those of us who might one day ask him for money. As it stands, we know only as much about Mr. Getty's internal motives as the court was able to wrench from Shylock on asking him why he should prefer a pound of flesh over repayment with interest of his loan. "It is my pleasure," he replied, refusing another syllable's amplification. It was, obviously, Mr. Getty's pleasure to gratify two supplicants in the course of a generation of supplication, even as it was his pleasure to deny the applications of thousands during the same period. So? *Epatex le bourgeois?*

Well, well, well. We can work ourselves up—can we not?—into a considerable lather against the rich. Not only can we; we do. I confess that I myself, who am if anything oversold on the capitalist system, get more exasperated by rich people than ever I do by poor people, for the obvious reasons (the rich should know better) and the less obvious reasons (the rich should know better how to enjoy themselves). But even so, what most *isn't* needed nowadays is a stupendous, redundant excoriation of the rich,

273

but rather a defense of the rich—and the sooner, the better, before they are made to disappear, which would be very bad news indeed.

The most far-out defense of the rich has been made by that most austere economist F. A. Hayek. In *The Constitution of Liberty,* he makes an empirical defense of liberty and, therefore, of capitalism and reasons the progressive feature of the income tax out of intellectual existence. He even goes so far as to say that if the rich did not exist, they should, quite literally, be invented. A society has an enormous stake in its rich—so much so that, assuming a society were starting from scratch, everyone equally poor, you would do well to pick 100 citizens and give them each $10,000,000. Because the rich are uniquely situated: Hayek explains what is obvious, yet what is obviously unrecognized—*e.g.,* by Norman Thomas—namely that the rich, because they are rich, are free to turn their attentions to other matters than getting and spending. Sometimes the rich will spend their money not to buy themselves the redundant wife (like Tommy Manville), or distribute silly books (like H. L. Hunt), or pay the bills of misanthropic revolutionists (like Friedrich Engels), but to commission another symphony from Mozart (like Lichnowsky), give money for medical research (like Roy Cullen), or pay the school bills of talented students (like Solomon Guggenheim).

The function of the rich as risk capitalists is so childishly easy to understand as to escape the attention of people who can think only in ideologized ellipses. The whole process of capital accumulation begins by the conception of the surplus. If there is to be civilization, there must be a surplus, and someone must have control of it. It comes down to the individual, or the state. In Russia it is (mostly) the state. In America it is (mostly) the individual. The way of life in Russia and the way of life in America are pretty rigorous inferences from the respective preferences for the one or the other means of acquiring and distributing capital accumulations.

And then I found myself saying to Norman Thomas, in defense of H. L. Hunt The Institution: What if it could be demonstrated that Mr. H. L. Hunt had by his own exertions reduced the price of a gallon of gasoline by a single penny? Isn't that an immense benefaction, considering the average family's consumption rate—worth at least the 2 billion he has accumulated? And isn't the existence of that accumulated 2 billion itself a part of the national patrimony inasmuch as it is constantly at work, supplying credit, employing people, paying tax bills? As a master of fact, didn't Cole Porter, in order to burn 25,000 candles, need to purchase them from candlemakers? And, in economic terms, would he have left Venice that much better off if he had given the money to the poor, rather than employed the poor? Not to mention Cole Porter's satisfactions, which just possibly were involved in fueling his creativity? Could he have written "In the Still of the Night" without candlelight?

But the arguments in defense of the rich are almost by nature defensive. "Let the rich be" is my motto. It is no more my burden to defend the rich than to excuse the poor. Some people *will* be rich. Some people *will* be poor. I have found myself in the past wishing that Mr. Rockefeller were not quite so rich as to assault me as frequently as he does with the cosmic imperative of electing him to public office, but I do not propose to do anything about it. Nobody goes around talking about the excesses of poor people as a *political* problem, or rather, nobody goes around saying that the poor should be forbidden their excesses as a *political* matter (could you imagine a law forbidding ghetto dwellers from drinking whiskey or conceiving illegitimate children? The Javits-Kennedy Act?). So why pick on the rich?

As a matter of fact, if one wanted to go to the trouble of collecting the accomplishments of the rich as a class, they would be considerable—in education, in art, in philanthropy, in continence, in modesty, in devotion to duty and to country and to God. But that *shouldn't* be the point; what should be the point is that the rich are a natural state of affairs, a healthy state of affairs, and we should carefully scrutinize our deeper motives when we talk about the buffoonery of H. L. Hunt or the Medicean gall of Nelson Rockefeller. Surely if we can survive free speech, which means Wayne Morse, and a free press, which means New York *Times* editorials, we can survive Mr. Hunt's self-subsidized utopianism and Mr. Rockefeller's flotillas of self-concern, which bombard our political defenses from time to time.

275

The rich are by no means entitled to a presumptive respect, though some of them who seem least respectable usually have hold of a very special skill. G. K. Chesterton said that he never understood the compunction to honor a man simply because at some point in his life he had contrived to corner the soybean market. On the other hand, there isn't any reason to disdain the particular skill and daring it takes to corner the soybean market. My guess is that the last man to corner the soybean market, whoever he was, put at least as much time and creative energy into the cornering of it as, say, Norman Mailer put into his latest novel and produced something far more bearable—better a rise in the price of soybeans than *Why Are We in Vietnam?* As long as the rich don't try to exact from us any special respect, we should give them such respect as, in each case, is the individual's due. There are the deserving rich and the undeserving rich, and we should as individuals treat them individually rather than as a class. But what we should do collectively is let them alone, stop scolding every time they give an expensive bash, tell them that the pressure on them will be social and moral and intellectual, not political, not coercive. Let them alone. They are valuable people. And they have their own problems. One of them is us. Let's relieve them of that.

ROBERT McNAMARA, CRIME SYNDICATE HEAD

March 9, 1965

A gentleman who teaches at a state college and who prefers to be anonymous (I shall call him Mr. Pestalozzi) has sent me the results of a poll he conducted among 100 students in the freshman class. He questioned them about current events, devising a simple poll—"Identify such-and-such"—and he listed the names of 25 persons prominent in politics, art, thought, and entertainment.

Brace yourself. The poll was conducted as the last Presidential campaign neared its climax. Who is William Miller? More than one-third (36) didn't know. Who is Robert McNamara? Two-fifths (39) didn't know. Dean Rusk—40 had no idea. The political campaign in England was at its peak; nearly one-half (46) couldn't identify Sir Alec Douglas-Home.

Ah, could this be the *avant-garde* new generation, interested not in workaday politics but only in literature and art ideology? Well, 67 had never heard of Jean-Paul Sartre; 39 had never heard of Walter Reuther; 40 of Lincoln Rockwell; 66 of Fellini; 67 of Thelonius Monk (what can the young generation be listening to?); 84 of Mary McCarthy (the silver lining); 91 of Walter Kerr.

The whole thing sounds like a leg-pull. It isn't. The professor noted, morosely, that not one of the students gave more than a single answer which might indicate a facetious mood—they all were obviously doing their plodding best. One student identified McNamara as "leads N.Y. crime syndicate." James Franciscus (confession from the author—I never heard of him) is "the new Pope"; William Miller, a venturesome student ventured, is "a local surgeon"; Felonius [*sic*] Monk is "head of the monks"; Mary McCarthy is "TV weather girl"; Mao is "a Japanese historian."

One young lady who submitted to the test nevertheless expressed her indignation at its being given. "Why *should* we be interested? We're just kids." The professor forbore replying that in a couple of years, said kids would be presenting themselves at the polls to decide whether or not they approve the defense policies of the head of the New York crime syndicate, whether they approve the medical techniques of the local surgeon Miller, and what is to be done about the aggressions of the Japanese historian Mao.

Can you blame the kids, as they call themselves? Yes and no. The system is, of course, primarily to blame. They are, to a very considerable extent, victims of the reigning notion that everybody is so very equal that no especial effort need be made to teach special people anything special, that what they don't get for and by themselves is undemocratic to suggest should be drummed into them.

It is not only easy, but largely correct, to blame our parents and teachers for their cultivation of ignorance in our youth. One might go so far as to say that Professor Pestalozzi's poll could not have yielded anywhere near the results he got if parents and teachers had done their undemocratic best to teach, by gawd, their students, instead of pandering to their slovenly desires to increase their ignorance.

But as much having been said, it should be said that it

is not altogether the fault of the adults. It is also the fault of some students who resent the mere fact of a questionnaire of this kind. Professor Hugh Kenner, who is probably the most eloquent critic in America, wrote last fall an article for the *Saturday Evening Post* entitled "Why Johnny Shouldn't Go to College," in which he insisted that for so long as we feel in America that every single boy and girl whose blood count is 80 and metabolism normal should matriculate in college, we are going to cut down the opportunities of those whose genes urge them on to excellence. These young people need to be told that the choice is open to them, to work for self-improvement or to yield the way to others, and let those who will, at any rate, pursue learning, without the albatross of egalitarian democracy to hold them back. It was once commonly supposed that what distinguishes the teacher from the student is the superiority of his experience and attainments. Now it is very widely supposed that the teacher is a sort of benign umpire in the dispensation of life adjustment and that everything is like everything else, that it doesn't really much matter whether Robert McNamara heads the Defense Department or New York's crime syndicate, that the difference between the two positions is of interest only to the political taxonomist, not to "us kids."

THE TELEVISION DISCUSSION SHOWS

June 7, 1967

What makes for successful television discussion (TD)? After a year's duty on the firing line I must report (a) that I don't know for sure and (b) that no one else seems to know either. There are four TD's being nationally syndicated at the moment. The canons of the profession frown on the explicit identification of a fellow toiler in the vineyard unless the purpose is to praise him. But students of TD will recognize that Mr. A. specializes in bringing on the kooks. His appeal, or so I am told by professional students of human misbehavior, is especially to those who yearn to see and hear someone on television in relation to whom they can feel an exalted superiority.

Yesterday, for instance, it was that paunchy little man who calmly announced that he was Napoleon Bonaparte, returned to deliver the armies of the West from their 150-year-old helplessness. Such a show is particularly appealing to those who are not absolutely certain of their own sanity but are *absolutely* certain that anyone who believes he is Napoleon is madder. than they, and Mr. A. will frequently adduce someone madder than they—that is his secret.

Tonight it's the lady who was accosted, as she was hanging out the wash, by the pilot of a flying saucer, who asked her where he might pick up a little gasoline, of which he was in short supply. *Hmmm.* The lady is utterly ingenuous, and you find yourself thinking: Well, stranger things *have* happened in history. What if it had been a television show in midsummer of 1492 and Mr. A. had presented a mad navigator who announced that he intended to sail west until he hit *land?* . . . Better reserve judgment on the lady of the wash.

And anyway it all is rather thrilling, in the quiet and security of your living room, to hear the talk of those who have had extraworldly experiences or who claim convincingly to have had them.

Mr. A. makes fun of his guest, and we see said guest strain with anxiety at the challenge to his dogma; but adamantly, like a Christian martyr facing the lions, he refuses to be shaken. You catch the fanatic's gleam in his eye. And that makes for good watching, in the same sense that the fresh wreck on the side of the highway makes for irresistible ogling. Such people crowd Hyde Park on Sunday afternoons in London to hear the waifs of the intellectual and ideological underworlds ply their nostrums and visions—some of them amiable ("Regain your health by eating only blackstrap molasses"); others mischievous ("Send the West Indians back to the Congo").

Not many converts are won, but that doesn't seem to matter. There are those who like to visit human zoos. Enough of them to sustain Mr. A. and also Mr. B., who on a lesser scale is also a kook-host, with, moreover, visions of himself as the Procrustean avenger who by elemental directness ("You are a very stupid man") or metallic derogation ("What makes you think you're so smart?") puts himself forward as the gyroscope of universal sanity. My own thinking is that Mr. B. quite undermines the intended effect. I walk away from his show prepared to enlist in Mr. Bonaparte's army and keep a can of gasoline at hand for straitened spacemen.

Then there is Mr. C. He doesn't specialize in kooks, though he does not always exclude them. He likes, as a general rule, to have a lot of people on his program, on the ground, one gathers, that any one person, save possibly himself, tends to get pretty boring. So that, typically, he will have a half dozen people on the show, representing a range of opinion, usually, from left liberal to left liberal.

Mr. C. has a lot of moxie, and that ain't bad in show biz. He is almost always a full-fledged participant in his own shows, which means, considering that among his guests one is likely to find the world's leading experts on aardvarks and zoometry, that Mr. C. has a hell of a problem boning up on aardvarks and zoometry sufficient to sound as though he had something relevant to say on the subjects—a difficulty compounded by his difficulty, in the opinion of some of his viewers, in saying anything relevant about anything. Shall we leave it that he doesn't entirely succeed? But then neither would anyone have succeeded since Erasmus, it being generally accepted that he was the last member of the human race to have mastered all the world's then available knowledge. Not, then, altogether Mr. C.'s fault. Though an occasional profession of ignorance, particularly in advance of some of his most cacophonous demonstrations of such, would perhaps add to the, uh, suspense of Mr. C.'s show.

Arrogance. Is it a hot property in TD? I cannot insinuate an arrogance in Mr. C. without acknowledging that my own critics assign that lamentable vice to me. There are various means by which public figures earn that particular reputation. Some people could be deaf, dumb, and blind and *still* appear arrogant. Dean Acheson, for instance. But mostly it has to do with the *way* you say things.

The correct way, if arrogance is to be safely avoided, is the circumlocutory way, via conversational zigs and zags, ellipses, obliquities, rhomboids, parallelograms, the cumulative effect of which is to commmunicate to the listener: "My dear friend, the point I am about to make is one which, if you find yourself disagreeing with it, means

280

that that is testimony to your superior skill, intelligence, loyalty, and compassion. If, on the other hand, you should agree with it, why you are dynamic, bold, adventurous, and the salt of the earth." Either way the listener can't lose.

Here, for instance, are three replies, in increasing order of objectionability arrogancewise, as Mr. C. would say.

Question: "Mr. Buckley, Senator Kennedy said on his return from Latin America that the poor people there are poor because the governments don't ensure them decent wages."

Answer I. "I have a great deal of respect for Senator Kennedy, and I don't doubt that he has learned a great deal from his personal observations during his extended trip through Latin America, but I do believe, though I grant I may be wrong—Senator Kennedy is far more experienced in these matters than I am—that the Senator may have neglected to put sufficient emphasis on nongovernmental factors that have contributed to Latin American poverty." Guaranteed to get by Bobbysoxers with impunity.

Answer II. "The Senator simply hasn't stressed other factors that, in my judgment, are at least as responsible as the failure of government action for the prevailing poverty." Acceptable, though a wee bit brinky.

Answer III. "Senator Kennedy's ignorance of economics perfectly qualifies him to act as a spokesman for the Democratic Party and solidly advances his imperial mission to confuse the world about the causes of poverty." Not good. Not good for your own image, if that is what you are out to cultivate. And, as a matter of fact, not particularly damaging to Bobby's, because the sympathy vote will flow to him like the baptismal waters to Sodom. In this respect Messrs. A. and B. run certain risks, as I have pointed out, of catalyzing the sympathy vote. But they don't really care. It is important to them that the listener should gravitate emotionally toward someone, whether the persecutor or the persecutee. Because identification causes the combative juices to stir, and the TD becomes a contest of sorts in which the listener is involved. And then it edges away from a purely informational type of program on over to polemics, to sport, to entertainment.

My own inclination over the years has been toward the third modality, for temperamental and other reasons I will not attempt to justify here. But I have found it difficult to maneuver within that modality in programs in which (as in *Firing Line*) I am not only adversary but also host. If you are merely the adversary, it is easier to be blunt, direct, even at the risk of enhancing your own reputation for arrogance and your opponent's human appeal. When you are so situated as to require that you spend, before the cameras roll, a half hour or so with your guest (who is usually attractive) blahing about this and that, knowing, moreover, that you will have to chitchat together during the commercial breaks with someone who, after all, is there in response to your own invitation—all that tends to dissipate such edges as are psychologically necessary for groin-and-eyeball adversary relationships.

Now it is generally supposed that the grudge meeting is the most satisfactory from the point of view of the listener, and there is at least a half-truth there. Nothing, but nothing, is more tedious than the debate between X and Y one-half of which is devoted to X's compliments to Y, and other half to Y's paeans on X's virtues. But then there are ways, not uninteresting to the public, of communicating one's disagreements sharply without taking every opportunity to void a dump truckful of abuse on the subject, *e.g.*, possible response IIIA to the question above: "Senator Kennedy regularly overstresses the role of government in the building of an economy. Latin American governments are no better situated to produce wealth than our own government was during the growth of American economic power over a period of a century." Less bombast, but perhaps, over the long haul, week after week, the rhythm is easier on the digestion. This doesn't rule out the possibility, here and there, of a good old atavistic sledgehammer, followed by a little controlled gore.

TD, like everything else worth submitting to, must have contrast. The principal contrast in TD is, of course, to be found among the visiting experts. Steve Allen's style is different from Sidney Hook's. The only similarity between John Williams and John Pastore is that they are both

Senators. But Pastore, if he yells all the time, will bore, and John Williams, if he never ever raises his voice, will, too—and so will the adversary in all likelihood bore if he treats every part of every exchange like a 100-yard dash. People can get out of breath just plain watching.

I repeat, then: I don't know what it is that makes for totally successful TD. Obviously, when the stakes are very high, the listeners will be very numerous—*vide* the audiences for the Kennedy-Nixon debates. The participation of a major world figure helps, but even that isn't enough to lure the dogged away from the old movies, as witness the exiguous ratings when Premier Khrushchev made his single public appearance, during his visit in 1960, on David Susskind's show.

Public relations technicians appear to know how to hypo a particular show so as to entice an audience larger than the average. But over the long term, promotion does not seem to pay off. The audience that counts is the steady audience, which will become accustomed to tuning in every week at the same time, barring superior distractions, on the assumption that the hour or the half hour is worth listening to, on the assumption that the guest, even if his name is unknown, will have something interesting to say and will say it interestingly; indeed, that that is why he was invited to appear.

Polling techniques are not yet so refined as to reveal distinctions in audience quality. Those who hover between TD and, say, late-night wrestling, are more easily won to the former if it is full of gore and a brilliant showcase for human conceits. Others are more interested, not exactly in information—information is much more concisely got from books or magazines—but in information produced under stress. It is the performance, then, that counts. And performance is often a matter of contrast. Quietness and unflappability are the best reply to bombast; liveliness to pedantry; charity to malevolence. But then I am scarcely preaching what I practice.

THE HYSTERIA ABOUT WORDS

June 15, 1963

Have you noticed that the use of an unusual word sometimes irritates the reader to such a point that he will accuse the user of affectation, than which there is no more heinous crime in the American republic? The distinguished political and social philosopher and columnist Russell Kirk used the word "energumen" to describe, in his Introduction to my book *Rumbles Left and Right,* whom it is I agitate against, and one reviewer fairly exploded with annoyance. Now the word in question means "someone possessed by an evil spirit" and fanatically addicted to a particular idea—can you think of a better word to describe certain kinds of people who seek to reorder public affairs according to their hypnotic visions? Should one refuse to use a venerable word for which there is no obvious synonym simply because it is a word that does not regularly appear in the diet of the average reader?

I raise the problem because I am often accused of an inordinate reliance on unusual words and desire—as would you in my shoes, I think—to defend myself against the insinuation that I write as I do simply to prove that I have returned recently from the bowels of a dictionary with a fish in my mouth, establishing my etymological dauntlessness. Surely one must distinguish between those who plunder old tomes to find words which, in someone's phrase, should never be let out, belonging strictly to the zoo sections of the dictionary, and such others as Russell Kirk, who use words because (a) the words signify just exactly what the user means and because (b) the user deems it right and proper to preserve in currency words which in the course of history were coined as the result of a felt need.

There is a sort of phony democratic bias against the use of unusual words. Recently I heard a young movie actress being interviewed on a radio station. She was asked by her interrogator what it meant to be an actress and replied that an actor's life was "multifaceted." "What are you trying to pull on me?" demanded the radio announcer. Sweetie pie ran, panicked, from the argument—what else,

284

in the democratic age, when it is deemed an effrontery on the democratic ideal to use a word that is not used twice a week by Little Orphan Annie? "I'm sorry I used such a fancy word . . . I guess I don't really know what it means . . . I should have said, there are lots of aspects to being an actress." Democracy won the day, and the show droned on.

Awhile ago I was on Jack Paar's program, and he asked me a number of questions having to do with this and that, which I tried, vainly, to answer as best I knew how. I wrote about that experience in *Rumbles* and described the ensuing tantrum of Mr. Paar and his associates, who steamed on and on about my ideological vices, expressing special outrage at my unintelligibility.

It is a curious thing, this universal assumption by a number of prominently situated opinion, or rather mood, makers that the American people are either unaware of the unusual word or undisposed to hear it and find out what it means, thus broadening not merely their vocabulary—that isn't the important thing—but their conceptual and descriptive powers. Those who say that the average American is incapable of appreciating the meaning of the word "energumen" are, in my humble judgment, nuts. The average American is, in Franklin P. Adams' phrase, above average, and his intelligence is not tied umbilically to Jack Paar's antiintellectualist muse. It is curious that a man who is offended by the use of the word "multifaceted" or "energumen" is perfectly capable of expressing a sentence of death-defying mechanical complexity. I am, unfortunately, innocent in the world of science, and I wish I knew what in the world the TV hawker is talking about when he reels off something having to do with a "double action injector system in the valve mechanism," but it does not occur to me to suggest that he is putting on airs; it occurs to me to rue my patently inadequate knowledge of my mechanical *abc*'s.

The point about unusual words is that they are as necessary to philosophy, economics, esthetics, and political science as they are necessary in the world of higher mechanics, in which so many people, displaying the natural American genius, are so much at home. It is possible, I suppose, to describe the refinements of an Astrojet fan-injection blah blah blah engine in words understandable to me, but the exercise is not often resorted to, because the manufacturers assume a certain level of mechanical literacy, as they assume that those who do not have it ought not to set the standards for those who do have it. So it is in other fields, which is why, in my judgment, when Mr. Russell Kirk uses the word "energumen," he should be allowed to use it, and the thing for book reviewers to do when they come upon it, if they are unfamiliar with it, is not to pout, but to open a dictionary and see if the word is one whose meaning they wish to learn. They must guard against going about like antiliterate energumens.

BOYS WILL BE HEROES

August 24, 1965

The best explanation I ever heard for man's compulsive race to get to the moon was offered by a shrewd and attractive lady, wife of a law school don at the University of Indiana. "Don't you understand?" she asked, after the company had worn each other down with elaborate scientific explanations. They wheeled toward her. "Boys will be boys."

The rhetoric, of course, can be escalated without difficulty, making the statement read: "Men will be men." That takes the hint of mischief out of it all, but it is much better with the mischief left in. Because there is a bit of mischief in adventure, and men who go off grandiloquently to meet their destiny often feel a trace of the excitement a boy feels when he goes out for the first time on an overnight hike. There is, of course, no fun at all in the pursuit of adventure if, as so often is the case, you die en route. No fun at all, when you feel fear, and loneliness, and helplessness. It is man's capacity to expose himself to the certainty that he will be lonely and afraid that makes possible great adventures of the human spirit.

And it takes a boyish zest for adventure for staid and middle-aged men to engage in such a dazzling adventure as Robert Manry's aboard *Tinkerbelle,* the 13½-foot converted dinghy in which he crossed the Atlantic Ocean, covering in eighty days 3,200 miles. The chances of surviving such a voyage were less than the chance our as-

286

tronauts will survive their orbits around the planet, covering, in one-tenth the time, a distance 1,000 times as long. The astronauts are to prove to us that heavenly rendezvous are possible between assorted flying objects and that man's body can endure eight days of weightlessness and immobility. Mr. Manry proved that a few planks of wood, none of them more than 13½ feet long, and strips of cloth, made by a single carpenter of moderate skill, can, using only nature's power, transport a man across the most treacherous ocean in the world.

One feels nothing but admiration for the astronauts. Theirs is, above all, a mission to press their fragile bodies against the unknown and in an experiment so mechanized that they are left with little to do except to obey the signals they hear. It must put a special tax on the spirit to be left with so little latitude. Mr. Manry, by contrast, had great latitude. He could point the nose of his boat in any direction he chose, except in the direction the wind was coming from, and he could leave both sails up, or take down one of them, or take down both of them, or trim one or both, or drag his sea anchor. An almost infinite number of possibilities. And if he made a serious mistake, he would drown. And he might have drowned anyway, because a truly determined sea will not respect the right of so frail a challenger to claim safe passage across the haunted area.

Mr. Manry, who is almost fifty and makes his living as a copyreader in Cleveland, knew enough of the literature of the sea to know that for every sailor the sea is the enemy, that it must be treated as the enemy, and that the enemy is formidable enough to have wrecked whole navies in her time. And the astronauts know that nothing in the world is more mysterious than science, that the most fastidious preparations, projections, and calculations are sometimes confounded by utterly inexplicable scientific backtalk or because someone didn't turn the screwdriver hard enough.

Even so, boys will be boys, and some boys have the makings of heroes: Astronaut Gordon Cooper has reported that "once, in the middle of the night, at an altitude of over 150 miles, over the middle of the Indian Ocean," he prayed. Mr. Manry may have had room in his cluttered dinghy for the thirty-third Psalm: By the word of

287

the Lord, the heavens were established, and all the powers
of them by the spirit of His mouth. Gathering together the
waters of the sea, as in a vessel, laying up the depths in
storehouses.

THE END OF THE LATIN MASS

November 10, 1967

In January of this year my sister died, age forty-nine,
eldest of ten children, and mother of ten children, the lot
of us catapulted into the dumb grief whence we sought
relief by many means, principal among them the conviction, now reified by desire, that our separation from her is
impermanent. It was the moment to recall not merely the
promises of Christ, but their magical cogency; the moment
to remind ourselves as forcefully as we know how of the
depths of the Christian experience, of the Christian
mystery, so that when one of us communicated with her
priest, we asked if he would consent to a funeral mass in
the manner of the days gone by, which request he gladly
granted. And so, on January 18, in the subzero weather of
a little town in northwestern Connecticut, in the ugly little
church we all grew up in, the priest recited the mass of the
dead, and the organist accompanied the soloist who sang
the Gregorian dirge in words the mourners did not clearly
discern, words which had we discerned them we would not
have been able exactly to translate, and yet we experienced, not only her family but her friends, not alone the
Catholics among us but also the Protestants and the Jews,
something akin to that synesthesia which nowadays most
spiritually restless folk find it necessary to discover in
drugs or from a guru in mysterious India.

Six months later my sister's oldest daughter—the first
of the grandchildren—was married. With some hesitation
(one must not be overbearing) her father asked the same
priest (of noble mien and great heart) whether this happy
ritual might also be performed in the Latin. He replied
with understanding and grace that that would not be possible, inasmuch as he would be performing on this occasion
not in a remote corner of Connecticut, but in West
Hartford, practically within the earshot of the bishop. We
felt very wicked at having attempted anything so

audacious within the walls of the episcopacy, and so the wedding took place according to the current cant, with everybody popping up, and kneeling down, and responding, more or less, to the stream of objurgations that issued from the nervous and tone-deaf young commentator, all together now, Who Do We Appreciate? Jesus! Jesus! Jesus! Je-*zus*—it was awful. My beloved wife—to whom I have been beholden for seventeen years, and who has borne with me through countless weddings of my countless relations, who was with me and clutched my hand during the funeral a few months earlier, whom I had not invited to my church since the vulgarizations of 1964, so anxious was I that, as a member of the Anglican Communion, she should continue to remember our services as she had known them, in their inscrutable majesty—turned to me early in the ritual in utter incredulity, wondering whether something was especially awry. Hypersensitive, I rebuked her, muttering something to the effect that she had no right to be so ignorant of what had been going on for three years, and she withdrew in anger. She was right; I was utterly wrong. How could she, an innocent Protestant, begin to conceive of the liturgical disfigurations of the past few years? My own reaction was the protective reaction of the son whose father, the chronic drunkard, is first espied unsteady on his feet by someone from whom one has greatly cared to conceal the fact. Let it be objected that the essential fact of the matter is that the sacrament of matrimony was duly conferred, and what else is it that matters? My sensibilities, that's what.

They do not matter, of course, in any Benthamite reckoning of the success of the new liturgy. Concerning this point, I yield completely, or rather almost completely. It is absolutely right that the vernacular should displace the Latin if by doing so, the rituals of Catholic Christianity bring a greater satisfaction to the laity and a deeper comprehension of their religion. There oughtn't to be any argument on this point, and there certainly isn't any from me—though I cherish the bodkin Sir Arnold Lunn so deftly inserted in the soft tissues of that argument: "If it is so," he said, arguing along with Evelyn Waugh and others for one (1) Latin mass each Sunday in the larger churches, "that the Latin Mass is only for the educated few, surely Mother Church in all her charity can find a little

289

place *even* for the educated few?" Indeed, when a most learned and attractive young priest from my own parish asked me to serve as a lector in the new mass, I acquiesced, read all the relevant literature, and, to be sure warily, hoped that something was about to unfold before me which would vindicate the progressives.

I hung on doggedly for three years, until a month ago, when I wrote my pastor that I no longer thought it appropriate regularly to serve as lector. During those three years I observed the evolution of the new mass and the reaction to it of the congregation (the largest, by the way, in Connecticut.) The church holds 1,000 people, and at first, four hymns were prescribed. They were subsequently reduced to three, even as, in the course of the experiment, the commentator absorbed the duties of the lector, or vice versa, depending on whether you are the ex-commentator or the ex-lector. At our church three years ago perhaps a dozen people out of 1,000 sang the hymn. (It is not much different with the prayers.) That is atypical, to be sure; the church is large and overawing to the uncertain group singer—*i.e.,* to most non-Protestant Americans. In other Catholic churches, I have noted, the congregations tend to join a little bit more firmly in the song. In none that I have been to is there anything like the joyous unison that the bards of the new liturgy thrummed about in the anticipatory literature, the only exception being the highly regimented school my son attends, at which the reverend headmaster has means to induce cooperation in whatever enterprise strikes his fancy. (I have noticed that my son does not join in the hymn singing when he is home, though the reason why is not necessarily indifference, is almost surely not recalcitrance, is most likely a realistic appreciation of his inability to contribute to the musical story line.)

I must, of course, judge primarily on the basis of my own experience; but it is conclusive at my own church, and I venture to say without fear of contradiction that the joint singing and prayers are a fiasco, which is all right, I suppose—the Christian martyrs endured worse exasperations and profited more from them than we endure from or are likely to benefit from the singing of the hymns at St. Mary's Church. What is troublesome is the difficulty one has in dogging one's own spiritual pursuits in the random cacophony. Really, the new liturgists should have offered training in yogi or whatever else Mother Church in her resourcefulness might baptize as a distinctively Catholic means by which we might tune off the Fascistic static of the contemporary mass, during which one is either attempting to sing, totally neglecting the prayers at the foot of the altar which suddenly we are told are irrelevant; or attempting to read the missal at one's own syncopated pace, which we must now do athwart the obtrusive rhythm of the priest or the commentator; or attempting to mediate on this or the other proper of the mass, only to find that such meditation is sheer outlawry, which stands in the way of the liturgical calisthenics devised by the central coach, who apparently judges it an act of neglect if the churchgoer is permitted more than two minutes and forty-six seconds without being made to stand if he was kneeling, or kneel if he was standing, or sit—or sing—or chant—or *anything* if perchance he was praying, from which anarchism he must at all costs be rescued: "LET US NOW RECITE THE INTROIT PRAYER," says the commentator, to which exhortation I find myself aching to reply in that "loud and clear and reverential voice" the manual for lectors prescribes: "LET US NOT!" Must we say the introit prayer together? I have been reading the introit prayer since I was thirteen years old, and I continue unaware that I missed something—*e.g.*, at the Jesuit school in England when at daily mass we read the introit prayers all by our little selves, beginning it perhaps as much as five seconds before, or five seconds after, the priest, who, enjoying the privacy granted him at Trent, pursued his prayers, in his own way, at his own speed, ungoverned by the metronomic discipline of the parishioners or of the commentator.

Ah, but now the parish *understands* the introit prayer! But, my beloved friends, the parish does not understand. Neither does the commentator. Neither does the lector. Neither, if you want the truth of the matter, does the priest—in most cases. If clarity is the purpose of the liturgical reform—the reason for going into English, the reason for going into the vernacular—then the reforms of the liturgy are simply incomplete. If clarity is the desideratum, or however you say the word in English, then the thing to do is to jettison, just to begin with, most of St.

Paul, whose epistles are in some respects inscrutable to some of the people some of the time and in most respects inscrutable to most of the people most of the time. The translation of them from archaic grandeur to John-Jane-Gyp contemporese simply doesn't do the trick, particularly if one is expected to go in unison. Those prayers, which are not exacting or recondite—are even they more galvanizing when spoken in unison? LET US NOW RECITE THE INTROIT PRAYER. *Judge me, O God, and distinguish my cause from the nation that is not holy; deliver me from the unjust and deceitful man.* Judge-me-O-God / And-distinguish-my-cause-from-the-nation-that-is-not-holy / Deliver-me-from-the-unjust-and-deceitful-man/ —Why? How come? Whose idea—that such words as these are better spoken, better understood, better appreciated, when rendered metrically in forced marches with the congregation? Who, thinking to read these holy and inspired words reverentially, would submit to the iron rhythm of a joint reading? It is one thing to chant together a refrain—Lord deliver us/Lord save us/Grant us peace. But the extended prayer in unison is a metallic Proscrusteanism, which absolutely defies the rationale of the whole business, which is the communication of *meaning*. The rote saying of anything is the enemy of understanding. To reduce to unison prayers whose meaning is unfamiliar is virtually to guarantee that they will mean nothing to the sayer. *"Brethren: Everything that was written in times past was written for our instruction, that through the patience and encouragement afforded by the scriptures we might have hope. I say that Christ exercised his ministry to the circumsized to show God's fidelity in fulfilling his promises to the fathers, whereas the Gentiles glorify God for his mercy, as it is written: 'Therefore will I proclaim you among the nations, and I will sing praise to your name.'"* These were the words with which I first accosted my fellow parishioners from the lector's pulpit. I do not even now understand them well enough to explain them with any confidence. And yet, the instruction manual informs me, I am to communicate their meaning "clearly" and "confidently." And together the congregation will repeat such sentences in the gradual.

Our beloved Mother Church. How sadly, how innocently, how—sometimes—strangely she is sometimes directed by her devoted disciples! *Hail Mary, full of Grace, the Lord is with you* . . . The Lord is with who! *Thee to you, Buster,* I found myself thinking during the retreat when first I learned that it is a part of the current edification to strip the Lord, His Mother, and the saints of the honorific with which the simple Quakers even now address their children and their servants. And the translations! *"Happy the Humble—they shall inherit. . . ."* One cannot read on without the same sense of outrage one would feel on entering the Cathedral of Chartres and finding that the windows had been replaced with pop art figures of Christ sitting in against the slumlords of Milwaukee. One's heart is filled with such passions of resentment and odium as only Hilaire Belloc could adequately have voiced. O God O God O God, why has thou forsaken us! My faith, I note on their taking from us even the canon of the mass in that mysterious universal which soothed and inspired the low and the mighty, a part of the mass—as Evelyn Waugh recalled—"for whose restoration the Elizabethan martyrs had gone to the scaffold [in which] St. Augustine, St. Thomas à Becket, St. Thomas More, Challoner and Newman would have been perfectly at their ease among us," is secure. I pray the sacrifice will yield a rich harvest of informed Christians. But to suppose that it will is the most difficult act of faith I have ever been called on to make, because it tears against the perceptions of all my senses. My faith is a congeries of dogmatical certitudes, one of which is that the new liturgy is the triumph, yea the resurrection, of the Philistines.

X. RIP

GEORGE LINCOLN ROCKWELL

August 31, 1967

Surely George Lincoln Rockwell was insane. And yet . . .
the problem is interesting not only for the moralists but
for the jurists, who struggle for a serviceable codification
of culpability. Was Rockwell personally responsible for
his genocidal writhings? Was he in the last troubled by
them?

I am at liberty to divulge a correspondence. I had
known Rockwell slightly, back before his mania hit him.
And so he was given, from time to time, to writing me
obscene communications and, publicly, to mocking what
he considered my pseudoconservatism. But in March,
1964, apparently stung by a public reference I had made
to him as a moral maniac, he wrote me: "I would be most
grateful if you would take the time to send me a reasoned
statement showing that what I preach and have fought so
hard for and have sacrificed so much for is a 'mania.' I
can assure you that I will not expose or print any such letter. If you convince me, I will not only quit but I will go
to work to repair such damage as I have caused by my
political efforts. . . . If you can do this much for me, Bill,
for God's sake please do it."

I was struck by this letter, so obviously what the psy-
chologists classify as "a cry for help," that cry which is so
often made by those in despair even if they do not themselves recognize it as such. The nontotalist tone suggested
the barest possibility of that revival of spiritual modesty
which necessarily precedes conversion.

I replied that I was unqualified to communicate with
authority the theological depths of Christian teachings on
race hatred and related matters and asked whether he
would consent to see a young priest, an old friend of mine,

brilliantly learned and persuasive, an adamantly anti-liberal—so as to ensure at least one common denominator.

I had expected Rockwell would turn down the suggestion. He didn't. "I will be most happy to talk with the priest and assure I will treat the matter most honorably and confidentially. . . . Is it possible the priest could come down here?"

I inquired, and Father Jude (as I shall call him) agreed, though specifying that the clandestine meeting should be at a rectory, not at Rockwell's headquarters. The meeting having been arranged, Rockwell wrote him: "I want to be sure you understand from the outset that in agreeing to discuss these matters with me, you are accepting a challenge which no other man before you has attempted. No matter what you think now, I am not an evil person, and am as sincere in my beliefs as any human being who ever walked the earth." And then a most extraordinary, though I think unintentional, condescension, revealing the depths of Rockwell's moral insanity and perverse innocence: "I cannot help feel that you will be hurt if you are unsuccessful in demonstrating error in our factual beliefs or reasoning. I despise hurting people—in spite of the propaganda about me."

The meeting took place. Two hours together. Rockwell wrote me: "I enjoyed the talk with Father Jude more than I am able to put into words, and it cleared up a lot of hazy areas in my thinking, at least. Sadly, it also exposed what is incontrovertibly an impassable chasm between our two worlds. I did not believe that was the case, or even possible—but if your thinking parallels the Father's then we are men of two different worlds."

And Father Jude wrote me a long letter. An excerpt: "G. R. is oddly personable, in a heavy, rude way, and not incapable of winning over single people of the same stripe. But that is the end of it. He is gross (I read his book on the way home), fanatical, and urges criminally insane suggestions on his readers. . . . On the surface he doesn't have any scruples about the morals of the Nazi movement. The only sign of hope is his desire to go on talking. He is a Nazi of the true, vulgar, 1937 variety. His mind is a disaster area, corrupted by snap verbal comparisons, *e.g.*, Jews are like termites, Hitler suffered for his people like

Christ. Under pressure he admits that the only relationship between his movement and *National Review* conservatism is that both are anti-Communist. I pointed out that if he causes one person to vote for him as a Nazi, he will have corrupted that person. I drew a blank."

Father Jude never heard again from Rockwell, which was discouraging, and neither did I, which was encouraging—he had evidently lost his appetite to write me his customary provocation. But the episode showed that even Rockwell had the glimmering of a conscience, and sometimes that conscience stirred like a three-month fetus, and that he might, just might, one day have turned on himself with the fury with which he assaulted others during his last years and thus might, just might, have won redemption.

JFK, THE MORNING AFTER

December 7, 1963

Norman Mailer, reviewing Victor Lasky's book on John Kennedy several weeks ago for the New York *Herald Tribune*, remarked that Kennedy's political genius rested in his apprehension of the main point in American politics toward the close of the fifties—namely, that the American people were ready, in Mailer's words, to turn away from the father image (Eisenhower) and accept as ruler someone cast in the role of the young hero—someone in the Hollywood image, as Mailer put it.

Mailer seems to have been right, as he very often is. What happened, two and one-half weeks ago, was the *morte d'Arthur*. The grief was that of a nation that had lost a young king, a young king whose own fairyland rise to power recapitulated the national experience, whose personal radiance warmed the whole nation—and whose great fiascoes were charitably disregarded, for were we not, really, forgiving ourselves? And are we not, really, grieving for ourselves? "A part of me has gone with him," one orator said, and a great chorus responds to the theme, and they all are exactly correct—they *have* lost a part of themselves. Much of America, the intelligentsia especially, succeeded in anthropomorphizing itself in the image of John Kennedy, whereon it had to follow that when he lay bleeding, they lay bleeding and that the great ache, the anxiety expressed so effusively, lay in the numbing realization that though their king was dead, they were still alive and would have to learn again to act for themselves. And, God help us, to think for themselves.

For it gives one the grues. The assassination itself, yes, obviously. We know what death is and what evil is in the twentieth century. We live with violence, and apocalypse is camped just over the horizon. We have lived with violent endings, for individuals, and for nations, and for races. We know the unyielding finality of death and one's helplessness before recurrent acts of individual and collective depravity. But what is this other thing that seems to be going on? Pay the man all the many compliments to which he is entitled, and sing the praises he is due. But not all this, no, indeed, and for the reason, first among the others, that it tends to undermine those qualities in national life that John Kennedy at his best exemplified: courage, dignity, fortitude, tough-mindedness, independence.

The rhetoric has gone quite out of control. The symbol of our emotional, if not neurotic, excess is the Eternal Flame at Arlington, a few hundred yards from the shrines we built to the memories of George Washington (86 years after he died), Thomas Jefferson (117 years), and Abraham Lincoln (57 years), who have no eternal flames. The lovely and tormented Mrs. Kennedy needs a gentle hand, lest in her understandable grief she give the air of the Pharaoh, specifying his own magnitude.

John F. Kennedy lived a life of tough controversy, and while it is correct that an individual's weaknesses should be buried with him, it is not ever possible to bury the public issues on which a public figure committed himself. Mr. Kennedy told us the fight would last beyond his lifetime, and his successor has pledged himself on the same side of those policies. It is sobering to recall that there was great dissension, left and right, in respect of John Kennedy's policies, up until the very moment he died. The issue of *Time* magazine dated the awful day of the assassination carried the news of a growing campus "disenchantment" with President Kennedy's policies, "now spread far and wide." "At conservative Georgia
297

Tech," said *Time*, "the complaint is that 'he's interfering with my personal life' through Big Government. At liberal Reed, where 'he doesn't inspire respect as Stevenson did,' the gripe is Kennedy's caution on the civil rights bill. At exuberant Wisconsin, 'he's liked in a negative way,' faulted for lack of political conviction." The restlessness, as we see, was not partisan, not only from the right.

Are we now being emotionally stampeded into believing that Kennedy was the incarnation and that respect for him requires that we treat his program like the laws of the Medes and the Persians?

What we need is a period of dignified mourning for a graceful human being, who passed through our midst with style and energy, a mourning more intense in virtue of the treachery of his end, but less intense than that which degenerates into abject pity for ourselves or that which asks that we place our personal grief above the best interests of our country as we understand them, which best interests many people thought of as calling for the retirement of Mr. Kennedy from public life one year from now. Jack Kennedy wouldn't want a caterwauling public besotted by its own tears for its own self or accepting his program for sentimentality's sake. He asked us to keep the torch lit. And that means work, each one of us according to his own lights, to keep this country at least as strong and as free, stronger, we can hope, and freer, by acting on his own idealism than it was when John Kennedy last knew it.

DOUGLAS MacARTHUR—MISSING BUT WELL ACCOUNTED FOR

April 5, 1964

The sad news has come in from Walter Reed Hospital. There never seemed really to be any doubt but that this time General MacArthur would die. But the news has shocked the public just the same, because we are once again reminded that even the imperishable perish.

MacArthur was the last of the great Americans. It isn't at all certain that America is capable of producing another man of MacArthur's caste. Such men spring from the loins of nations in whose blood courage runs, and we are grown anemic. That is why so many have spoken of an age that would die with MacArthur. An age where, occasionally, heroes arose, acknowledging as their imperatives that duty, honor, and country which MacArthur cherished, but which the nation that rejected him has no stomach for, preferring the adulterated substitutes of our age of modulation.

I have often thought that it is a key to the understanding of what has happened to this country that Dwight Eisenhower became President, rather than Douglas MacArthur. This is not the time to slight Mr. Eisenhower, whose principal fault, after all, lies in his being quintessentially a part of his age: The age is at fault, not Eisenhower; the age was not imaginative enough for MacArthur. The age was afraid of MacArthur, and well might it have been, because he stood above it, as De Gaulle stands above his own time. In France they turned, at last, to De Gaulle but only because the monstrous inefficiency of the French finally prevented recourse to yet one more mediocrity. We in America, being more efficient, more conservative, than the French, never felt the need to reach beyond a mediocrity, so we elected the affable Eisenhower, and let MacArthur go to his Colombey-les-deux-églises at the Waldorf Towers, there to fade away.

Even while he did that, he managed to retain his grandeur. It is an unfortunate image—fade away—as if, as the years went by, the general had grown paler and paler ending up in a pastel insipidity from which all the vital colors of his manhood had drained. He grew, eventually, physically weak, but his powers were undiminished, his august presence unmistakable. When, as recently as a year ago, he walked into the meeting of the jaded celebrities from all over the world that *Time* magazine had convoked to celebrate an anniversary, he, and only he, produced that throat-catching sense of excitement which Henry Luce, subsequently introducing him, was prepared, honestly and boyishly, to acknowledge as an almost metaphysical property of that man.

It did not matter that he lived as a recluse in the Waldorf Towers, his presence was felt right up until the last minute, when messages of grief and concern stormed the Walter Reed Hospital, on a scale that overwhelmed hospital officials, who had never seen the like of it. A lot of us felt that for so long as he lived, the nation drew, somehow, from his great strength. And now we are—we are—sad, and lonely, and grateful. If we as a nation must die, we can find no better words to die by, this side of Scripture, than his, given at his last public appearance at West Point:

"The shadows are lengthening for me. The twilight is here. My days of old have vanished—tone and tint. They have gone glimmering through the dreams of things that were. Their memory is one of wondrous beauty, watered by tears and coaxed and caressed by the smiles of yesterday. I listen vainly, but with thirsty ear, for the witching melody of faint bugles blowing reveille, of far drums beating the long roll. . . . But in the evening of my memory . . . always there echoes and reechoes: Duty, honor, country."

HAIL TO THE CHIEF (HERBERT HOOVER)
June 22, 1963

When Herbert Hoover entered on his terminal sickness, one of his closest friends remarked that he hoped the Chief (as they all called him) would live forever—but not one day after he stood to lose control of his faculties. Hoover, without that prodigious brain wouldn't have been Hoover at all, just as the pathetic Churchill, except during his (fortunately frequent) moments of lucidity, is not Churchill at all. Where great men are involved, senility is a matter of special consequence, for what is at stake is not merely one's relationship to someone one has loved, but one's relationship to someone one has greatly relied on intellectually and morally. When his mind is gone, the emptiness is like that which fell on Greece when the rumor went out that the oracle at Delphos was dead.

It is impossible to catalogue the achievements of this extraordinary man, and anyone who suffers (who is the exception?) from a sense of personal impotence should read a good biography of Mr. Hoover (*Our Unknown Ex-President* by Eugene Lyons, qualifies) to discover what in fact one *can* do in the course of a twenty-four-hour day, if only one puts one's mind to it. Granted there are few who are born with Mr. Hoover's miraculously retentive mind, which served him the way whole libraries serve the rest of us. (Once, at Mr. Hoover's dinner table, I slurred a decision Woodrow Wilson made in 1915, and my host descended on me with an encyclopedic thoroughness, as though he had been studying nothing else than the career of Mr. Wilson over the past fifty years.) But few Americans cultivate their character, and it is the character, rather than the congenital intellectual potential, that determines whether our minds will be harnessed. Hoover tapped all the resources of his mind. And lavished them on his family, his friends, and his country.

All of us are very much in the grip of contemporary historical judgments. History selects its heroes and its villains, and few of us resist participation either at the parade or at the guillotine. Have you noticed that, in recent months especially, Harry Truman is being lifted up by the hagiographers to the status of hero? The gentleman has his strengths, no doubt about it, and this is not the moment to dwell on his weaknesses; but have you noticed that *it* is happening, without scrupulous examination of the historical conscience? So it went in reverse, with Mr. Hoover. No doubt about it, when he left the White House in 1933, he was the most despised lame duck in American history. For one thing, he was caught up in an impersonal economic tragedy, of which he became the embodiment ("Mr. Hoover's Depression"). For another, Franklin Roosevelt urged the majority of the electorate along to believe that Mr. Hoover took personal pleasure in the tribulations that befell the working class.

Not many are aware that the great humanitarian Mr. Roosevelt personally refused to give Mr. Hoover a Secret Service escort when he left Washington after the inauguration of his successor. Mr. Hoover went away unguarded, discredited, unloved, and—and continued to work as he had done during the preceding twenty years, as a public servant, only this time inconspicuously. Slowly, ever so slowly, the people began to realize that up there, high in the Waldorf Towers, a man lived who was totally incorruptible, whose concept of public service, although he lacked the capacity to theatricalize his involvement in it, was about the purest thing to be seen in major national politics. And in due course he got up to speak at a Republican National Convention, in 1948, and was given

301

the kind of ovation reserved for those whose personal heroism is altogether convincing. The people at last outgrew the myth of Hoover the misanthropic shopkeeper who took pleasure in bankrupting the customer whose debt was thirty-one days old. They began to see him for what he was: a gentle, firm, diligent, wise, unflashy, resourceful, devoted patriot. Americans, unlike Latins at a bullfight, are slow to turn against an unconvincing matador. And they are slow to reverse their judgment. It is to the American people's credit that they reversed their judgment on Herbert Hoover.

His strengths were numerous, his weaknesses few. One of these, no doubt, was his failure to communicate to the people the true meaning of the mechanized welfarism which is a great semantical and economic imposture: the chimera, which is the demagogic mainstay of liberal politics, that it is possible for the majority of Americans (a) to receive benefits from the federal government without (b) paying for them. The Chief failed. But so, too, have all others failed. It may have been his own personal failure as a political dramatist. It may be—historians, one supposes, will one day rule on the question—the failure of the American people to comprehend the economic actions of the free society. It could be that historians of the future will rule the failure of Mr. Hoover and the American people to reach a political rapport was an index not of the personal failure of this kind and intellectually rigorous man, but of the failure of the people to understand, or want to understand, the requirements of freedom. In which case it was not Mr. Hoover's fault. He will sleep the sleep of the just man, whose troubles were not that he didn't speak out, but that the people would not listen.

EVELYN WAUGH

April 14, 1966

I once encountered a very angry lady in Dallas, Texas, who announced herself as head of a vigilance committee to keep dirty literature out of the local libraries, and we talked a bit. I forget just how the conversation moved, but at one point I said that to pull out all the salacious

302

passages from modern literature would require the end of individual reading. All of us would have to have private readers, like the old eccentric who forced his prisoner to read to him the works of Charles Dickens in the novel by Evelyn Waugh. Who, asked the lady book critic, is Evelyn Waugh? The greatest English novelist of this century, I ventured; but, on ascertaining that he was not a dirty writer, she lost all interest and went off to look for more dirty books to rail against.

I wrote Waugh and told him about the episode. My letter did not include any reference to any business matter, so I knew he would not reply to it; but I knew the little story would appeal to his sense of satire, so strongly developed as to make him, in the judgment of the critic Edmund Wilson, the "only first-rate comic genius the English have produced since George Bernard Shaw." (Waugh's reply, several years later to an interviewer who asked what was his opinion of Edmund Wilson: "Is he American?" End comment.) But Waugh was much more than that, though millions of his readers, who read only *Handful of Dust,* and *Scoop,* and *The Loved One,* did not know about the other dimensions, did not know that Evelyn Waugh, the great satirist, was a conservative, a traditionalist, a passionately convinced and convincing Christian, a master stylist routinely acknowledged during the last decade, as the most finished writer of English prose.

He died at sixty-two, having completed only one volume of long autobiography. In it he recorded, dispassionately, the impressions of his early years, something of the lives of his ancestors, many of them eccentric, and of the chaos of his undergraduate career at Oxford, from which he was duly expelled, as so many interesting Englishmen are expected to be. He decided, in his mid-twenties, that the thing to do was to commit suicide, and he described, as he would in a novel, his own venture in this dramatic activity—the verse from Euripides about water washing away the stains of the earth, neatly exposed where it could not be missed by grieving relatives and meticulous coroners; wading out into the ocean, thinking diapasonal thoughts; then running into a school of jellyfish; and racing back to the beach, putting on his clothes, tearing up Euripides, and resuming his career, for which we thank God's little jellyfish.

He was an impossible man in many respects. At least as far as the public was concerned. Like J. D. Salinger and James Gould Cozzens, he simply refused to join the world of flackery and televised literature. On one occasion when he did consent to grant an interview to a young correspondent from the *Paris Review,* because he was related to an old friend, Waugh thoroughly disconcerted the interviewer by arriving at the hotel suite, taking off his clothes, and getting into bed, lighting a huge cigar, and breaking open a bottle of champagne, and then uttering: "Proceed."

Rather than live a public life, he situated himself in a large old house in the country, surrounding himself with a moat that was proof against all but his closest friends and the vicar. The piranhas made a specialty of devouring all first-class mail asking for interviews, comments, suggestions, whatever. I confess to having successfully swum across that moat, after several fruitless assaults. I discovered that the squire felt an obligation to reply to all letters concerning questions of commerce, so that if you wanted a comment or two on a matter of literature or philosophy or politics, you could hope to get it by dropping into your letter a trivial question relating to business.

But he was a man of charity, personal generosity, and, above all, understanding. He knew people, he knew his century, and having come to know it, he had faith only in the will of God and in individual man's latent capacity to strive toward it. He acknowledged the need to live in this century, because the jellyfish will not have it otherwise, but never, ever, to acclimate yourself to it. Mr. Scott-King, the classics teacher, after his tour through Evelyn Waugh's "Modern Europe," comes back to school, and there the headmaster suggests that he teach some popular subject, in addition to the classics—economic history, perhaps, for the classics are not popular. "I'm a Greats man myself," the headmaster says. "I deplore it as much as you do. But what can we do? Parents are not interested in producing the 'complete man' any more. They want to qualify their boys for jobs in the public world. You can hardly blame them, can you?" "Oh yes," Scott-King replies, "I can and do." And deaf to the headmaster's entreaties, he declares, shyly but firmly, "I think it would be very wicked indeed to do anything to fit a boy for the modern world."

ADLAI STEVENSON

July 20, 1965

Alongside him, they all were illiterate, depending for their aura on professional ghosts, on entire departments of great universities, on a conscript American Academy of Arts and Sciences. But Adlai Stevenson was the genuine article. They all ghosted for him at one time or another—Archibald MacLeish, Bernard De Voto, Arthur Schlesinger—but they were ghosting for a man who, they knew, could, in his own field, outwrite every one of them. So that when he spoke, the words were truly his, in a sense that they never were truly Roosevelt's or Kennedy's.

How great a contribution is that? It is inestimable, and it is altogether detachable from the burden of Adlai Stevenson's day-to-day political thought, which oscillated from the banal to the mischievous. Mr. Stevenson was devoted to a means of communicating his thought to the people, which, because it was based on the assumption of human intelligence, was, therefore, based on the assumption of human nobility. It is ironic that at the time he spoke, the most educated men in the country tended to be the most addled politically, while the least educated were those the momentum of whose vision was sufficient to penetrate to the essential specifications of a problem. The majority didn't get lost in the maze of refractions that Stevenson the ambiguist got lost in—for which we have Providence to thank—on his way to the Presidency. But Adlai Stevenson, at least during his 1952 campaign and from time to time thereafter, verbalized an innate intelligence, idealism, and wit which were a credit not only to him, but to his countrymen.

He spoke to me once, with vast enjoyment, of his long relationship with Harry Truman, whom he had known well beginning in the forties, when Truman was a Senator. During that period, Stevenson was the closest assistant of Secretary of the Navy Knox, who was a frequent witness before the Truman Committee. He and Truman had come to know each other well. In March, 1952, Mr. Stevenson recalled, President Truman called him to Blair House (the White House was being rebuilt) for dinner at eight. Stevenson arrived promptly, and Truman immediately told him that he must run for President, announce on such-and-such a day, and select so-and-so as his campaign manager. Stevenson replied that he was greatly flattered, but that the answer was no, he was committed to running again for governor of Illinois, he did not want to run for President, thanks very much. "Truman paid no attention, but repeated his exhortations, whereupon I repeated my demurrals, and this went on literally until one in the morning, at which point Truman got up and said: 'Adlai, you're the most indecisive man I ever met!' "

Stevenson roared with pleasure, and I did, too; but no doubt it crossed his mind, as it certainly did my own, that Truman, of course, had been proved right. From a "firm decision" not to run, Mr. Stevenson swung over and became an ardent candidate. Meanwhile, Truman had switched over to opposing him. Why? The reasons given are the worst: that Truman didn't like the *kind* of campaign Stevenson had waged. The *kind* of campaign Stevenson had waged was a paradigm—around which any candidate of the future should conjugate his own campaign. But then again, just possibly, it may have been that that disqualifying indecisiveness in Stevenson was apparent to Mr. Truman by 1956 in a way it hadn't been in 1952 and that rather than cite it as the reason for transferring his allegiance from Stevenson, he chose instead to disparage Stevenson's "fancy talk" to his close associates.

I doubt that Mr. Stevenson's thought is hard enough to endure in its own right. Indeed, it is hard even now to recall it. But he was a bird of paradise, and the scene is drearier for his going.

HENRY R. LUCE

March 11, 1967

Mr. Luce, who was the greatest journalist, well, maybe ever, would have admired the moxie in *Newsweek*'s current cover, which is a facsimile of its archrival *Time* and with a cover picture of Henry Robinson Luce, 1898-1967. *Newsweek* was not pandering to a dead journalist for the sake of subtly advancing the prestige of the breed, in the way that provincial kings and princes turn up for royal funerals of their Augustan cousins in order to remind the

306

world and themselves of the unity of the breed. At the moment of his dying Luce was less a journalist than something else. His journalistic prodigies were matters of the past; the corporate succession had been established, all in orderly manner. But Luce was a continuing entity, and for that reason continuingly newsworthy, and never more so than at the moment when he died and it was suddenly realized by the entire professional community that he would no longer be around, even in retirement, to give the edge of his opinions or make felt the weight of a weighty presence.

Mr. Luce was not a lot of things, and what he principally was not was a crusader. It wasn't any lack of courage or any dilution in his own convictions, but rather a quality of resignation to reality that caused him to give windmill tilting a wide berth. He could, and often did, mount sustained campaigns in pursuit of objectives big (*e.g.,* U.S. entry into World War II) and small (*e.g.,* the election of Eisenhower); but the goals were carefully chosen, and above all they were realizable. Luce had an aversion to lost causes. Far better to let a cause disappear than to espouse it hopelessly. His thinking in this respect was Calvinist: The world is as it is because that is the way God made it, and although there is plenty of scope within which to exercise our minuscule capacities for self-improvement, one must not speak imperiously to the elements, because the elements do not listen, not even if you put them on the cover of *Time.* That sense that one must beware of futility seemed to grow into a kind of professional nervousness.

The good journalist knows that people are quick to tire, and it is important to tire ahead of them, so as to devise in good time new means of attracting their attention. Mr. Luce told a former aide on one occasion that the secret of his success was to stay six weeks ahead of the people. Five weeks ahead, and he would not be exercising his capacity for leadership, which a creative journalist must do. Seven weeks ahead of the people, and you are a prophet, and prophets are bores. And go broke. "I'm tired of anti-Communism," Harry Luce told a friend in the summer of 1953. "I knew then with the force of revelation," the friend later said, "that Joe McCarthy was through." Luce was, as usual, six weeks ahead of the people.

Mr. Luce was born a Presbyterian and died a Presbyterian—born when practicing Protestants of every denomination literally believed in every nuance of the Apostles' Creed; died at a moment when leading Protestant theologians are wondering whether the Apostles' Creed could even be trusted with the assertion of Christ's divinity.

He was born and died a practicing, committed capitalist. Born into an age when capitalism was an economic system and a social philosophy; died when capitalism was, as a social philosophy, all but extinct and, as an economic arrangement, looking less the kind of thing Adam Smith had sculpted than something that had grown up out of the notebooks of Beatrice and Sidney Webb.

Mr. Luce continued to be comfortable in the folds of his evolutionizing faiths, and yet he did so without ever striking anyone as a vicar of Bray. There was a no-nonsense Scotch toughness there that managed to convey the impression that things might look bad to us orthodoxists, but you should see what they'd be like if H. R. Luce didn't have his finger in the dike. And in his own way, he did keep his finger in the dike, though he chose his dikes carefully, and they were never more than man-sized.

He was fond of asking startling questions. "Why have you never asked me for a favor?" he demanded to know at dinner one time. I replied that he had indeed done me a favor. One night he came back from a meeting with the Foreign Policy Association and found his talented wife wrestling with a form letter to be sent out inviting sponsors to attend a dinner for the editors of *National Review*. He threw himself at the letter, and the two of them wrestled with it for a half hour, while I mused that this surely was the most expensive editorial attention a 150-word letter had ever received. I reminded him of the incident as we sat there, surrounded by the swells who had been seduced into attendance by the galvanizing prose of Henry and Clare Booth Luce. "You know," he said, "I'm a pretty good promotion man." "No," I said, "I didn't know." "How do you think I built a $500,000,000 empire?" "Editorial talent," I hazarded. "Nonsense!" As always, the practical man.

Five weeks ago I dined with him in Phoenix, and he

told me he wished to appear on my television program in the spring but not to talk about the press or the American proposition—but on another subject. He was being mysterious. "What?" I asked. "Well, you're not to say, because that would spoil it. But what I want to say is this— say it to the professional churchmen—the Council of Churches gang. Look: if you're really interested in relieving poverty, you've got an obligation to defend the system that works best at relieving poverty. See what I mean?"

Yes, I said, and promised to keep it quiet, and he grinned in anticipation of the day in the spring when he would wield the Lord's sword and have a little scoop while he was at it. All that and, now, heaven, too.

FRANK CHODOROV

January 24, 1967

(The eulogy delivered at Mr. Chodorov's funeral.)

Most of you know, some of you better than I, the biography. He was born in New York, poor, the son of Russian immigrants, and he lived on the lower West Side, even as it was slowly becoming fashionable. "They painted the fronts white and the shutters green," he wrote fifty years later, "and invested the section with profitable romance by reviving its ancient name of Greenwich Village."

He finished high school and enrolled at Columbia University, where, during his first year, his principal interest was football, and he made the varsity squad. He graduated, and married, and went out to make his way in commerce, "having," as he wrote, "given up as hopeless for a Jew the ambition of becoming a professor of English." He worked, and made a modest living, for himself, his wife, and his two children. And then, in the thirties, his two children grown, he turned one day to his wife and asked her permission to leave his life and the little security it had given him in order to teach. Up until then, like Paul Gauguin, he had mostly seen, and now, like Gauguin, he wanted to express himself. Her consent, to that as to every request he ever made, was instantly given. And he began the career, quietly, studiously, passionately,

309

which made him friends among so many people who never laid eyes on him.

During all the years he had worked as a salesman and in advertising he had continued to read, and early in his post-graduate career he had fastened on Henry George as the object of his primary fascination. At first he was drawn to George because of the literary style. "Here," he once recalled, "was something of the cameo clarity of Matthew Arnold, a little of the parallel structure of Macaulay, the periods of Edmund Burke. I know I was more interested in how this man Henry George—some fellow who, I had heard, had run for mayor of New York—said it than in what he had to say. Probably a nineteenth century essayist, I surmised, whom I had missed and the deficiency had to be made up. I borrowed [*Progress and Poverty*] for a week or two."

Now, having for many years cultivated what he grew to believe was the unique social vision of George, he became the director of the Henry George School. But in due course there was a falling out, and he resigned. One cannot truly understand Henry George, he once remarked, without understanding his antipathy toward socialism. But George's most modern exegetes, he feared, were disposed to traduce George, to put his social philosophy at the service of the state. And it was the centralized state that Frank Chodorov was born, and lived, to oppose.

He had a go at journalism. During those years he had met Albert Jay Nock. Once again, in his admiration for Nock, he could unite his passion for prose and for a philosopher of the individual. Nock, the stunning belletrist, the author of *Our Enemy the State,* the founder of the renowned journal the *Freeman.* The two of them had a go—unsuccessful—at reviving the ancient *Freeman.* He turned then to individual journalism, rented a dingy little office downtown near where he grew up, and founded a personal monthly four-page journal which he called *analysis.* I met him there, where he wrote, edited, copyread, published, distributed, and merchandised the little journal which got under the skin of those, comparatively few, who recognized that all, or seemingly all, of America, in a fit of opportunism, had lost hold of the ancient moorings. *analysis* was, for those who saw it, the testimony of a single man against the spirit of an age

310

which had become infatuated with the possibilities of the central solution for the problems of society. In *analysis* the old fires burned, or rather were kept flickering. "Lenin," John Chamberlain wrote in 1952, "said it long ago: to make collectivism stick in a land that has known the blessings of individualism, you must catch a whole generation in the cradle and forcibly deprive it of tutors who have learned the bourgeois alphabet at their mothers' knees. In a land of republican law this is impossible; no matter how clever or omnipresent the collectivist propaganda may be, a few culture-carriers of the old tradition will escape. They may be reduced to publishing broadsheets like *analysis* instead of books; they may be compelled to conduct their straggling classes in dingy rooms in old brownstone fronts. Certainly they will have a hard time getting posts on a university faculty. But they will be still hanging around—and still talking—when the tinsel begins to wear off the latest Five Year Plan or government-sponsored Greenbelt colonization scheme. Their books and pamphlets, ready for the chance encounter that sparks all revolutions or 'reactions,' will fan the revival of the old tradition that periodically displaces the callow presumptions of the 'new.' "

The sparks were struck. He accepted a post with *Human Events,* which in those days was four pages of sparkling news commentary by Frank Hanighen and four pages of philosophy by him, alternating with Bertrand de Jouvenel, with William Henry Chamberlin, and, on the fourth week, with a guest. From there he went once again to the resurrected *Freeman,* which he served as editor, in association with Leonard Read. He left it to freelance, joining the staff of *National Review,* and then the tragedies, in rapid succession, struck.

His wife died, shortly after they celebrated their fiftieth wedding anniversary. He was inconsolable, lost; a mild rebuke, this individual powerlessness, some would say, to the spirit of total individualism—some, but only those who misunderstood the nature of the individualism he believed in, which called for aloofness from remote and synthetic and involuntary associations, but which flowered in the giving of oneself to one's family, and friends, and philosophical soul mates. He went to Europe, for the first time, and was able to report exultantly on the collapse of

311

rigid Marxism in Germany, the end of that demonic ideology that had elevated to religious faith the necessity to subordinate the individual. He returned to New York happy to conclude that dogmatic socialism was on the wane, but pessimistic, in his gentle, yet obdurate, way, that the forms would outlive the substance and that the inertia of statism would continue to erode the individual and the free society. And he kept on preaching.

And then, at the Freedom School in Colorado, he was struck down. His daughter, Grace, went to him, and he was barely able, after the stroke, to talk. But he did, in near delirium, mention that his faith in Henry George was whole, that George, above all others, understood. She brought him back to New York, and he recovered his powers of speech. But he could not write again, and as he grew worse, he could not read, and not to write, not to read were consignments to an insanity from which he was saved only by his devotion to Grace and her husband, Herbert, and to his grandchildren, Lisa, and Erik, and Francine. After a while he needed professional nursing care, and the first summer he stayed in the country, near Grace. I saw him there, and puffing his fugitive pipe, he leaned over to me and said grumpily: "You know what this place is? It's a die-in." His eyes twinkled, but he was not greatly amused—without his typewriter, his books, without even, for long hours of the day, his family. But he was resigned. He had been resigned ever since Celia died.

That fall he returned to New York, to the Mary Manning Walsh home, run by Catholic sisters, and there nursed first by Sister Fidelis, then—when she was transferred to Boston on the grounds that her miraculous attentions could not be monopolized by a single city—by Sister Bernadette Mary, who gave him attention and love. And always Grace, and Herbert, and the children. And the forbidden cigarette lighters, sneaked in to him like hacksaw blades to men in a death house, and the wicked gleam of appreciation at this final defiance of authority. Individualism to the end. And finally, last Wednesday, a crisis, and a merciful death.

After I met him at *analysis,* we were frequently together. He came to Yale to speak while I was still an undergraduate. His manner was diffident, slightly didactic, firm, gentle—always gentle. Dr. Opitz reviewed one of his books and remarked that an extraordinary feature of it was that he united a polemical passion with an apparent incapacity to utter any meanness toward anyone, dead or alive. He spoke from a heart full of belief, enlightened by a mind keen and observant and understanding. He spoke thus, in style resolutely undemagogic, on every occasion. He thought it somehow profane, by the force of oratory, to seduce any listener toward positions with which he wasn't, somehow, organically oriented. "The purpose of teaching individualism," he wrote, "is not to *make* individualists but to *find* them. Rather, to help them find *themselves*. If a student takes readily to such values as the primacy of the individual, the free market place, or the immorality of taxation, he is an individualist; if he swallows hard, he must be counted a recruit for the other side." There are those, he was saying—and he took his thought from the Book of Job and later from the immortal essay of Albert Jay Nock on the Remnant—who are latently capable of understanding. Those who aren't, well, they aren't; but do what you can for those who are.

Whether a point of view about the political redeemability of the non-Remnant so morose is realistic doesn't much seem to matter somehow. It is quite enough for any man to do to stir the sentiments and thought of those who are predisposed to listen. And so at a relatively late age he swung into high gear. Among the enterprises he started was, in 1952, the Intercollegiate Society of Individualists, whose goal it is to undo the damage done a half century ago by the Intercollegiate Socialist Society. I was the ISI's first president, but I was purely a figurehead, as I was soon reminded. In short order I had a letter from him: "Am removing you as president. Making myself pres. Easier to raise money if a Jew is president. You can be V-P. Love. Frank."

And then he started to write his books, his wonderful books of essays, innocent—and that was their strength —of the entangling complexities of modern life. It simply didn't matter that there had been an Industrial Revolution, that economists had made finicky examinations of the business cycle, that E had been discovered to be equal to mc squared. Because he dealt in personal and social truisms in his books, and he did not ever entertain

313

the question that a world, whatever its conceits and ef-fronteries, would conceivably presume to justify the subor-dination of the individual.

During the years immediately after he left Columbia, he was greatly infatuated with atheism. On reading and rereading Henry George, he abandoned his faith in non-faith, though he never joined a religion; indeed, he or-dained that no service said over his grave should be religious. He came to believe in "transcendence," a con-fession he wrote into an essay which he entitled—and the elision is his, not his editor's or his publisher's—"How a Jew Came to God." Many people, he penetrated, are un-witting believers. "Even the ultra-materialistic socialists," he wrote, "in their doctrine of historical inevitability, are guilty of transcendentalism. Admittedly, I reasoned, this is a flight of the finite mind from its own limitations; it is a search for security in an invariable; it is mining for bedrock in the infinite." As for him, he could only bring himself to say that religion, the kind of religion he believed in, is a "faith in the possibility of an explanatory pattern of constancies." John Chamberlain called him a mystic—"but only," said Chamberlain, "in the sense that all men of insight are mystics. His mystical assumption is that men are born as individuals possessing inalienable rights."

"These rights of man," his daughter, Grace, wrote me yesterday, "stem from a source higher than man and must not be violated. To him this *was* a religion. It was a be-lief handed down to his son and daughter as a religious concept—even though he did not consciously mean it thus. . . . He refused to think about spiritual freedom or the freedom gained through the spiritual life; but in his con-cept of man's right to himself he unknowingly carried and tried to spread a message from the spiritual world."

We are gathered here today to affirm that knowing Frank Chodorov or even knowing his works was a spiri-tual experience. We weep at the loss of a father and a grandfather, a personal friend and teacher to those who knew him and his writings, a friend of the human race, whose faith in it—and love for its individual mem-bers—ennobles mankind. As a Christian, I postulate that today he is happy and serene in the company of the angels

and the saints and his Celia. We who have time left to
serve on earth rejoice in the memory of our friend and
teacher, a benefactor to us all, living and unborn. May he
rest eternally in peace.

WILLIAM FRANK BUCKLEY, 1881-1958

October 25, 1958

The vital statistics are that he grew up in Texas and, as
the oldest son, undertook, upon the premature death of his
father, to look after the health and welfare of his mother
and the education of his three brothers and sisters. He did
this, and educated himself at the University of Texas by
teaching Spanish, which he had mastered while living as a
boy on the frontier. He went to Mexico to practice law,
and saw the revolution against the benevolent and auto-
cratic Porfirio Díaz and what followed in its wake, and
learned, and never forgot, his distrust of the revolutionary
ideology.

There are not many alive who knew him then, but those
who did remember keenly the intelligence, the wit, the
largeheartedness and—always—the high principle, which
brought him a singular eminence in the community. That
eminence the American government repeatedly acknowledged, as when three successive Secretaries of State
called on him for guidance; as when the Wilson administration offered him the civil governorship of Veracruz (he
refused indignantly); as when the Mexican government
appointed him counsel at the ABC Conference in Niagara;
as when he was called by the Senate Foreign Relations
Committee as the premier American expert on the tangled
affairs of Mexico. And in 1921, the end of the line: exile
from Mexico. At that, he was lucky. For he had indeed
materially aided a counterrevolutionary movement. The
fact that the counterrevolutionists were decent men, and
those in power barbarians, does not alter the political
reality, which is that it is a very dangerous business indeed
to back an unsuccessful insurrection, and he knew it and
barely escaped with his skin.

He had married, and had three children, and would
have seven more, all ten of whom survive him. He
launched a business in Venezuela, and his fortunes fluctu-

315

ated. But as children, we were never aware of his tribulations. We knew only that the world revolved about him and that whether what we needed was a bicycle, or an excuse to stay away from school for a day, or the answer to an anguished personal problem, he was there to fill the need, and when he thought the need exorbitant or improper, he would, by a word, bring us gently to earth. He worshiped three earthly things: learning, beauty, and his family. He satisfied his lust for the first by reading widely and by imposing on his lawless brood an unusual pedagogical regimen. The second impulse he gratified by a meticulous attention to every shrub, every stick of furniture that composed his two incomparable homes. The third he served by a constant, inexplicit tenderness to his wife and children of which the many who witnessed it have not, they say, often seen the like.

In his anxiety for the well-being of his country his three passions fused. Here in America was the beauty, the abundance, that he revered; here in the political order was the fruit of centuries of learning; here his wife, and his ten children, and his thirty-one grandchildren, would live, as long as he lived and years after. So he encouraged us to stand by our country and our principles. To his encouragement, moral and material, *National Review* owes its birth and early life. It was only two weeks ago that, crippled and convalescent in Austria, he registered, in turn, joy, and indignation, and amusement, and sadness, as his wife read aloud to him from the latest issue of this chronicle of America's glories and misadventures.

My father died last week at seventy-seven, and we take leave of him in the pages of the journal which had become his principal enthusiasm. We pray God his spirited soul to keep.

MAUREEN BUCKLEY O'REILLY

August 11, 1964

Shortly after *National Review* was launched, in the fall of 1955, a young girl one or two years out of Smith College approached us, volunteering to work for the magazine without pay. She had been doing as much, during the preceding period, for the Christophers, the altruistic organization of the Maryknoll priest Father James Keller, and we had had word of her success there as private secretary, amanuensis, and scriptwriter for "F.K.," as she affectionately, if a little irreverently, referred to her revered friend and boss. But by nature argumentative, she sought an activity that would tax a little bit less her exhaustive capacity for Christian charity and so sought out our worldly journal, where, under certain circumstances, she might be permitted, provided the formulation was cautious, to point out to some of her fellow citizens that their political behavior was straying dangerously close to that of Racca, the fool. She took a normal person's pleasure out of an occasional indulgence in this liberty and wrote from time to time a coruscating editorial paragraph which would not have won an imprimatur from the Christophers, although, because her wit was leavened by charity, would have got an amused smile from her old mentor F.K. She got as much from her associates on *National Review,* but it was never patronizing, because we were no more immune than the *pomposi* of the political world from her evenhanded barbs. She simply would not tolerate stuffiness, and all of us learned, in those moments when we tended to give way to our little vanities, that we were running the danger of committing our self-esteem to her chastening hands. An offhand remark from her, a casual note to a colleague, a facetious memorándum to the staff were sufficient to remind us that the law against taking oneself too seriously was being rigorously enforced by a young Smith ('54) graduate, Phi Betta Kappa, twenty-three years old (who knew better than anyone we had ever seen how to laugh wholesomely, cleansingly. How many mean and self-important little devils she drove in despair from our offices during that period by her incorruptible laughter—).

She took on the most menial and exacting chores, and for three whole years, in addition to her other duties, managed the crank mail department. Soothingly she would write Mrs. Jones that *National Review*'s refusal to credit the theory that Alaska was being prepared as a concentration camp for all those who had voted against the censure of Joe McCarthy was not, in and of itself, sufficient reason to conclude that *National Review* was a Communist Plot. Depending on the tone of the correspondent, she was commensurately generous, considerate, impossible. If the plaintiff proved to be invincibly hoarse, unimpeachably and vindictively ignorant, her answers would sharpen. One lady, who could not understand *National Review*'s innocence of such palpable Communist operations as fluoridated water, Roy Cohn, the income tax, and Russell Kirk, was constantly canceling her subscription, conjoining to her cancellation notices vivid manifestos of disapproval of *National Review* and all its subversive works, and then, cooling off, would cautiously renew. Maureen would take her gently by the hand and explain patiently why Russell Kirk could simultaneously teach at the New School for Social Research and yet remain outside the Communist Party, but one time, after the lady had canceled for maybe the fifteenth time, Maureen, overtired, took her at her word and sternly forbade the circulation department to reinstate her subscription. For weeks the lady tried, clandestinely, to put her subscription back in force, but however deviously she approached the circulation department, she would run into the unremitting ukase against her. Finally, in despair, she sent a postcard: "Maureen, dear, I surrender." She got the next and, I suppose, succeeding issues. One gentleman had a dreadful time unraveling his subscription problem—partly our fault, partly his. Maureen worked for weeks trying to sort out his difficulties, but no matter how much she put herself out, he grew more and more heated, more and more refractory, to the point where she finally wrote to him: "Dear Mr. Smith: It occurs to me that it makes no sense for us to conspire together any longer to straighten out your difficulties with the Circulation Department. My suggestion to you is that you start again from scratch and take out a fresh subscription under an assumed name."

She became engaged in 1958 to an apolitical Irishman of great gentleness, with a sense of humor equal even to her own and a personal charm against which she was, for once, totally helpless. The prospect of losing her was more than her colleagues could endure, and so we persuaded her to stay on even after her marriage, until she was very large with child—and then she went and did not return. At home, between children (she had five in five years), she

318

did odd work for us, editing the two volumes *An Evening with National Review* and *Relaxing with National Review*. She had a bias against hanging on, as an ex-hand, and was consistently unwilling to step foot in her old offices, although on the rare occasions when she would do so, it was always cause for spontaneous celebration for all who had known her and worked side by side with her. Because "she was the essence of what it means to be alive; even physical objects were brighter and more wonderful when she was there," as a veteran editor of *National Review* remarked, concluding, "She was the sweetest girl I ever knew."

Maureen was struck down by a cerebral hemorrhage—on the day Senator Goldwater was nominated—and died two days later without regaining consciousness. On behalf of the original staff of *National Review,* who owe her such a very great deal, I bid her good-bye, and commend to the care of Our Lord one of His most precious creations, my beloved sister:

MAUREEN BUCKLEY O'REILLY
1933-1964

ALOISE BUCKLEY HEATH

February 7, 1967

"For her," an august and worldly professor of the social sciences called in when the word leaked out that she was in coma, "I have to confess I have said a prayer, for the first time in many years even though I never met her." His prayer, and others, were unavailing. Aloise Buckley Heath died on Monday, January 16, 1967, ten days after an unsuccessful operation, which was performed a few hours after she had complained of a bad headache and was driven, by her husband, to the hospital in Hartford. Unconsciousness and partial paralysis gradually set in, and when the doctor did operate, it was only because as he put it, he would have done so on his own wife under similar circumstances—he gave her only 1 or 2 chances out of 100. And then a few minutes later, when he actually observed the damage done by the cerebral hemmorhage, he simply stitched her back together and waited, as the family did—her husband, her ten children, her mother, her eight brothers and sisters—for the inevitable end. It came later than the young doctors had predicted. "They don't realize," said one doctor, "that at forty-eight the heart is strong. It goes right on beating for a while, a good while. What happened to her brain is the kind of thing that usually happens to people in their late sixties or seventies. That's why she isn't dead—yet. But there won't be any pain, any consciousness." She was buried at St. Bernard's Cemetery, in Sharon, Connecticut, on Wednesday, January 18, alongside two of her sisters, who had died at age three days and thirty-one years. At the service, said as she would have wanted, in Latin, a memorial card was distributed, a small photograph, the dates of birth and death on one side, and on the other a passage from François Mauriac's *Ce Que Je Crois* that she had seen and expressed admiration for—as a young girl, she had been schooled in France, and she knew the language as a native—only a month ago, Mauriac wrote: *"Faites, Mon Dieu, que je me recueille dans la paix de votre présence, afin que quand mon heure sera venue, ja passe par une transition presque insensible, de vous à vous, de vous, pain vivant, pain des hommes, à vous amour vivant déjà possédè par ceux de mes biens-aimés qui se sont endormis avant moi dans votre amour."* ("Grant, O Lord, that I might commune in the peace of Your presence, so that when my hour is come, I shall pass through a transition all but insensible, from You to You; from You, the Living Bread, the Bread of Man, to You, the Living Love, already possessed by those of my beloved friends who, in that love, have gone before me to sleep.")

"Though I never met her," one reader wrote, "I felt along with thousands of *National Review* readers, I'm sure, the force of her personality; her vibrant, joyous spirit sang out of her seasonal articles for *National Review*." "Of all the writers on your magazine, over the past eleven years," an attorney wrote, "she must surely have been the most lovable." And from a minister: "My wife, my children, and I feel something of a personal loss in the death. . . . As she has on several occasions in the past, she added to the joy of our Christmas celebration with her most recent article, [giving us] that sense of thankful and

320

lighthearted appreciation of the mercies of God which we are trying to nurture in those whom He has given us to love."

Aloise Heath wrote for the very first issue of *National Review* and had an article in the issue that was on the stands when she took sick. She did not, however, write frequently. There was, of course, the handicap of her motherhood of ten children and the very special care she took of them. Besides that, she was notoriously disorganized, so much so that generations of editors clamored, unsuccessfully, for her articles, and when she died, she had on her desk, as usual unanswered, a letter from the editor of a prominent monthly begging for copy. She had excited, at Smith College, the admiring attention of the academicians, as sharply distinguished from the administrators, who at one point got so fed up with her dilatory habits they suspended her for a year (she graduated with the class of 1941, instead of 1940)—a lever against her which unfortunately no editor inherited. But the professors gave her all the ritual honors of a very bright young writer. She was married in 1942 and got around to writing an article about her first child five years later. It was published in the *Ladies Home Journal*, and with her check for $500 she bought expensive presents for all her brothers and sisters, resolved to write regularly, and didn't—not even when the agent for Somerset Maugham—who thus announced himself—offered to handle her material. She was always acquiescent; she would agree to write anything in the world any editor asked her to write and simply did not do so—she was too busy with her growing family. She did produce a piece for *NR* at Christmastime, the ordeal of whose parturition was an annual agony—bits and pieces would come in by notepaper, telegram, telephone. But they were the most applauded pieces we ever published, even though they seldom touched on politics. Seldom, but not never . . .

She complained in one of them that her children had been overpoliticalized. For instance "the kindergartner of unshakable opinion—what we can't shake in Janet is her firm opinion announced thirty seconds after she heard of the President's assassination last year that Senator

Goldwater shot him. 'Janet, you *mustn't* say that!' her horrified older brothers and sisters exclaim when the subject comes up from time to time. 'I won't. I won't tell *anyone,*' she reassures them. 'Shall it be our two's secret?' "

Janet wasn't the only problem. A year later there was Timothy, with his paraplegic leg: "Six-year-old Timothy, who has been standing aloofly in the background watching you with great concentration, has apparently now accepted you. He whispers in my ear that he has something important to tell you. I transmit the message and Timothy stands before you shortly and informs you somberly that his message is about Communism. The Communists, he thinks you ought to know, are against us and we are against Communists, and they plan to beat us up but, man, are they going to be surprised, because they don't even *know* about Timothy Heath yet! And with modest pride, Terrible Timothy sticks one skinny little leg in the air and shows you his heavy brace and boot. 'One kick with *that* foot,' he grits from clenched teeth; and while you ponder the appalling fate in store for the Communists, Tim smiles and the serious little face breaks into whole galaxies of twinkles and dimples. . . ."

And there was always, in the household, the problem of distinguishing politics and theology. Sometimes, she admitted, she was herself responsible for the confusion. Let her speak for herself on the matter of Mrs. Major and her eternal soul:

"Did I really tell Timothy that Tommy Major's mother was going to Hell because she voted for Johnson? No. I DID NOT. Once and for all.

"What happened was this. One day Timothy said: 'Would you go to Hell if you voted for Johnson?'

"I said: 'Do you mean *me* or do you mean *people*? If you mean me, the answer is yes because I'm an educated voter and I'd be committing a mortal sin if I voted for him. If you mean "people," no, because they are not as smart as your dear, dear mother, you lucky boy.' Tim looked at me gravely. 'Will Tommy's mother go to Hell? She's going to vote for Johnson.'

" 'Oh, I don't think so, Tim,' I said, not terribly interested in the whole subject. 'She doesn't know enough to know what she's voting for. But wouldn't she be surprised if she *did* go to Hell!'

"It was then that I made my big mistake. You remember those lovely warm days last fall. Well, they affect me very badly. They increase my euphoria to the point of mania. I was near the piano while I talked to Tim and I sat down and played and sang, *'Tommy's mother went to Hell/On the Donkey ticket/Now she knows a Johnson vote/Is very, very wicked.'* Timothy thought it was charming and rushed out to collect his friends Brian and Billy to hear it. Billy called in his sister Beth who was playing with Pammy Shepherd from the next street over. In about ten minutes there were over a dozen children in the house bawling out at the top of their lungs the news that 'Tommy's Mother went to Hell.' And what was I doing? Big fat fool that I am. I was sitting there at the piano bawling it out with them and playing different versions of the piano accompaniment and setting up duets and interesting arrangements and in general behaving not at all like a woman whose living room windows face onto the Major driveway. And that's absolutely all there is to it.

"I don't blame her for thinking it was a rehearsal. I don't even blame the children for telephoning her the next few days and nights to sing it. I drummed it into their heads so hard they probably still can't think of another tune. And that I swear is the whole story. It is absolutely what happened. And don't believe any other version."

But her madcap problems were not usually political. She was sharply observant and, therefore, sharply critical—the curse of the whole class of the pretentious, because she had a jeweler's eye for cant, for silliness (which, however, if it was unaffected, she loved), for hokum, political and nonpolitical. One of her weapons was literalness. She wrote several times with vast amusement about some of the practical problems posed by writers in ladies' magazines. There was the article warning the wife against "Becoming Less Appealing," which cautioned against making long social telephone calls or "talking more loudly than her husband." "In certain isolated circumstances," she mused, "doing so would be justified; chronic laryngitis on the part of the husband, for instance; or the case of a man who might be worried about *his* Becoming Less Appealing, and therefore refusing to talk more loudly than his wife at the very same identical moment that his wife refused to talk more loudly than her

323

husband. We can all see where *this* sort of situation would end, I am sure."

And there was the article that caught her eye, instructing wives on how to be more romantic with their husbands: "There was a *very* moving love scene [in the article] in the course of which a woman stood 'with her hands clasped on Loren's neck, her red hair pressed against his chin, her lips ardently uplifted.' The trouble is, when *I* clasp *my* hands on my husband's neck, press my interestingly graying hair against his chin and ardently uplift *my* lips, all I get is a mouthful of Adam's apple."

She was as amused by all aspects of language. Traveling in France with her sister Priscilla she found herself stuck in the elevator. "I cried: 'To the help!', which is what you cry when you are trapped in an Alpine pass in a blizzard at midnight and wolves are attacking you; and Priscilla shouted: 'The ascendor does not march!', which means that the elevator isn't working. After a while, pausing for a cigarette, we noticed the sign on the door. 'By means of a telephonic apparatus which finds itself at the interior of the ascendor, *ladies* and *gentlemen,*' the sign said pointedly, 'may inform the concierge with all calm that a mechanical anomaly has passed itself.' There is more to this message than meets the eye, we found. And you will find, if you try to say *'Anomalie mécanique' without* all calm."

Her strength was the children she loved—to the extent, she always made clear, that that was possible for anyone who truly understands children. One time she received a letter from an irrepressibly attractive and utterly impossible thirteen-year-old boy, friend of one of her sons, asking her whether she would recommend him to a school into which he sought admittance. (The entire, hilarious correspondence caught the eye of the *Reader's Digest,* which published it in its entirety.) She wrote, copy to the applicant, to the headmaster: "[Peter] is more sophisticated today than three years ago, when, at the age of ten, he frequently urged me not to get my liver in a quiver. Today, when Peter and I have what he refers to as 'a difference of opinion,' he retires with complete equanimity to his own back yard until such time as my ill-humor subsides. My change of mood is apparently picked up by Peter's extrasensory perception within the hour, for whenever I decide that the time has come for forgiving and forgetting, he appears at my front door within fifteen minutes, to assure me *he* has forgiven and forgotten. By way of proof (penance?) he then resumes without rancor his status as our daily visitor. . . ."

She knew children, and knew the duty of the parent to try to dominate children, but knew also the limits of any such ambition, children being . . . children. "If they start throwing books at each other," she wrote in a piece about carpools, "it is best to park the car on the side of the road and exhibit emotional stability until they've stopped. Even this is unnecessary if the books are being thrown by Fourth, Fifth, or Sixth Form boys. Their aim is invariably excellent, and you are in no danger whatsoever. Occasionally there may be stationed on one of your carpool routes a policeman who does not like it when a child sticks his head out of the car and shouts: 'What's old pennies made of?' and all the others shriek, *'Dirty Copper!'* At least he doesn't like it twice a day for nine months of the year, which is when the children like it. If this should be the case, humor him. I myself find that the easiest thing to do is to work out a detour around him, though I understand some mothers make the children stop it."

But she always found her own children (and everyone else's), whatever the generic menace, individually fascinating, individually challenging, individually superior. "Timothy is five years old. He is small, handsome, stern, rather conceited, we suspect; and he has the kind of passion for accuracy which so unduly prolongs even the simplest of bedtime stories. When he comes home from kindergarten, we meet; we do not reune, as did his poor be-mom-mèd eldest brother and I twelve years ago. Nor do I ask for a detailed accounting of Timothy's morning; I say 'Have fun?' and then I say 'That's good!' before he answers. . . .

"Timothy was home from school with a cold, and we were glad to see each other, so to speak. We sat alone together in the kitchen over a plateful of plums, and I said, as a gesture of friendship: 'Tim, what's two and two?' Between Heaths, this is not a question; it is the opening gambit of an old routine which ends in 'What's twelve and twelve?' to which the (always) killingly funny answer is, 'Twenty-four. Shut your mouth and say no more.' Furthermore, it is Timothy's absolutely favorite joke; so I felt a little rebuffed when he asked gravely: 'What's two?'

And thus was his mother introduced to the new math, in which numbers are second-class citizens, and it all depends on colored rods . . .

Always she insisted on the realisms. There was the Christmas when she announced to her children that they would attempt a Trapp Family Christmas, the distinguishing feature of which was that each child would select another child (by ballot) as his special protégé (*Christkindl*), and proceed to shower (anonymously) special favors on him or her until Christmas day, when the *Christkindl*'s benefactor would identify himself. The idea was heroically launched. But her children didn't appear to be exactly Trapp-minded:

"That afternoon they were all in the coat closet (well they *were,* that's all. They *like* the coat closet) making out their Christmas lists. Pam, who can spell, was helping the ones who can't write; and Alison, who is magic, was helping the ones who can't talk. I had my ear at the crack, listening, because I'm still trying to hear one of those childhood conversations whose innocent candor tears at your heartstrings. You've read about them, I'm sure. What I heard was my dear little ones calculating how much more each of them would get for Christmas if they didn't have so many brothers and sisters. They named, giving reasons therefor, their choice—those they would gladly do without. They catalogued the children they would trade for hockey skates or an electric organ with four octaves, or seven Betsey-Wetsies with seven different-colored hairs. From what I could hear through the crack, *nobody* kept Buckley and Timothy, which is understandable, but not nice. . . ."

Undaunted, she went on with her resolute plans for a Trapp Family Christmas.

"I didn't see how the *Christkindl* custom could go wrong, though. I *still* don't. In the Trapp family, everyone writes his name on a piece of paper and the papers are put in a basket which is passed around as soon as the children have finished singing: '*Ye heavens, dew drop from above.*' Everybody picks a name from the basket, and the pickee, if you follow me, becomes the picker's secret *Christkindl,* and the idea is, you do your *Christkindl* a good turn every day until Christmas without ever letting him know who you are. . . ." But at her house it was, as usual, chaotic—the children found themselves picking themselves, or prematurely divulging their identities, or whatever. Finally, she contrived a means by which the children would pick out their *Christkindl* and be picked out. It was not altogether democratic and by no means left to chance. She reserved a *droit de mère:* All the children were *given* a specified piece of paper. "The baby ate her paper; but it was all right, because I knew whose name she had eaten. I had arranged for us to draw each other, because we're in love. Everybody was getting pretty tense, not to mention bloody, until one of them—I haven't asked which—found a solution: every Sunday now, they each buy seven penny lollipops, and every night they slip a lollipop under their *Christkindl*'s pillow. Well, I *know* that doesn't sound so terribly spiritual, but it's better than what they used to do. What they used to do was steal each other's lollipops. I wouldn't want anybody to think that the baby and I have sunk to such a mundane relationship, though. We haven't had to change our routine at all. Every morning my *Christkindl* allows me to rock her a little; and every evening I rock my *Christkindl* a little."

The last Christmas, never daunted, she had experimented with group singing, which meant the children as a body, rather than as individuals, and that, as ever, was something else again, and, as ever, she wrote about it hypnotically:

"Gay my children unquestionably are. They rollick into the house from school, burst into paroxysms of laughter at the extraordinary coincidence of their reunion with various carpools, plan their far-flung wickedness in gales of muffled giggles, are scolded with eyes twinkling above insufficiently suppressed grins, and fall asleep in the midst of a choked chuckle at 8, 9, or 10 P.M., according to whether their bedtime was at 7, 8, or 9. . . .

"Do you know what 'afforient' is? Neither did I till I heard Priscilla, who is fifteen and who should know better, sweetly warble that the three kings afforient were. . . .

"And has anybody ever wondered where the Ranger is on Christmas Eve? . . . Well, Betsey Heath has. '*Away* is the Ranger,' she will inform you, if you listen carefully.

And obviously, he is away because there is no crib for his bed. . . .

"Janet, canny little Janet, all of whose sins are premeditated and blatant, sang exactly what she intended to sing. *'No L, No L the angels did say.'* It was a matter of the angels' alphabet, she explained to me a little tiredly. . . . I eyed her suspiciously, because more humor in the family we do not need, but I let it pass. . . .

"Have you ever wondered, in the long watches of the night, what Child is this who laid to rest on Mary's lap is sleeping? Well, it is the Child whom angels greet with Ann the Sweet, while shepherds' watches keeping. Well, St. Ann was Mary's mother, certainly sweet and probably dead, argued Alison. Why *wouldn't* she be with the angels? As for the shepherds, what with their setting off for Bethlehem, well-known for its good and bad thieves, keeping their watches was a very friendly gesture on the part of the angels. Ann the Sweet probably thought of it. . . .

"Some of them were taking an individual called 'Good Heed' to the angels' ward; many of them with the jellied toast proclaimed. . . .

"Pam, even Pam, kept announcing in her clear, sweet contralto that God and sin are reconciled. . . .

"But I was too weary to go on. 'Children,' I said. 'Let's just do one song absolutely *perfectly*. Let's concentrate on "Silent Night," because that's the one we know best anyway. . . .'

"They lined up, looking very clean and handsome and holy, Jim and John at the back, Timothy and Janet on either side of Pam at the piano, and the middle echelon sensibly and unquarrelsomely distributed in the middle according to heights. *Just like the Trapp Family,* I thought to myself happily. Pam turned and gave them all a long and, I hoped, stern look, before she played the opening measures.

" *'Silent night, holy night,'* nine young voices chanted softly, and I noticed Jennifer and Betsey beginning to break up in twinkles and dimples. *'All is calm, all is bright,'* they went on, John's recorder piping low and clear. Buckley and Alison clapped their hands briefly over their mouths. *'Round John Virgin, Mother and Child,'* the chorus swelled sweetly, and I rapped hard on the piano.

'Just *who*,' I asked, in my most restrained voice, 'is Round John Virgin?'

" 'One of the twelve opossums,' the nine young voices answered promptly, and they collapsed over the piano, from the piano bench onto the floor, convulsed by their own delicate wit.

"And that's why we didn't have *this* year's Christmas carol program."

"One of the reasons—I say one of the reasons because I could easily think of another if I put my mind to it—that I kept on having babies for years after all my classmates had worked up to president of the State PTA was that I always thought a big family would be such fun at Christmas. Which who doesn't, including people like me, who know? I know why my husband Ben has the spirit of Christmas around Thanksgiving and the Spirit of Ash Wednesday around Christmas. I keep telling him I know. 'I know,' I say. 'I know. I know. I know.'

"I know we always get more glitter and glue on the floor than on the candles and that I never remember to wipe it up until the dining-room carpet is permanently (though interestingly) spangled. I know I look absolutely insane, crawling around in the snow for weeks before Christmas, putting candy canes on window sills and then galloping madly off into the dark, jingling sleighbells and shouting 'Ho! Ho! Ho!' I know the newsboy would rather have two dollar bills than a $1.95 flashlight wrapped in green paper and silver ribbon, with 'MERVYN' spelled out in red Scotch tape. I know no one can eat those Cut'n'Bake cookies after the children have decorated them with green sugar and cinnamon hearts (Christmas tree) and then with more cinnamon hearts and melted marshmallow (Santa Claus) and then with more melted marshmallow and pink crayon (angel). I know it's un-Gesell and not even altogether Spock to look a ten-year-old square in the eye and say: 'But Sweetie, how should *I* know why Polly's Santa Claus is really her father? Maybe her father *has* to be her Santa Claus, poor little thing! Maybe Santa Claus just doesn't *like* Polly. Did you ever think of that? . . .' "

Stuff and nonsense? Well . . . "Some day"—she wrote on Christmas, 1964, taking off with her striking literary skill on the ladies' type of magazines that tell you how to be a perfect wife, promising, in her own caricature, to be "even more emetic," but somehow accomplishing something quite different. She wrote: "Some day, though, I will have a fling at becoming a perfect woman, nobly planned, which, the way I dope it out, means spending absolute hours making love your whole existence, and keeping silent in the churches, and weeping while men work, and trying to be a better smoke than a good cigar, and constantly widening the gap between your price and rubies', and being good and letting who will be clever, and while your babes around you cling, showing Wordsworth how divine a thing a woman may be made.

"In my case, though, it will have to be while my grandbabies around me cling, because right now, and for the next fourteen and a quarter years, I'm going to be too busy. . . ." Celebrating Christmas in the usual way.

On Christmas Eve last, with only twelve and one-half years to go, she was busy, at the apogee of her yearly cycle, stuffing the stockings of her children with candies and puzzles and games and toys, when suddenly she stretched out under the tree and slept. This was not totally surprising. The difference was when she woke an hour later. She did not resume her duty, her joy—even though there were still four stockings left to fill. She went, without saying a word, to bed, and so her husband and eldest child, astonished, worried, finished the work of the Christmas maker extraordinary. She didn't know what it was that had happened, and the doctors didn't seem to know, and two weeks later the Christmases were, for her, forever ended. And little Janet, her *Christkindl* of the year of the Trapps, when she got the news, responded that "Nothing will ever be fun again," which is exactly how others felt, who knew her when we all were children together.

INDEX

332

Jefferson, Thomas
  on conspiracies, 54
  on justifying revolutions,
    120
John Birch Society
  and Communist
    conspiracy, 53
  and conservatism, 19-22
  and Ronald Reagan, 73
Johnson, Lyndon B.,
  Crime Commission, 177
  criticism of, in *Partisan
    Review*, 46
  defeat of Goldwater, 27
  in *Glamour* poll, 32
  and Great Society, 34
  invitation to Robert
    Lowell, 217-18
  and plan to bomb
    Communist China, 219
  sanity of, 202-04
  and Vietnam, 46

Kempton, Murray, 58
Kennedy, Edward "Teddy,"
  198, 200
Kennedy, John F.
  consideration of Fulbright
    as Secretary of State, 50
  essay following death of,
    296-98
  Gore Vidal on, 196-98
  and Peace Corps, 247
  and plan to bomb
    Communist China, 218
  "popularity," 248
  and religion issue, 61
  on U.S. moon program, 69
Kennedy, Joseph P., 201
Kennedy, Robert F.
  approval of, in *Partisan
    Review*, 45

in *Glamour* poll, 32
as monarch, 200-01
as President, 198-200
on race and Vietnam
  issues, 129-30
and Ronald Reagan, 85
Kenner, Hugh, 259, 278
Kerr, Clark, 72, 74-76, 78
King, Martin Luther
  and civil disobedience,
    118-20, 137
  death of, 122-25
Kirk, Russell,
  at *National Review* and
    New School, 318
  and "religiosity," 26
  use of unusual word, 284
Knowland, William, 73
Kopkind Andrew
  on Martin Luther King,
    118-19
  on Ronald Reagan, 73, 74,
    78, 83, 87

Labor law, suggested
  revisions, 65
Labor unions
  and death of New York
    World Journal Tribune,
    63-65
  influence on public affairs,
    28
  and public inconvenience,
    131-33
Lane, Mark, 176, 183, 184
Latin America, poverty in,
  192
Lee, Mayor Richard, 114-16
Lenin, 20
Lennon, John, on Beatles'
  popularity, 248-50
Lens, Sidney, 110

336

340